Montezuma Amish

Mennonite Cookbook

**A Collection Of Recipes,
Ideas And Helpful Hints To
Nourish You And Yours**

1st Printing	April, 1985	500 copies
2nd Printing	November, 1986	500 copies
3rd Printing	September, 1987	1,000 copies
4th Printing	March, 1988	5,000 copies
5th Printing	December, 1988	5,000 copies
6th Printing	November, 1989	5,000 copies
7th Printing	November, 1990	10,000 copies
8th Printing	September, 1991	10,000 copies
9th Printing	August, 1993	10,000 copies
10th Printing	December, 1995	10,000 copies

ISBN: 0-9630704-0-1

Printed
By

FATHER&SON
ASSOCIATES, INC.

4909 North Monroe Street
Tallahassee, Florida 32303
800-741-0907

TABLE OF CONTENTS

SUBSTITUTIONS

FOR...	YOU CAN USE...
1 tablespoon cornstarch	2 tablespoons flour OR 1½ tablespoons quick cooking tapioca
1 cup cake flour	1 cup less 2 tablespoons all-purpse flour
1 cup all-purpose flour	1 cup plus 2 tablespoons cake flour
1 square chocolate	3 tablespoons cocoa and 1 tablespoon fat
1 cup melted shortening	1 cup salad oil (may not be substituted for solid shortening)
1 cup milk	1/2 cup evaporated milk and 1/2 cup water
1 cup sour milk or buttermilk	1 tablespoon lemon juice or vinegar and enough sweet milk to measure 1 cup
1 cup heavy cream, whipped	2/3 cup well-chilled evaporated milk, whipped
Sweetened condensed milk	No substitution
1 egg	2 tablespoons dried whole egg and 2 tablespoons water
1 teaspoon baking powder	1/4 teaspoon baking soda and 1 teaspoon cream of tartar OR 1/4 teaspoon baking soda and 1/2 cup sour milk, buttermilk or molasses; reduce other liquid 1/2 cup
1 cup sugar	1 cup honey; reduce other liquid 1/4 cup; reduce baking temperature 25˚
1 cup miniature marshmallows	About 10 large marshmallows cut-up
1 medium onion (2-1/2 dia.)	2 tablespoons instant minced onion OR 1 teaspoon onion powder OR 2 teaspoons onion salt; reduce salt 1 teaspoon
1 garlic clove	1/8 teaspoon garlic powder OR 1/4 teaspoon garlic salt; reduce salt 1/8 teaspoon
1 tablespoon fresh herbs	1 teaspoon dried herbs OR 1/4 teaspoon powdered herbs OR 1/2 teaspoon herb salt; reduce salt 1/4 teaspoon

HANDY CHART OF KITCHEN MATH WITH METRIC

KITCHEN MATH WITH METRIC TABLES

Measure	Equivalent	Metric (ML)
1 Tbsp.	3 tsp.	14.8 milliliters
2 Tbsp.	1 oz.	29.6 milliliters
1 jigger	1-1/2 oz.	44.4 milliliters
1/4 cup	4 Tbsp.	59.2 milliliters
1/3 cup	5 Tbsp. plus 1 tsp.	78.9 milliliters
1/2 cup	8 Tbsp.	118.4 milliliters
1 cup	16 Tbsp.	236.8 milliliters
1 pint	2 cups	473.6 milliliters
1 quart	4 cups	947.2 milliliters
1 liter	4 cups plus 3½ Tbsp.	1,000.0 milliliters
1 oz. (dry)	2 Tbsp.	28.35 grams
1 lb.	16 oz.	453.59 grams
2.21 pounds	35.3 oz.	1.00 kilogram

THE APPROXIMATE CONVERSION FACTORS FOR UNITS OF VOLUME

To Convert from	To	Multiply by
teaspoons (tsp.)	milliliters (ml)	5
tablespoons (Tbsp.)	milliliters (ml)	15
fluid ounces (fl. oz)	milliliters (ml)	30
cups (c)	liters (l)	0.24
pints (pt)	liters (l)	0.47
quarts (qt)	liters (l)	0.95
gallons (gal)	liters (l)	3.8
cubic feet (ft^3)	cubic meters (m^3)	0.03
cubic yard (yd^3)	cubic meters (m^3)	0.76
milliliters (ml)	fluid ounces (fl oz)	0.03
liters (l)	pints (pt)	2.1
liters (l)	quarts (qt)	1.06
liters (l)	gallons (gal)	0.26
cubic meters (m^3)	cubic feet (ft^3)	35
cubic meters (m^3)	cubic yards (yd^3)	1.3

SIMPLIFIED MEASURES

dash = less than 1/8 teaspoon
3 tsp. = 1 Tbsp.
16 Tbsp. = 1 cup
1 cup = 1/2 pt.
2 cups = 1 pt.

2 pt. (4 c.) = 1 qt.
4 qt. (liquid) = 1 gal.
8 qt. (liquid) = 1 peck
4 pecks - 1 bushel
16 oz. = 1 lb.

If you want to measure part-cups by the tablespoon, remember:

4 Tbsp. = 1/4 cup
5⅓ Tbsp. = 1/3 cup
8 Tbsp. = 1/2 cup

10⅔ Tbsp. = 2/3 cup
12 Tbsp. = 3/4 cup
14 Tsbp. = 7/8 cup

CONTENTS OF CANS

Of the different sizes of cans used by commercial canners, the most common are:

Size	Average Contents
8 Oz.	1 cup
picnic	1¼ cups
No. 300	1¾ cups
No. 1 tall	2 cups
No. 303	2 cups
No. 2	2½ cups
No. 2½	3½ cups
No. 3	4 cups
No. 10	12 to 13 cups

Foreward

Today I must have Martha's hands, for there's so much to do that if I miss a minute of time I never shall get through the many tasks that wait for me. And so, Dear Lord, I pray, for strength and swiftness. Give to me "Martha's hands" today.

Today I must have Mary's heart. There are so many things that must be done today and time goes by on rapid wings; and so, lest I engrossed with work, should lose that better part, I pray keep me close to Thee, and give me a "Mary's heart."

By Lorie C. Gooding
Selected by Mrs. Ruth Yoder

We wish to sincerely thank all those who shared their favorite recipes. Special thanks goes to Irene and Mari Yoder for their art work and the support and encouragement from Irene. We appreciate (Mom) Mrs. Levi Kauffman, Alta and Linda Kauffman, Edna, Mary Lois, Irene, Bertha and Vera Yoder, Viola and Bertha Swartzentruber and Lorene Plank for contributing much of their time. Also Sandy Cheeves and Macon County Extension Service for their help. God Bless You All.

Sincerely,

Mrs. Ruth Yoder

COMMON CAUSES OF FAILURE IN BAKING

BISCUITS

1. Rough biscuits caused from insufficient mixing.

2. Dry biscuits caused from baking in too slow an oven and handling too much.

3. Uneven browning caused from cooking in dark surface pan (use a cookie sheet or shallow bright finish pan), too high a temperature and rolling the dough too thin.

MUFFINS

1. Coarse texture caused from insufficient stirring and cooking at too low a temperature.

2. Tunnels in muffins, peaks in center and a soggy texture are caused from over-mixing.

3. For a nice muffin, mix well but light and bake at correct temperature.

CAKES

1. Cracks and uneven surface may be caused by too much flour, too hot an oven and sometimes from cold oven start.

2. Cake is dry may be caused by too much flour, too little shortening, too much baking powder or cooking at too low a temperature.

3. A heavy cake means too much sugar has been used or baked too short a period.

4. A sticky crust is caused by too much sugar.

5. Coarse grained cake may be caused by too little mixing, too much fat, too much baking powder, using fat too soft, and baking at too low a temperature.

6. Cakes fall may be caused by using insufficient flour, under baking, too much sugar, too much fat or not enough baking powder.

7. Uneven browning may be caused from cooking cakes at too high a temperature, crowding the shelf (allow at least 2" around pans) or using dark pans (use bright finish, smooth bottomed pans).

8. Cake has uneven color is caused from not mixing well. Mix thoroughly, but do not over mix.

PIES

1. Pastry crumbles caused by over-mixing flour and fat.

2. Pastry is tough caused by using too much water and over mixing dough.

3. Pies do not burn - for fruit or custard pies use a Pyrex pie pan or an enamel pan and bake at 400°-425° constant temperature.

BREADS: (YEAST)

1. Yeast bread is porous - this caused by overrising or cooking at too low a temperature.

2. Crust is dark and blisters - this is caused by underrising, the bread will blister just under the crust.

3. Bread does nto rise - this is caused from over-kneading or from using old yeast.

4. Bread is streaked - this is caused from under-kneading and not kneading evenly.

5. Bread baked uneven - caused by using old dark pans, too much dough in pan, crowding the oven shelf or cooking at too high a temperature.

OVEN TEMPERATURES

Slow	300°
Slow moderate	325°
Moderate	350°
Quick moderate	375°
Moderately hot	400°
Hot	425°
Very hot	475°

* * * * *

DEEP-FAT FRYING TEMPERATURES WITHOUT A THERMOMETER
A 1-inch cube of white bread will turn golden brown:

350° to 355°	65 seconds
355° to 365°	60 seconds
365° to 375°	50 seconds
375° to 385°	40 seconds
385° to 395°	20 seconds

BEEF

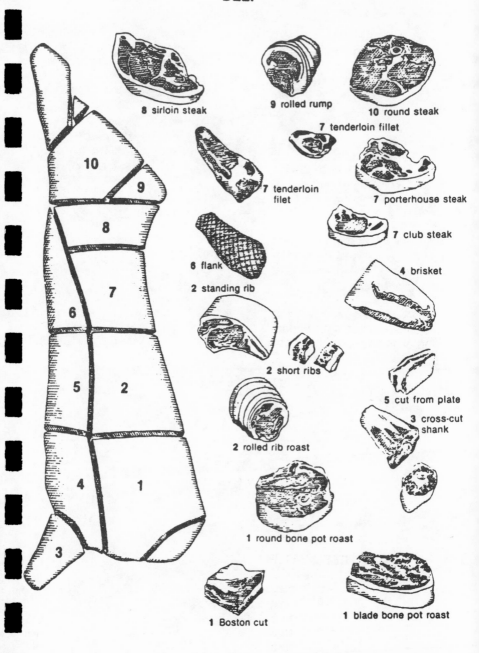

8 sirloin steak

9 rolled rump

10 round steak

7 tenderloin fillet

7 tenderloin filet

7 porterhouse steak

7 club steak

6 flank

2 standing rib

4 brisket

2 short ribs

5 cut from plate

3 cross-cut shank

2 rolled rib roast

1 round bone pot roast

1 Boston cut

1 blade bone pot roast

VEAL

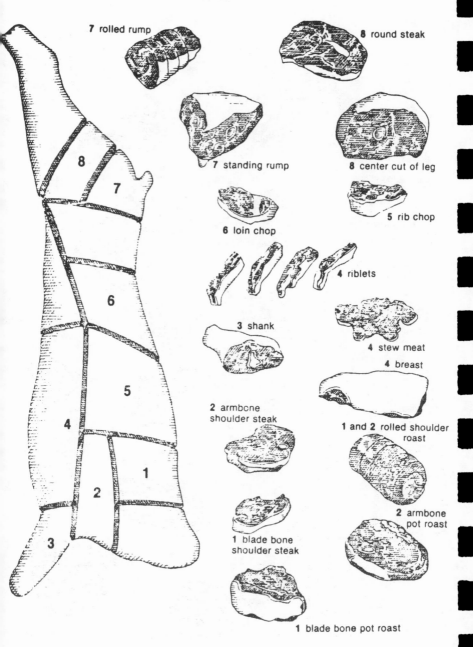

7 rolled rump

8 round steak

7 standing rump

8 center cut of leg

6 loin chop

5 rib chop

4 riblets

3 shank

4 stew meat

4 breast

2 armbone shoulder steak

1 and 2 rolled shoulder roast

2 armbone pot roast

1 blade bone shoulder steak

1 blade bone pot roast

PORK

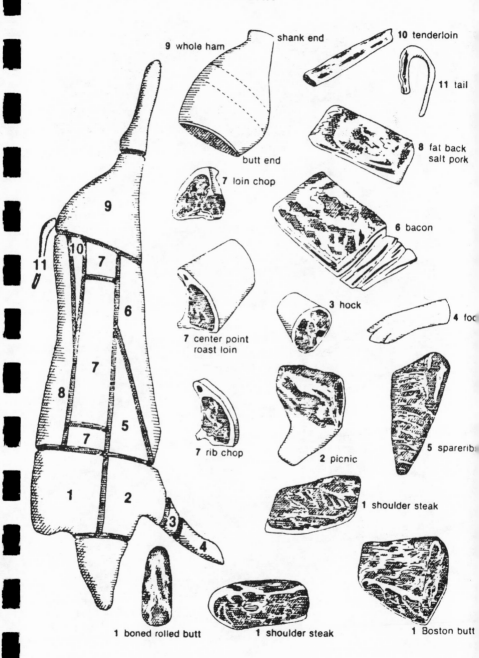

9 whole ham — shank end
butt end

10 tenderloin

11 tail

8 fat back salt pork

7 loin chop

6 bacon

7 center point roast loin

3 hock

4 foot

7 rib chop

2 picnic

5 spareribs

1 shoulder steak

1 boned rolled butt

1 shoulder steak

1 Boston butt

LAMB

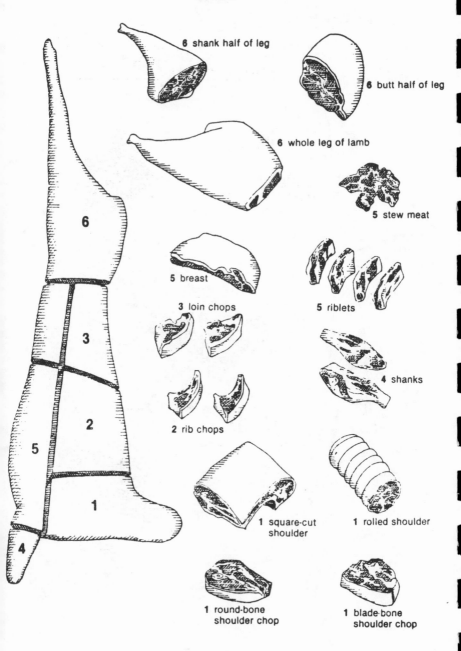

6 shank half of leg

6 butt half of leg

6 whole leg of lamb

5 stew meat

5 breast

3 loin chops

5 riblets

2 rib chops

4 shanks

1 square-cut shoulder

1 rolled shoulder

1 round-bone shoulder chop

1 blade-bone shoulder chop

APPETIZERS & BEVERAGES

CHEESE BALL
Irene Yoder

2-8 oz. cream cheese
1 tube hickory smoked cheese
2 t. Worcestershire sauce

1 t. minced union
1 T. Lawry's seasoning salt
1 pkg. dried beef

Cut dried beef into small bits. Add the rest of the ingredients and beat well. Roll in chopped pecans. Serve with crackers.

CHEESE BALL
Linda Yoder

2-8 oz. pkgs. cream cheese
1 pkg. chipped beef

1/2 t. salt

Mix and form ball. Refrigerate. This ball may be frozen.

CHEESE BALLS
Mrs. Bertha Yoder

2 c. shredded sharp processed
   cheese
1/2 c. soft butter

1 c. flour
1 t. chives
1/2 t. seasoning salt

Mix cheese and butter, stir in flour, chives, and salt. Mix well. Shape in 1" balls and place on an ungreased cookie sheet. Bake until set or light golden brown. 400° 15-20 min.

CHEESE BALL
Mrs. Loretta Brenneman

1-8 oz. pkg. cream cheese
1/3 lb. mild Cheddar cheese
6 slices American cheese
6 slices dried beef

1/4 c. pecans
1 T. salad dressing
1/2 t. Worcestershire sauce

Chop Cheddar cheese, American cheese, dried beef and pecans in blender, or put through a food grinder. Beat cream cheese and add blender-chopped things, salad dressing and Worcestershire sauce. Form into a ball and roll in additional chopped nuts.

1

PARTY CHEESE BALL

Miriam Brenneman

16 oz. cream cheese
2 c. (8 oz.) shredded sharp
   Cheddar cheese
1 T. chopped pimento
1 T. chopped green pepper
1 T. finely-chopped onion

2 t. Worcestershire sauce
1 t. lemon juice
Dash of cayenne pepper
Dash of salt
Chopped pecans

Combine softened cream cheese and Cheddar cheese, mixing until well-blended. Add pimento, green pepper, onion, Worcestershire sauce, lemon juice and seasonings; mix well. Chill. Shape into ball; roll in nuts.

VARIATION: Omit pecans; roll in finely-chopped fresh parsley.

STUFFED CELERY STICKS

Bertha Swartzentruber

7 medium stalks celery
1/2 c. shredded Swiss cheese
   (about 2 oz.)

1/2 c. finely-chopped, fully-cooked
   ham
1/3 c. mayonnaise or salad
   dressing
1/2 t. prepared mustard

Cut celery into 3" pieces. (Make sure celery is completely dry.) Mix remaining ingredients. Spread about 1 T. in each piece of celery. Cover and refrigerate 1 hr. Makes 14 appetizers.

FRESH FRUIT DIP

Mrs. Harley Yoder

1-8 oz. pkg. cream cheese

1-7 oz. jar marshmallow creme

Combine softened cream cheese and marshmallow creme; mix till well-blended. Serve with fresh fruit.

VEGETABLE DIP

Mrs. Chris L. Miller, Irene Yoder

1 c. Hellmann's mayonnaise
1 c. sour cream
1 T. dry onion flakes
1 T. parsley flakes

1 t. Lawry's seasoning salt
1 t. dill weed
1/2 t. Worcestershire sauce
1/2 t. Accent

Mix all together and refrigerate.

FINGER JELLO

Mrs. Paul E. Yoder, Becky Plank

3 or 4 envs. Knox unflavored gelatin

3-3 oz. pkgs. any flavor jello
4 c. boiling water.

Mix and pour into baking pan and cool until firm. Cut into squares and serve.

EGGNOG

Mrs. Harley Yoder

1-32 oz. can eggnog
12 eggs, separated
1½ c. sugar

1 qt. milk
1 qt. whipping cream
Nutmeg and vanilla

Pour can of eggnog in bowl and freeze; get out 30 min. before serving, to soften. Beat egg yolks, slowly add sugar, cover and chill 1 hr. Stir in milk, fold in whipped cream. Beat egg whites till stiff; fold in mixture. Add nutmeg and vanilla to taste. Put in frozen eggnog to keep cold while serving.

HOT MOCHA MIX

Mrs. Elmer M. Yoder (Esther)

2 c. instant nonfat dry milk
1½ c. sugar
4 c. non-dairy coffee creamer

¾ c. cocoa (scant)
¾ c. instant coffee

Combine all ingredients in mixing bowl; stir well. Store mix in an airtight container. For each serving, place 3 T. mix in a cup. Add 1 c. boiling water and stir well. Yield: about 75 servings.

(I usually add some extra coffee.)

LEMONADE

Esther Ruth Yoder

4 lemons
2 ½ c. sugar

1 gal. water

Juice 3 lemons. Put 1 lemon in blender with a little water and blend well. Strain and add lemon juice, water and sugar. Add ice and serve.

ORANGE JULIUS
Alta Kauffman, Ruth Yoder

6 oz. orange concentrate
4 T. sugar
1 c. milk

16 to 18 ice cubes
1 t. vanilla or maple
1 c. milk

Put first 5 ingredients in blender and blend well. Add remaining cup of milk and serve immediately. Delicious served with popcorn.

PUNCH
Mrs. Marlene Swartzentruber

2 pkgs. cherry Kool-Aid
2 pkgs. raspberry Kool-Aid
2 pkgs. orange Kool-Aid
3 c. sugar

1 sm. can pineapple juice
1-6 oz. can frozen orange juice
1-6 oz. can frozen lemonade

Mix and add enough water to make a gallon or just enough to suite your taste.

PUNCH
Mrs. Alva Yoder

3 lg. cans pineapple juice
4 lg. pkgs. strawberry jello
2 lg. cans frozen orange juice

4 sm. cans lemonade
3 c. sugar
1½ gal. water

Mix together and add ginger ale just before serving. Makes 4 gal.

Save leftover fruit juices until there's enough to freeze in an ice tray. The cubes add extra flavor to lemonade or iced tea.

PUNCH
Mrs. Eli Kauffman, Mrs. Bertha Yoder

1 pkg. cherry Kool-Aid
1 pkg. strawberry Kool-Aid
2 c. sugar
3 qts. water

1-6 oz. can orange juice
1-6 oz. can lemon juice
     concentrate
1 qt. ginger ale

Mix all ingredients together and serve. Makes 1½ gal.

PUNCH

Mrs. Ivan Yoder

1 gal. fruit drink   1 qt. ginger ale
1/2 gal. orange sherbet

Beat frozen sherbet into drink, add ginger ale just before serving.

MAUI MILK PUNCH

Ruth Yoder

1 1/2 qts. vanilla ice cream   1 t. lemon juice
3 c. chilled pineapple juice   4 c. cold milk
1/3 c. orange juice

In a mixing bowl, while beating softened ice cream, gradually add fruit juices, then milk. Pour into chilled container. Makes 3 qts.

WEDDING PUNCH

Miriam Brenneman

1 1/2 c. sugar   1/4 c. lemon juice
3 c. water   2 qts. ginger ale
46 oz. can pineapple juice   3 bananas
1 1/2 c. orange juice

Mix sugar, water, pineapple juice and orange juice. Put lemon juice and bananas in blender and blend until smooth. Add banana mixture and ginger ale just before serving.

ROOT BEER

Ellen R. Brenneman

1 gal. warm water   4 t. root beer extract
1 3/4 c. sugar   1 T. yeast

Mix all ingredients together and set in sun for 3 or more hrs. Chill in refrigerator overnight.

Notes

BREADS

HONEST WEIGHT

ANGEL BISCUITS

Ruth Yoder

5 c. flour
3 t. baking powder
1½ t. salt
1 t. soda
¼ c. sugar

1 c. shortening
¼ c. warm water
1 pkg. yeast
2 c. buttermilk

Mix dry ingredients. Cut in shortening like pastry. Dissolve yeast in warm water and mix with buttermilk. Add to dry ingredients, mix until smooth. Roll out like biscuits. Dip in melted butter and bake. 400° 12-15 min.

BISCUITS

Ruth Yoder

4 c. self-rising flour
2 T. sugar
2 T. baking powder

7 T. Crisco
2 c. buttermilk

Mix all together except buttermilk, until crumbly, then add buttermilk. Roll out and cut. Put on cookie sheet and bake. 425° 8-10 min. Makes 30 to 35.

BUTTERMILK BISCUITS

Mary Lois Yoder
Mrs. L.D. Kauffman

2 c. plain flour, sifted
¾ t. salt
2 t. baking powder

½ t. baking soda
3 heaping T. Crisco
1 c. buttermilk

Sift dry ingredients together, and cut in Crisco. Make a well in center of flour mixture, pour in buttermilk, and mix lightly with a fork. Place on a floured cloth, and knead for about 1 min. Roll dough out to aboue ½" thickness and cut with a cutter. Place ½" apart on ungreased cookie sheet. Bake 450° 10 min. Makes 24.

Be patient - in time the grass becomes milk!

7

QUICK BUTTERMILK BISCUITS

Verda Overholt

¼ c. warm water
1 T. yeast
¾ c. lukewarm buttermilk
¼ t. soda

1 t. sugar
1 t. salt
3 T. cooking oil
2½ c. bread flour

In bowl, dissolve yeast in water. Measure flour. Stir rest of ingredients (except half of flour) into yeast mixture. Add remaining flour. Mix with hands. Turn onto floured board. Knead until smooth. Shape as desired. Let rise until double in size, about 1¼ hrs. Bake at 400° 15-20 min. Makes 1½ doz.

SOUTHERN GAL BISCUITS

Becky Plank

4 c. sifted flour
8 t. baking powder
1 t. cream of tartar
1 t. salt

1 c. shortening
2 eggs, unbeaten
4 T. sugar
1⅓ c. milk

Sift dry ingredients into bowl, blend in shortening till it looks like cornmeal. Pour in milk slowly. Mix with fork. Add eggs. Stir to a stiff dough. Roll out to ½" thick. Cut with cookie cutter. Bake at 400° 10-15 min.

BREAD

Mrs. Daniel Swartzentruber

½ c. warm water
1½ T. white sugar
4 T. yeast
6 c. very warm water
1 c. Cane Patch syrup

1½ T. salt
3 lbs. whole wheat flour
1 c. corn oil
3 lbs. white flour

Mix warm water, white sugar, and yeast and let dissolve. Mix very warm water, Cane Patch syrup, salt, and whole wheat flour well in mixer bowl. Next add yeast mixture and mix well. Next add corn oil. Mix well. Add white flour. Work with mixer till dough is plenty thick, then put it on the table and work by hand for 10 min. Set in a warm place and let rise ½ hr. Work down and put in pans. Let rise in pans till ready to put in oven. 350° 20 min. Will make ten 1-pound loaves.

HONEY BREAD
Vernie Brenneman

3 T. yeast
1 c. warm water
2 c. hot water
1/2 c. honey
1/2 c. brown sugar

4 t. salt
4 T. shortening
2 1/2 c. cold water
4 c. whole wheat flour
10 c. white flour

Dissolve yeast in warm water. (Add 1 T. sugar.) Use 2 c. hot water to dissolve honey, brown sugar, salt and shortening. Then add cold water. Add yeast water, whole wheat flour and 3 c. white flour. Beat with beater. Then add the rest of the flour. You may have to use more flour if dough is too thin. Knead well. Let rise. Knead again. Let rise again. Shape and put into pans. Let rise again. Bake 325° 35 min. Makes about 9 loaves.

After bread has been baked, remove from pans and cover with cloth and plastic to get soft bread.

RAISIN WHEAT - HONEY BREAD
Elsie N. Yoder, Becky Plank

1/4 c. or 4 pkgs. yeast
1 T. sugar
2 c. warm water
3 c. white flour
1 c. raisins
1 c. water

1/2 c. honey
1/2 c. lard or shortening or oil
2 eggs
1 T. salt
8 c. whole wheat flour
1/4 c. wheat germ (optional)

Dissolve yeast and sugar in warm water. Add white flour. Let rise for 10-20 min. Blenderize raisins and water. Add yeast mixture together with raisins, honey, lard or shortening, eggs, salt, and 2 c. whole wheat flour. Mix well with mixer. By hand put in the rest of the whole wheat flour. Knead well. Let rise twice. Shape and put into greased pans. Let rise and bake 350° 20-25 min.

For 4 batches, put in 3 times everything except yeast. Use 1/2 c. or 8 packages yeast for 4 batches.

WHEAT BREAD   Mrs. Crist Yoder Sr.

5¹/₂ c. water   5¹/₂ c. whole wheat flour, sifted
3 T. yeast   11¹/₂ c. white flour, sifted
¹/₂ c. honey   1¹/₂ t. salt
¹/₂ c. oil

Dissolve yeast in 1 c. warm water, then add this to the rest of the
water, oil, honey and salt. Add sifted flour gradually, makeing dough
stiff enough so that it can be easily handled. Knead dough until it is
smooth and elastic. Let rise double in bulk, then punch down and let
rise again. Put in pans until double in bulk. Makes (3 med. and 3 lg.
pans). Bake until a golden brown 350° 20 min.

I use a portable mixer till dough is plenty thick.

WHEAT BREAD   Mrs. Robert Paul Yoder

6 c. very warm water   4 T. yeast
¾ to 1 c. honey   1 c. oil
3 lbs. wheat flour   1½ to 2 T. salt
3 lbs. white flour

First dissolve yeast in 1 c. water. Take the 5 c. water and add salt,
honey, and wheat flour; beat well. Add yeast water and beat. Next
add oil and beat well. Add white flour and knead well. Let rise till
double, about 1¼ to 1½ hrs. Shape and put in nine 1¼ lb. loaf pans
and let rise again, about 1 to 1½ hrs. Bake at 400° 20 min.

WHEAT BREAD   Mrs. Stanley Yoder

2 c. milk (scalded)   15 c. white flour
4 c. water   5 T. salt
¹/₂ c. oil or lard   2 eggs (beaten)
¹/₂ c. honey   4 T. yeast and 1 T. sugar
6 to 8 c. wheat flour   dissolved in 1¹/₂ c. warm water

Mix all ingredients together, except flour, adding yeast mixture last.
Beat well; then add 6 to 8 c. wheat flour, 1 c. at a time. Slowly add
around 15 c. white flour, kneading well after each addition. Let rise
1¹/₂ hrs. Punch down and shape and put into greased bread pans.
Let rise 1¹/₂ to 2 hrs. again. Bake 325° 25-30 min. Makes about ten
1¹/₄ lb. loaves.

WHITE BREAD
Mrs. Raymond Weaver

1/4 c. yeast	5 c. warm water
2 T. salt	1/2 c. oil
2 T. sugar	1/2 c. sugar
	15 1/2 c. white flour

Dissolve 1/4 c. yeast and 2 T. sugar in 2 c. warm water. Put 2 T. salt, 1/2 c. oil, 1/2 c. sugar and 3 c. warm water in large pan. Mix 3 c. flour into yeast mixture. To this, add the rest of the flour-about 12 1/2 c. (For wheat bread, use 5 c. wheat and 1/2 c. brown sugar.) The loaves are from 1 1/4 to 1 1/2 lbs. each. Let rise around 1 1/2 hrs, then put in pans and let rise again for about 1 hr, or until about the size you like it. Bake 350° 25 min. Makes 6 loaves.

WHOLE WHEAT BREAD
Elsie N. Yoder

3 pkgs. dry yeast	1 T. salt
1 c. warm water	2 1/2 c. cold water
2 T. sugar	3 c. whole wheat flour
2 c. hot water	10 c. white flour
1/2 c. honey or molasses	4 heaping T. shortening, melted
1/2 c. brown sugar	

Dissolve yeast in warm water. Add 2 T. sugar. Dissolve honey in 2 c. hot water; and yeast mixture. Add 3 c. wheat flour and 4 c. white flour. Beat well with beater. Add shortening and beat well. Add 6 c. white flour and knead well. Add more flour if needed. Let rise till double in size. Knead well. Let rise till double in size. Knead lightly and shape into loaves. Put into greased bread pans and let rise till double. Makes nine 1 lb. loaves. Bake at 350° for 20 min.

Be kind, for everyone you meet is fighting a hard battle.

WHOLE WHEAT FREEZER BREAD   Miriam Brenneman

3 c. warm water
3 pkgs. yeast
1/4 c. honey
1/4 c. molasses

1/2 c. butter, melted
1/3 c. powdered milk
7 to 8 c. whole wheat flour

Dissolve yeast in warm water. Add honey, molasses and butter. Add powdered milk and flour, a few cups at a time, until you get a stiff dough. Knead about 10 min. Cover and let dough rest abuot 15 min. Divide dough into 3 pieces, form into loaves, put in pans and brush with butter. Let rise until double and bake 350° 35 min. To freeze the dough, don't wait for it to rise. Cover each pan with plastic wrap and put in freezer. The pans can be removed when the loaves are frozen. Rewrap loaves and freeze up to 1 month.To use, put loaf into pan, cover and let thaw at room temperature for 4 to 5 hrs. Do not let rise higher than a normal loaf or it may collapse in the oven. Bake 350° 35 min. 9x5" pans

BANANA NUT BREAD   Mrs. Isaac Plank

3 bananas
2 c. flour, sifted
1/2 c. nuts
1 t. soda

1 c. sugar
1/2 c. shortening
1 t. salt
1 t. baking powder
2 eggs

Mix shortening and sugar, add eggs, add mashed bananas. Dissolve soda in 1 T. water, add to the mixture and beat thoroughly, add dry ingredients and nutmeats, stir only until mixed. Bake at 350° in greased loaf pan for 50 or 60 min.

Contentment is not found in having everything
but in being satisfied with everything you have.

ZUCCHINI BREAD

Mrs. Elmer M. Yoder (Esther)
Mary Lois Yoder

3 c. flour
1/2 t. baking powder
2 t. soda
1 t. salt
1 1/2 t. cinnamon
3 eggs

1 1/2 c. sugar
1 c. oil
2 t. vanilla
2 c. shredded zucchini
1-8 oz. can crushed pineapple,
   drained well
3/4 c. nuts, chopped

Beat eggs, add sugar, vanilla and oil. Stir in zucchini and pineapple. Mix in dry ingredients and nuts. Bake 350° for 1 hr. Yield: 2 bread pans.

ZUCCHINI BREAD

Mrs. Sarah Weaver
Mrs. Rufus L. Yoder

3 eggs
1 c. brown sugar, packed
1 c. granulated sugar
1 c. vegetable oil
2 c. grated zucchini
1 t. vanilla

3 c. all-purpose flour
1/2 t. cinnamon
1 t. baking powder
1 t. soda
1 t. salt
1 c. chopped nuts

Beat eggs until frothy. Stir in sugars, oil, zucchini, and vanilla. Combine dry ingredients. Stir into zucchini mixture until well mixed. Stir in nuts. Pour into 2 well-greased pans. Bake 325° for 1 hr. Two 9x5x3" pans. Cool 10 min. in pan; remove to wire rack. Cool thoroughly before slicing.

ZUCCHINI BREAD

Sadie A. Yoder

3 lg. eggs
3/4 c. sugar
1 c. vegetable oil
2 c. zucchini (peeled & grated)
1 T. vanilla

3 c. flour
1 t. salt
1 t. baking powder
1 t. soda
3 t. cinnamon
1 c. nuts

Combine in mixer bowl first 5 ingredients, and beat well. Sift together flour, salt, baking powder, soda and cinnamon. Add zucchini mixture, and stir until blended. Add 1 c. chopped nuts. Pour batter into 2 greased 8" bread pans. Bake 350° for 1 hr. and remove from pans. Cool on racks.

CORN BREAD

Mrs. Robert Paul Yoder

1 c. wheat flour
1 c. cornmeal
3 t. baking powder
1/2 t. salt

1/3 c. brown sugar
2 eggs
1/2 c. cooking oil
1 c. milk

Mix dry ingredients. Add remaining ingredients. Mix well and bake 350° 25-30 min. 9" square pan.

This is very good with strawberries and cold milk. Or with creamy navy beans.

SOUR CREAM CORN BREAD

Ruth Yoder, Lila Yoder

3/4 c. cornmeal
1 c. flour
1 t. soda
1 t. cream of tartar
1 t. salt

2 1/2 T. sugar
1 egg, well beaten
2 T. melted butter
1 c. thick sour cream
4 T. milk

Sift flour and cornmeal, add soda, cream of tartar and salt. Add beaten egg, cream, milk and melted butter. Beat thoroughly. Pour into greased 9" square pan. Bake 425° for 20 min. Serve with strawberries and milk, or beans (your choice) with a thin white sauce.

OATMEAL PONE

Ruth Yoder

1 pt. whole wheat flour
1 pt. oatmeal
1 pt. sweet milk
1 T. baking powder

1 t. salt
1/4 c. oil
1/4 c. honey

Mix all ingredients together. Bake 400° 20-25 min. Serve with strawberries or peaches and milk.

You cannot do a kindness too soon
because you never know how soon it will be too late.

CINNAMON ROLLS

Mrs. Raymond Weaver

2 c. milk
14 T. butter
1 T. yeast
2 T. sugar
6 eggs
1 c. sugar
2 t. salt
12 c. flour

SYRUP FOR PANS:
2 c. water
2 c. brown sugar
Bring to boil, then add:
4 T. butter
2 t. vanilla

Scald 2 c. milk and butter. Soak yeast and 2 T. sugar in 2 c. warm water. Mix eggs, sugar, and salt together, then add yeast mixture with eggs, mix. Then add milk and butter. Add flour until dough is sticky. Let rise 2 hrs, then punch down and let rise 30 min. Roll out and cover with melted butter (1 stick) and cinnamon and nuts. Roll up and cut 1/2" or 3/4" thick. Put a little syrup in bottom of pans, then put rolls in pan. Let rise again. Bake 325° 20 min. Put white or caramel icing on. Makes 10 or 12 pans.

Put towels under rolls right after they get out of the oven and a wet towel over the top.

CINNAMON ROLLS

Kathy Yoder, Mrs. Floyd E. Yoder

1 c. milk
1 c. butter
5 T. yeast or 5 pkgs. yeast
7 eggs

1½ c. sugar
3 t. salt
7 c. warm water
5 lbs. + 5 c. flour

Heat milk and butter. Dissolve yeast in 1 c. warm water. Beat eggs and add sugar and salt. Beat well. Put 6 c. warm water in large bowl and add all above ingredients. Mix in flour and beat or knead for 5 min. Add more flour if needed. Let rise twice and roll out. Put on melted butter, cinnamon and brown sugar and roll up - cut, put in pans and let rise. Bake 325° for 16 min. Frost with white or caramel icing.

CINNAMON ROLLS

Verda Overholt

2½ c. scalded milk
1¼ c. oleo
2½ c. lukewarm water
2½ T. yeast
2½ T. sugar

1½ c. sugar
1¾ T. salt
5 eggs
1½ c. mashed potatoes
15 c. flour

Melt butter in milk; let cool. Soak yeast and 2½ T. sugar in lukewarm water. Mix other 4 ingredients together and add milk and yeast mixtures with it. Add flour until mixture is just sticky. Let rise until double, punch down, roll out and cover with melted butter, brown sugar, and cinnamon. Roll up and cut ½" to ¾" thick.

SYRUP FOR PANS: 2 c. water, 2 c. brown sugar; bring to a boil, then add: 4 T. oleo, 2 T. vanilla. Put syrup in bottom of pans, put rolls on syrup; let rise till double. Bake 325° 10-15 min. Frost with white or caramel icing.

If you don't have cake flour, measure the required amount of all-purpose flour and take out 1 T. from each cup, replacing with 1 T. cornstarch to each cup.

WHITE HOUSE CINNAMON ROLLS

Mrs. Crist Yoder, Jr.
Mrs. Norman Yoder

2 T. yeast
1 c. warm water
3 T. butter
5 to 6 c. flour

1 c. sugar
1 t. salt
1 c. warm milk
2 eggs

Mix yeast and ½ c. sugar and 1 c. warm water; set aside. Warm milk and add butter. Add beaten eggs and remaining ½ c. sugar, salt. Add yeast mixture, then slowly add flour till smooth. Let rise till double in bulk (about 1 hr.), punch down; let rise again. Roll out on greased surface in oblong shape, about ½" thick and spread with melted butter. Sprinkle with brown sugar, cinnamon, nuts, and raisins (optional) - as much as desired. Grease fingers and roll like a jellyroll. Cut slices ½" thick and put in greased tin ¼" apart. Let rise in warm place about 45 min. and bake 350° for 25 min. Cool, frost with caramel or white icing, and sprinkle with nuts (optional).

The stickier the dough, the better the rolls will be. I find that a long thread cuts my dough more evenly.

CINNAMON SWIRL LOAF

Elsie Yoder

7 to 7½ c. all-purpose flour
2 pkgs. active dry yeast
2 c. milk
½ c. sugar
½ c. shortening
2 t. salt
2 eggs
½ t. ground cinnamon
½ c. sugar

CONFECTIONERS' ICING:
Stir together:
1 c. sifted powdered sugar
¼ t. vanilla
Enough milk to make drizzling
    consistency (about 1½ T.)
Use spoon to drizzle over loaf, or
    spread it with a spatula.

Soften active dry yeast in ¼ c. water. In a saucepan, heat milk, ½ c. sugar, shortening and salt just till warm, and shortening is almost melted; stir constantly. Add yeast and eggs. Stir in 2 c. flour; beat well. Add enough of remaining flour to make a moderately stiff dough. Continue kneading till smooth and elastic (3-5 min.). Shape into a ball. Place in lightly-greased bowl. Cover; let rise in warm place till double in size (about 1 hr.). Punch dough down; turn out onto lightly-floured surface. Divide in half. Cover; let rise 10 min. Roll each half into a 15x7" rectangle. Brush entire surface with water. Combine the ½ c. sugar and cinnamon. Sprinkle each rectangle with half the sugar-cinnamon mixture. Roll up jellyroll style, beginning with narrow end. Seal long edge and ends. Place sealed edge down in 2 greased 9x5x3" loaf pans. Cover; let rise till almost double (35-40 min.). Bake 375° 30-40 min. or till done. (If crust browns too quickly, cover with foil last 15 min. of baking.) Remove from pans; cool. Drizzle with Confectioners' icing. Makes 2 loaves.

HANDICAPPED

I'd like to tell him how my love
Burns fervent and I try—
But words sound flat, and so today
I'll bake his favorite pie.

The words beat for expression, but
They sound so dull when said . . .
I'll sew a button on his shirt,
And sweep, and make his bed.

If only speech of gold were mine
I might this love express . . .
I'll make a pudding that he likes . . .
And may be he can guess!

17

SWEET ROLL DOUGH

Becky Plank

1 c. scalded milk	1½ t. salt
1 c. lukewarm water	2 eggs (beaten)
2 T. yeast	6½ c. flour
½ c. shortening	½ t. nutmeg
½ c. sugar	1 T. real lemon

Scald milk and pour over sugar, salt and shortening. Dissolve yeast in water and 1 T. sugar. Add eggs, nutmeg and lemon. When milk has cooled to lukewarm, add yeast. Beat well. Add flour gradually. Knead lightly, working in just enough flour so dough can be handled. Place dough in a greased bowl, cover and let rise 2 hrs. Flatten dough on floured surface to ¾" thick. Melt butter enough to cover dough well. Mix ½ c. sugar and 3 t. cinnamon and ½ c. chopped nuts (nuts optional). Sprinkle on dough. Roll together, cut and place in greased pans. Let rise till ⅔ desired thickness of baked roll. Bake 400° 18-20 min. Frost with icing of your choice.

APPLE FRITTERS

Laura K. Yoder

1 c. flour	1 egg
1½ t. baking powder	½ c. milk + 1 T.
½ t. salt	2 medium apples
2 T. powdered sugar	

Combine dry ingredients. Beat egg and milk together; stir into dry ingredients. Stir in apples that have been peeled, cored, and finely diced. Drop batter by heaping teaspoonfuls into deep, hot fat. (I like to flatten them a little.) Fry until brown, turning once. Drain on paper towel. Glaze with thin powdered sugar icing, or roll in powdered sugar. Makes 12.

One way to be angry and not sin is to be angry at nothing but sin.

ORANGE TWISTS

Ellen R. Brenneman

2 c. scalded milk
2 T. yeast
2 T. sugar
1 c. orange juice
4 eggs, beaten
1 c. heaping sugar

1 t. salt
1/2 c. melted shortening
Yellow coloring
Lemon flavoring
8 c. flour
Orange flavoring
Orange rind

Dissolve yeast in 1/3 c. warm water. Add 2 T. sugar. When milk is cool, add yeast. Add orange juice. Put in enough flour to make a spongy dough. Let rise. Add eggs, sugar, salt, shortening, coloring, flavoring. Add flour, but not enough to make it stiff. Let rise. Roll out, cut and twist into an 8 shape. Let rise. Fry in hot oil; drain. Glaze with the following:

1/2 c. water
1 box powdered sugar

Orange flavoring
Orange rind

If this is not enough flour, add a little more.

DOUGHNUTS

Lorene Plank

2 c. lukewarm milk
1/2 c. sugar
2 t. salt
2 T. dry yeast dissolved in
   warm water

2 eggs, slightly beaten
1/2 c. soft shortening
7 to 7 1/2 c. flour

Mix sugar and salt to lukewarm milk. Add eggs. Beat well. Add shortening and yeast and water mixture. Beat well again. Slowly add flour. Cover and let rise. After second rising, roll out 1/2" thick and cut with 3" doughnut cutter. Let rise until very light (about 30-45 min.). Drop into hot fat (375°). After they are browned on both sides, drain on absorbent paper. Glaze in very thin powdered sugar and milk mixture while doughnut is still warm. Makes 60.

Horse sense dwells in a stable mind.

DONUTS Mrs. William N. Yoder, Mrs. Robert Paul Yoder
(Yoder's Bakery recipe)

5 c. milk	5 t. salt
5 T. yeast or 5 pkgs.	5 eggs, beaten
1¼ c. shortening	17½ c. flour
1¼ c. sugar	1¼ c. warm water

Scald 5 c. milk; cool to warm. Dissolve 5 T. yeast in 1¼ c. warm water; add to milk. Stir in 7½ c. flour; beat, cover and let rise in warm place till double in size. Cream shortening, sugar, salt, and eggs. Add to yeast mixture, then add 10 c. flour. Knead. Let rise till double in size. Knead. Roll out to ¼" to ½" thick. Cut with cutter. Let rise till double in size. Fry and glaze.

GLAZE:
1 lb. confectioners' sugar   6 T. water
1 T. vanilla

GLAZED POTATO DOUGHNUTS Alta Kauffman

1 pkg. active dry yeast	¼ c. sugar
¼ c. warm water	1 t. salt
1 c. milk, scalded	¾ c. mashed potatoes, instant
¼ c. shortening	may be used
2 eggs	5 to 6 c. sifted flour

GLAZE:
1 lb. confectioners' sugar   6 T. water
1 T. vanilla

Dissolve yeast in warm water. Combine milk, shortening, sugar and salt. Cool until lukewarm. Stir in yeast, potatoes, and eggs. Gradually add enough flour to make soft dough. Turn onto floured surface. Knead until smooth and satiny. Place in lightly greased bowl, turn over to grease top. Cover. Let rise in a warm place until doubled, 1 to 1½ hrs. Roll to ½" thickness; cut with doughnut cutter. Cover; let rise until doubled, about 30 min. Meanwhile, stir confectioners' sugar, water, and vanilla together. Mixture will look like very thick cream. Fry doughnuts in deep, hot fat, 375°. Drain on absorbent paper. Drop hot doughnuts into Glaze. Place on cooking rack until Glaze is set. Makes about 3½ dozen.

FILLED COFFEECAKE   Ruth Yoder

1 c. milk   CRUMBS:
1 stick oleo   1/2 c. brown sugar
1/2 c. sugar   1/2 c. flour
1 t. salt   3 T. butter
1 T. yeast in 1/2 c. warm water   1 T. cinnamon
3 1/2 c. flour   1/2 c. pecans
2 eggs
FILLING:
1 c. milk   2 t. vanilla
3 T. flour   2 1/2 c. powdered sugar
1 c. shortening

Mix oleo and sugar; add eggs and salt. Slowly add flour, yeast mixture, and milk. Pour into 3 well-greased cake pans. Put Crumbs on top and bake 350° 20 min. Put in 3 cake pans.
FILLING: Cook together milk and flour; cool. Add shortening, powdered sugar, and vanilla. Cut coffeecake in half and spread with filling. Put tops back on bottom layers. Makes 3.

HUSH PUPPIES   Lorene Plank

2 c. cornmeal   1 egg (beaten)
1 T. flour   3 T. onions (chopped)
1/2 t. soda   1 c. buttermilk
1 t. salt

Mix dry ingredients. Then add egg, onions, and buttermilk. Mix thoroughly. Drop by teaspoonful into hot fat - around 300°. Yields 3 to 4 dozen.

APPLE MUFFINS   Lela Brenneman

BEAT: COMBINE:
1 egg   1 1/2 c. flour
STIR IN: 2 t. baking powder
1/2 c. milk   1/2 t. salt
1/4 c. melted shortening   1/2 c. sugar
1 c. coarsely-chopped, unpeeled   1/2 t. cinnamon
  apples

Add dry ingredients all at once to liquid ingredients. Stir only enough to moisten. Spoon batter into greased muffin cups 2/3 full. Sprinkle sugar over each and bake 400° 20 min.

BLUEBERRY - LEMON MUFFINS

Ruby Swartzentruber

1¾ c. flour
½ c. sugar
2½ t. baking powder
¾ t. salt
¾ c. milk

⅓ c. vegetable oil
1 egg, beaten
1 c. blueberries
2 T. sugar
1 t. grated lemon rind

Combine flour, ½ c. sugar, baking powder and salt in a large mixing bowl. Make a well in center of mixture. Combine milk, oil and egg; add to dry ingredients, stirring just until moistened. Add blueberries with 2 T. sugar and lemon rind; gently fold into batter. Spoon into greased muffin tins, filling ⅔ full. Bake 400° 25 min. until golden brown.

BRAN MUFFINS

Beulah Yoder

½ box (or 9 oz.) Bran Buds
1 c. boiling water
½ c. corn oil
1 c. sugar
2 eggs, beaten

1 pt. buttermilk
2½ c. plain flour
2½ t. soda
1 t. salt

Pour boiling water over Bran Buds. Stir and let stand until cool. Add all other ingredients and mix well. Bake 400° 15-20 min. Store, covered, in refrigerator and use as desired. Keeps 4 weeks.

BRAN MUFFINS

Mrs. Crist Yoder, Jr.
Mrs. Harley Yoder

1-15 oz. box Raisin Bran
5 c. flour
3 c. sugar
5 t. soda

2 t. salt
1 c. oil
4 eggs, beaten
1 qt. buttermilk

Combine first 5 ingredients. Add rest of ingredients. Fill muffin pans ¾ full. Bake 400° 12-15 min.

This mixture will keep in refrigerator for 1 month.

A lot of kneeling keeps you in good standing with God.

HEIRLOOM RAISIN MUFFINS
Verna Mae Wingard

1 c. raisins
1 c. water
1/2 c. soft butter
3/4 c. sugar

2 eggs
1 1/2 c. flour
1 t. baking powder

Combine raisins and water in saucepan. Bring to a boil, cover and simmer 20 min. Drain raisins and reserve water. Add enough water to reserved liquid to make 1/2 c. Cool well. Cream butter and sugar until fluffy. Add eggs and beat 2 more min. Stir flour and baking powder. Add flour mixture alternately with 1/2 c. raisin liquid, beating well. Stir in raisins. Spoon into greased muffin pan. Fill 2/3 full. Bake 400° for 18 min.

CLOUD LIGHT PANCAKES
Mrs. Levi Kauffman, Ruth Yoder

1 c. Pillsbury flour
2 T. sugar
2 T. baking powder (yes T.)

1/2 t. salt
1 egg
2 T. melted shortening
Milk, enough to make batter
pour easily

Combine dry ingredients. Add egg, shortening, and milk. Mix lightly - mixture will be foamy. Bake on greased griddle. Serve with syrup - liver pudding or sausage. Serves 4.

HOTCAKES
Mrs. Eli Hostetler

1 c. oats (uncooked)
1 1/2 c. buttermilk
1/4 c. brown sugar
2 eggs

1/4 c. butter
1 c. flour
1 t. baking soda
1 t. salt

Place oats and buttermilk in a mixing bowl; let stand 5-10 min. Stir in brown sugar. Beat eggs; add butter; stir into oat mixture. Stir slightly with wooden spoon until combined; do not beat. Makes 16-4" pancakes.

PANCAKES
Mrs. Noah Yoder

2 c. flour
4 t. baking powder
2 eggs

2 c. milk
1/2 t. salt

Beat together and drop by large spoonfuls into hot greased skillet. Serves 8

PANCAKE MIX
Vernie Weaver

5 lbs. whole wheat flour
12 T. sugar
16 T. baking powder

5 lbs. plain flour
6 T. salt

PANCAKES:
2½ c. mix
2 c. milk

2 eggs
4 T. cooking oil

We freeze the mix until ready to use. Serves 8 to 10.

PANCAKE MIX-N-SYRUP
Malinda Wingard

1 c. all-purpose flour
1 egg
2 T. sugar
2 T. baking powder
⅓ c. oil (Crisco) - corn oil will stick
½ t. salt
⅔ c. milk

SYRUP:
1 c. white sugar
1 c. brown sugar
1 white Karo
1 c. water
Pinch of salt
½ t. vanilla
⅓ t. maple flavoring

Mix together flour, sugar, salt and baking powder. add oil, egg and milk and beat. Bake as pancakes or waffles.
SYRUP: Mix together white sugar, brown sugar, water, and salt; bring to a boil only. Add Karo and flavorings. Avoid cooking after Karo is added. The syrup will serve more than 4, but can be kept until another time. Pancake recipe seves 4.

WHOLE WHEAT PANCAKES
Mrs. Robert Paul Yoder

3 c. wheat flour
4 t. baking powder
¼ t. soda

½ t. salt
1½ c. buttermilk
1½ c. milk
2 eggs (optional)

Mix dry ingredients, then add milk and buttermilk. Bake on hot griddle. Serves 10 to 12.

WHOLE WHEAT PANCAKES

Mrs. Samuel Nisly

2 c. whole wheat flour
2 T. brown sugar
2 t. baking powder
1 t. soda
1 t. salt

2 eggs
2 c. buttermilk*
4 T. melted butter

*If no buttermilk on hand, use 2 c. milk and 2 T. vinegar.

Combine the first 5 ingredients, add eggs, milk and butter; beat well. Bake on hot griddle. Serves 8.

FRENCH TOAST

Ruby Swartzentruber

4 eggs
1 c. milk
1 T. sugar

1/2 t. salt
8 slices day-old bread
1 t. shortening

Beat eggs, milk, sugar and salt together in shallow dish. Heat shortening in skillet or on griddle. Dip bread slices, one at a time, into egg mixture. Fry on both sides till lightly browned.

FRENCH TOAST

Mary Lois Yoder

1 egg
1/3 c. milk
1/2 t. sugar

1/8 t. vanilla
Dash of salt
1/8 t. nutmeg

For every 2 slices of bread you use, beat 1 egg, plus 1/3 c. milk, 1/2 t. sugar, 1/8 t. vanilla, salt and nutmeg. Dip bread in mixture, just to coat both sides. Melt just enough Crisco (not butter or margarine as it will burn) to cover bottom of skillet. Brown one side, spoon egg mixture into center of bread until it is absorbed. Continue to add egg mixture, until about 1 T. of it remains on top of the unbrowned side; carefully invert bread to brown other side. Remove when evenly browned. Serve with syrup or Tomato Gravy.

To cut fresh bread easily, cut with a hot knife.

WAFFLED FRENCH TOAST   Mrs. Elmer M. Yoder (Esther)

½ c. milk
4 eggs
1 T. sugar
¼ t. salt

1 T. butter or margarine, melted
2 t. cinnamon
8 slices day-old bread

Combine first 6 ingredients in a shallow bowl, beating well. Dip bread slices, one at a time, into egg mixture, coating well. Bake in preheated oiled waffle iron 2 min. or until browned.

WAFFLES   Mrs. Chris L. Miller

3 c. sifted flour
5 t. baking powder
1 t. salt
2 t. sugar

⅔ c. melted butter
2 c. milk
4 eggs, separated

With mixer, beat egg yolks, add milk, beat 1 min. longer. Add sifted dry ingredients to this and beat 1 min. Add melted butter and beat again. Fold in stiffly-beaten egg whites. Bake in preheated oiled waffle iron until browned. Served about 10.

FRUIT FLAVOR SYRUP (for pancakes)   Mrs. Chris L. Miller

1 sm. box fruit-flavor gelatin
½ c. sugar

2 T. cornstarch
1 c. water

In saucepan, mix gelatin, sugar, cornstarch and water and boil. Pour into pitcher and serve hot on pancakes!

MAPLE SYRUP   Mrs. Marlene Swartzentruber
                                  Mrs. Loretta Brenneman

2½ c. sugar
2 c. light corn syrup

1¼ c. water
1 t. maple flavoring

Mix all ingredients except maple flavoring. Stir. Bring to boil, remove from heat; add maple flavoring. This can also be made in much greater quantities and sealed in sterilized jars.

Use half brown sugar, if desired.

PANCAKE SYRUP

Elsie N. Yoder

1 c. brown sugar
1 c. white sugar
1 c. water
A little salt

1 c. Karo
Vanilla flavoring
Maple flavoring

Mix first 4 ingredients together. Bring to rolling boil. Remove from heat; add vanilla and maple flavorings to taste. Add Karo.

PANCAKE SYRUP

Mrs. Noah Yoder

1 c. white sugar
2 1/2 c. water

1 c. brown sugar

Stir together in pan, bring to full rolling boil. Serve warm over pancakes. If desired, add maple flavoring to taste.

BISQUICK PIZZA CRUST

Ruth Yoder

5 1/2 c. Bisquick

3 T. melted butter

1 pkg. yeast in 1 1/2 c. warm water

Mix all ingredients together. Grease pans and press mixture in 4 pizza pans. Bake 350° 8-10 min.

PIZZA CRUST

Irene Yoder

2 c. Bisquick
1/2 c. milk

2 t. mustard

Mix all ingredients together, grease pans, press mixture into 2 pizza pans. Bake at 350°.

PIZZA CRUST

Ruth Yoder

2 c. flour
1 T. baking powder

1 t. salt
2/3 c. milk
1/3 c. oil

Mix ingredients together, press into 2 pizza pans. Bake at 350° 8-10 min.

PIZZA DOUGH

Mrs. Loretta Brenneman
Lorene Plank

1 c. warm water
1 pkg. yeast
1 t. sugar

1 t. salt
2 T. oil
2½ c. flour

Measure water into bowl and sprinkle in yeast, stirring until dissolved. Stir in additional flour. Turn out on lightly-floured board and knead until smooth and elastic, working in more flour if dough is sticky. Allow dough to rest 5 min. before patting out on pans. Bake 425° for 20 min. It makes two 13-1/4x9" pans.

For thicker crust, take this recipe 1½ times for 2 pans.

BROWN AND SERVE ROLLS

Miriam Brenneman

2 c. milk
¼ c. sugar
2 t. salt
3 T. shortening

1 pkg. yeast
¼ c. warm water
5 to 6 c. flour

Scald milk, add sugar, salt and shortening. Cool to lukewarm. Dissolve yeast in water. Add to milk mixture. Add enough flour to make a soft dough. Knead lightly and put into a greased bowl. Let rise until double in bulk. Turn dough out onto a floured board. Shape into rolls and brush with butter. Let rise until double in size. Bake at 250° for 20 min. Remove from pan, cool, wrap and freeze. To use, thaw and bake at 375° until brown. Makes 3 dozen.

Can be baked at 350° till done.

COCKTAIL BUNS

Mrs. Marlene Swartzentruber

COMBINE:
2¼ c. flour
½ c. sugar
2 t. salt
2 T. yeast
ADD:
½ c. soft butter

GRADUALLY ADD:
2 c. hot tap water
ADD:
1 egg - beating slowly for
 approximately 2 min.
BEAT IN:
4½ c. flour (or to make
 soft dough)

Turn dough onto floured surface - knead smooth (approximately 10 min.). Place in greased bowl - grease top and let rise until double in size, approximately 1½ hrs. Punch down and cover and refrigerate overnight or until dough is cold. Two hours before serving, shape into balls the size of a silver dollar, place on cookie sheet; brush top with a beaten egg and sprinkle seeds on top, either poppy or sesame seeds. Bake 325° 10-15 min., cool, and cut in half and use for party sandwiches.

DINNER ROLLS

JoAnn Inhulsen

½ pt. water
1 qt. milk
2½ c. sugar
2 T. salt
12 to 15 c. flour

4 or 5 pkgs. dry yeast
3 potatoes with enough water
 to cover
2 eggs
3 sticks margarine

Scald milk and add margarine. Cook potatoes till tender and mash, do not drain water. Dissolve yeast in a little water. Cool liquids before adding yeast. Mix all ingredients and add 5 c. flour to make sponge. Let rise for ½ hr. then add enough flour to make smooth and elastic. Knead. Let rise until light; about 30 min. Bake 350° 20-25 min. Makes 10 to 12 dozen.

Wisdom is knowing what to do next; virtue is doing it.

Use plastic disposable bottle liners for recipe card covers.

NEVER FAIL DINNER ROLLS
Irene Yoder

2 pkgs. yeast
2 c. lukewarm water
1/2 c. shortening
1/2 c. sugar

2 t. salt
3 eggs
6 1/2 c. flour

Dissolve yeast in water, add sugar, salt and 3 c. flour. Beat until smooth. Add shortening and eggs and beat well again. Then stir in the rest of the flour or enough to make easily handled dough. Knead well and place in greased bowl. Cover and set in warm place. Let rise until more then doubled in size (2 hrs. or longer). Shape into rolls and place in a well-greased pan. Cover and let rise until light (20-30 min.). Bake 375° for 25 min. 9x13" pan. Makes 2 1/2 to 3 dozen.

For brown rolls, use 2 c. whole wheat flour and 4 1/2 c. white flour.

Unbaked rolls store indefinitely in freezer thus are quite handy for unexpected company.

OATMEAL DINNER ROLLS
Mrs. Alva Yoder

1 c. quick oatmeal
1 c. buttermilk
1 egg
1/2 c. brown sugar
1 c. flour

1 t. salt
1 t. baking powder
1/2 t. soda
1/4 c. melted shortening

Combine oatmeal and buttermilk. Set aside 5 min. Add egg and sugar to oatmeal; mix well. Add flour, baking powder, salt, and soda; mix. Add shortening last and mix lightly. Fill muffin pans half full and bake 400° for 20 min.

The way to break a habit is to drop it.

SILLA'S DINNER ROLLS   Ruth Yoder

1 stick butter
1/2 c. Crisco
1/4 c. oil
1 heaping c. sugar
3 t. salt
3 c. boiling water
4 c. buttermilk
4 T. instant potatoes

8 eggs
1 c. warm water
1 T. sugar
1/4 c. yeast
5 lbs. flour
2 c. wheat flour
1 1/2 c. unprocessed bran

Dissolve yeast in 1 c. warm water and 1 T. sugar; set aside. Mix together first 8 ingredients. Mix well and cool liquids before adding yeast. Add eggs, then gradually add flour and bran. Mix well. Let rise till double, shape into rolls and place in well-greased pans, cover and let rise until light, about 30 min. Bake 350° for 25 min. Makes 9 dozen.

OVERNIGHT BUNS   Alma Yoder

1 pkg. yeast
1 c. lukewarm water
1 T. sugar
1 1/2 c. sugar
1 c. shortening

1 T. salt
4 eggs
4 c. lukewarm water
Flour

Combine first 3 ingredients and set side. Mix the 1 1/2 c. sugar, shortening, salt, water and eggs thoroughly - electric mixer may be used. Start adding flour, then yeast mixture. Keep adding flour until dough reaches desired consistency for easy handling. Set this in the refrigerator in the evening. Knead every hour (3 or 4 times) until time to retire. Shape into buns, the size of walnuts or larger - let rise until morning. Bake on cookie sheet at 350° for 15 min. or until done.

"A good recipe for busy people." Makes 72 rolls plus 24 sweet rolls.

If a nail in a plastered wall loosens, wrap a little cloth around the nail, saturate it with glue, and replace in the hole; when the glue hardens, it'll hold firmly.

REFRIGERATOR ROLLS

Mrs. Harley Yoder

1 c. shortening
1 c. sugar
1½ T. salt
1 c. boiling water

2 eggs
2 pkgs. or 2 T. yeast
1 c. warm water
6 c. flour

Pour boiling water over first 3 ingredients, blend and cool. Add beaten eggs. Sprinkle yeast into 1 c. warm water and stir until dissolved. Add to mixture. Add flour. Mix well. Cover and place in refrigerator at least 4 hrs. Keeps up to 1 week. Shape and let rise 3 hrs. Bake on greased pan 400° 12-15 min. Makes 36 rolls.

FAVORITE QUICK SUPPER

Mari Yoder

Measure 3 c. flour into bowl; answer telephone; take large bowl off small son's head; sweep up flour. Measure 3 c. flour into large bowl. Measure ¼ c. shortening; answer doorbell; wash shortening from son's hands and face. Add ¼ c. of shortening to flour. Mix well; rock crying baby for 10 min. Answer telephone. Put son in tub and scrub well. Scrape flour and shortening mixture from floor, adding enough tears to relieve tension. Open 1 can of beans and serve with remaining strength.

CANNING & FREEZING

Do you have excess cantaloupes? Cut fresh into balls, pour a light syrup over it, then freeze. Serve partially thawed.

APPLE BUTTER   Mrs. L.D. Kauffman

1 gal. applesauce   2 t. cinnamon
3 c. light brown sugar   1 t. nutmeg
1 qt. apple cider, or   1 t. cloves
  1/2 c. vinegar

Mix above ingredients and cook slowly, until it begins to thicken, stirring frequently. If you like a light colored apple butter, you can thicken with clear gel or cornstarch before it gets too dark. Yield: 6 or 7 pints.

FIG JAM   Mrs. Floyd E. Yoder

3 c. figs, blended   2 sm. boxes raspberry jello
3 c. sugar   1 pkg. Knox gelatin

Wash figs and put through the blender. Mix ingredients together and cook for 15 min. Pour into containers and let cool. Place jam in freezer.

MOCK GRAPE JELLY   Mrs. Alva Yoder

3 c. beet juice   1 pkg. grape Kool-Aid
1 pkg. Sure-Jell   4 c. sugar

Combine beet juice, Kool-Aid and Sure-Jell. Bring to boil and add 4 c. sugar. Bring to boil again and boil 10 min. Pour in jars and seal.

STRAWBERRY FREEZER JAM   Naomi Yoder

4 c. (prepared) strawberries   2 boxes Sure-Jell (fruit pectin)
8 c. sugar   1 1/2 c. hot water

Remove caps from strawberries. Crush berries. Measure 4 c. into large bowl. Add sugar and stir thoroughly. Let stand 10 min. Mix hot water and Sure-Jell in a saucepan, bring to a boil and boil 1 min. Stir constantly. At once stir into fruit. Continue stirring 3 min. Immediately ladle into containers. Wipe top with damp cloth. Cover at once with lids. Let stand at room temperature 24 hrs. Store jam in freezer. Yields 9 cups.

FREEZING STRAWBERRIES
Mary Lois Yoder

Strawberries to fill 5, 1½ pt.
containers
4 c. sugar

2 c. mashed strawberries with juice
1 pkg. Sure-Jell
¾ c. water

Fill containers with strawberries (whole or sliced). Add sugar to 2 c. mashed strawberries. Boil Sure-Jell and water for 1 min. (timed after mixture comes to full boil). Remove from heat, add mashed berries, stirring well until all sugar is dissolved. Divide this evenly into the 5 containers. Work crushed mixture in and around whole berries.

KETCHUP
Mrs. Levi Kauffman, Mrs. Raymond Weaver

8 qts. tomato juice
1½ qts. vinegar
7 c. sugar
2 c. ground-up onions
½ c. salt

1 t. EACH:
cinnamon
cloves
red pepper
ginger
nutmeg

Clear gel mixed with water

Cook slowly for 1 hr. Thicken with clear gel or cornstarch and put in blender and then put in jars to process in hot water bath for 40 min.

Put onions in blender. Add more spice if you like.

MINCEMEAT
Mrs. Lydia Yoder

1 qt. ground or chopped meat
6 qts. chopped apples
1 qt. broth
1 qt. apple cider or 1 pt. vinegar
1 qt. Karo

2 qts. sugar
4 t. cinnamon
2 t. cloves
2 t. nutmeg
1 T. salt
1 lb. raisins

Cook meat and rind. Add remaining ingredients. May be canned or frozen.

CANNED BOILED PEANUTS
Vernie Weaver

Fill quart jar with washed fresh peanuts and 4 t. salt. Fill with water and pressure cook for an hour at 10 to 15 pounds of pressure.

PICKLED BEETS
Miriam Brenneman

3 qts. cooked beets, peeled
   and cut up
4 c. white sugar

3 c. vinegar
1½ c. water or beet brine
2 T. salt

Heat last 4 ingredients to boiling. Pack cooked beets into jars. Pour boiling syrup over beets to cover. allow ½" head space in jars. Put lids on jars and process in boiling water for 30 min.

PICKLED OKRA
Chris Inhulsen

Wash and prepare 2 lbs. of young okra pods and pack tightly into hot sterilized jars. Add 1 clove of garlic per jar. Mix together as a brine and boil: 2 c. vinegar, 2 c. water, 2 T. dill seed, 2 T. salt, and 3 hot pepper pods (optional). Pour brine over okra and process in boiling water for 5 min. Let stand for 1 month before opening.

PICKLED SQUASH
Chris Inhulsen

8 c. thinly-sliced small yellow
   squash
2 c. sliced onions
4 bell peppers, sliced
2 c. vinegar

3 c. sugar
2 t. celery seed
2 t. mustard seed
1 jar pimento peppers
½ c. salt

Combine squash and onions in large container. Cover with ice and salt and set aside for 1 hr. Put bell peppers on ice the last 5 min. of the hour. Drain and rinse well. Combine vinegar, sugar, spices, and bring to a boil. Add squash, onions, and both peppers and bring to a full boil. Pour into sterilized jars and seal.

CINNAMON CANDY PICKLES
Mary Kauffman

1 gal. cucumbers
SYRUP:
2 c. vinegar
2 c. water
1 pkg. cinnamon red hot hearts

2 c. lime

8 c. sugar
8 sticks cinnamon
Red cake coloring

Peel cucumbers. Cut in ¼" slices. Soak 24 hours in water to cover, with 2 c. lime. Drain and wash. Soak in clear water 3 hrs. Mix syrup ingredients, boil and pour over cucumbers. Reheat for 2 more mornings and process in boiling water for 20 min. on the fourth day.

BEST EVER DILL PICKLES

Mrs. Stanley Yoder

6 cucumbers
1 c. sugar
1 c. water

1 pt. vinegar
1/4 c. salt

Soak cucumbers whole in ice water 3 or 4 hrs. Slice and put in hot jars. Add generous amount of dill and onions on top - boil sugar, water, vinegar and salt - pour over pickles. Bring water to a boil in a canner and put jars in, counting time as soon as you put jars in. Process 20 min.

GARLIC DILL PICKLES

Mrs. Harley Yoder

3 pts. vinegar
4½ qts. hot water

1½ c. sugar

Bring to boil. Put ½ clove garlic in bottom of jars and small amount of dill seeds, then fill with cucumbers. Fill with boiling vinegar mixture. Seal jar.

SWEET GARLIC DILL PICKLES

Mrs. William N. Yoder,
Alta Kauffman, Esther Ruth Yoder,
Viola Swartzentruber

3 c. sugar
2 c. vinegar
Garlic

2 c. water
2 T. salt
Dill

Make syrup of sugar, vinegar, water, and salt. Put 1 garlic bud and 1 head dill in quart jars. Slice medium-sized peeled cucumbers (1/4" thick) into jars and pour the syrup over them. Cold pack with water to top of jars, bring to boil. Remove from heat, remove lid and let cool in the water. Ready to eat in 2 weeks.

FREEZER PICKLES

Mary Lois Yoder, Irene Yoder

2 qts. **very thinly** sliced,
   unpeeled cucumbers
1 lg. onion, sliced

2 T. salt
1½ c. sugar
½ c. vinegar

Mix first 3 ingredients with hands until salt is dissolved. Let set 2 hrs., then drain and add vinegar and sugar mixture. Mix well, put in containers and freeze.

LIME PICKLES
Lorene Plank

7 lbs. cucumbers - sliced
  1/4" thick
1 c. lime
4 1/2 lbs. sugar
1 1/2 qts. vinegar
1 c. water

1 t. celery seed
1 t. whole cloves
1 t. pickling spice
1 t. salt
Green food coloring

Soak sliced cucumbers 24 hrs. in 1 gal. water with 1 c. lime. Then drain and wash lime off and soak in clean water 3 hrs. Drain and cover with clear water every hour. Drain. Mix sugar, vinegar, water, and spices. Mix well and pour over cucumbers and let stand overnight. Next morning, simmer 35 min. Add enough food coloring to make nice and green. Put in hot jars and seal.

MIXED PICKLES
Sadie A. Yoder

3 qts. shelled beans
1 1/2 qts. snap beans
2 qts. celery
2 qts. cucumbers
2 qts. corn
3 qts. carrots
6 onions

6 red peppers (for color)
3 T. dry mustard
3 T. turmeric
2 pts. white sugar
3 pts. vinegar
1 c. flour mixed with water to
  thicken brine
Salt to taste

You can vary the amount of vegetables. Cook each vegetable separately, except onions and cucumbers don't cook. Just put them in with the rest of the cooked vegetables. Can hot. Makes a good 3 gallons.

PEPPER RELISH
Lela Brenneman, Viola Swartzentruber,
Lorene Plank, Naomi Yoder,
Ruby Swartzentruber

24 green sweet peppers
12 onions

2 1/2 lbs. sugar
1 pt. vinegar
2 t. salt

Grind together peppers and onions. Cover with cold water for 20 min. Then drain and squeeze out water. Mix sugar, vinegar, salt together. Add peppers and onions. Bring to a boil and simmer for 30 min. Put into jars and seal.

PICKLE RELISH

Mrs. Chris L. Miller

1 gal. ground cucumbers
1 pt. ground onions
½ c. salt (scant)

6 c. sugar
3 t. celery seed
3 t. turmeric
1 qt. vinegar
Green food coloring

Mix first 3 ingredients and let stand 2 to 3 hrs., then drain. Bring next 5 ingredients to a boil, add pickles and let come to a boil, then put in jars and seal.

GREEN TOMATO PICKLES

Lila Yoder

7 lbs. green tomatoes, sliced
3 gals. water

4½ c. pickling lime

SYRUP:
5 lbs. sugar
3 pts. vinegar
1 t. whole cloves
1 t. whole allspice

2 sticks cinnamon
1 t. celery seed
2 t. salt

Slice tomatoes and soak in pickling lime and water for 24 hours. Drain and soak 4 hrs. in fresh water, changing every hr. Bring Syrup to a boil. Pour over tomatoes and let stand overnight. The next morning, simmer for 1 hr. Pour in jars and seal.

BRUNSWICK STEW

Lila Yoder, Linda Kauffman

1-14 lb. pork shoulder
1-7 to 8 lb. hen
1 gal. tomatoes
1 gal. cream-style corn
3 cans tomato soup

1 c. brown sugar
1 stalk celery
4 lg. onions
5 lg. potatoes
Sugar, salt, red pepper
½ c. vinegar

Grind celery, potatoes, onions in food chopper. add to cooked and ground meat. Simmer all together. add sugar, salt and red pepper to taste; also ½ c. vinegar. Cool and freeze - or can under pressure like meat.

Put a freezer container in the freezer part of your refrigerator and put your leftover vegetables in until you have enough to make a quick vegetable soup. You may want to add tomato juice or anything to your liking.

DEER BOLOGNA

Irene Yoder

30 lbs. ground deer meat
1 lb. Tender Quick
1 oz. black pepper
1/2 c. sugar

1/4 oz. salt
1 t. garlic salt
1 1/2 t. mace
3 T. liquid smoke flavoring

Mix Tender Quick, pepper, sugar, salt, garlic salt, and mace. Add this and Tender Quick to ground meat. Mix real well. Then put through grinder again. Press in wide-mouth jars and cook for 3 hrs, or 10 lbs. pressure for 90 min. for qts., or 10 lbs. pressure for 75 min. for pts. Makes 30 lbs.

BARBECUED HAM

Mrs. Floyd E. Yoder

1 ham
3/4 lb. oleo
1 sm. onion
7 oz. hickory smoked barbecue sauce

36 oz. "Pop's" barbecue sauce
1/2 bottle hot sauce
1 c. catsup

Bake ham, then add the other ingredients. Put in jars and cook for 4 hrs.

FREEZER POTATOES

Malinda Wingard

Use only small to medium-size potatoes, best when just dug. Wash and cook in boiling water not over 2 min. Drain. Put in cold water and peel. Chill in refrigerator before running through the Food Master to avoid sticking together. After they have been shredded, put in containers and store in freezer. This makes a handy vegetable dish. Prevents spoiling, sprouting and wrinkling.

FRENCH FRIED POTATOES (FROZEN)

Alta Kauffman

6 medium potatoes (peeled)
Cold water

Oil for frying
Salt

Cut potatoes into strips. Rinse in cold water; dry thoroughly between towels. Fry small amounts in deep, hot oil (370°) about 5 min., until tender, but not brown. Drain on paper toweling. Cool to room temperature. Package and freeze. To serve: Arrange potatoes on baking sheet. Put in hot oven, 425° for 10 min., or until brown, turning once. Season with salt. Serves 6.

PIZZA SAUCE

Mrs. Noah Yoder

1/2 bu. tomatoes
3 lbs. onions
2 green peppers
3 hot peppers
Add 2 bulbs garlic (separated)
1 pt. oil

1 1/2 c. sugar
1/2 c. salt
2 T. oregano
8-6 oz. cans tomato paste
2 T. basil leaves
2 T. parsley flakes
6 bay leaves

Chop vegetables and blend in blender. Mix remaining ingredients together and boil 1 hr., stirring frequently. Remove bay leaves before canning. You may also hot water bath 15 min. Remove garlic before using.

PIZZA SAUCE

Lena Yoder

6 qts. tomatoes, cooked
2 green peppers
4 onions
3 T. oregano
4 t. basil leaves
1 t. garlic powder
4 t. pizza seasoning
2 t. celery salt

1 t. pepper
2 t. rosemary leaves
1/2 c. sugar
1 T. salt
2 t. chili powder
3 bay leaves
2 T. hot sauce

Blend tomatoes in blender. Chop onions and peppers in blender. Combine all ingredients, cook to blend flavors. Add 8 T. cornstarch (in a little water) to thicken, if desired. Put hot in jars to seal.

SUGAR SYRUPS FOR CANNING

Alta Kauffman

THIN SYRUP:
2 c. sugar
4 c. water
Yields 5 c. syrup.

HEAVY SYRUP:
4 3/4 c. sugar
4 c. water
Yields 6 1/2 c. syrup.

Boil sugar and water together 5 min. You will need from 3/4 to 1 c. syrup for each quart jar.

STEWED TOMATOES
Mrs. Marlene Swartzentruber

4 qts. tomatoes, peeled & cored ¼ c. chopped bell peppers
(approximately 2 doz. large)   1 T. sugar
1 c. chopped celery   2 t. salt
½ c. chopped onion

Combine all ingredients; cover and cook 10 min., stirring occasionally to prevent sticking. Pour hot into hot jars, leaving 1/2" headspace. Adjust caps. Process pints 15 min.; qts. 20 min. at 10 lbs. pressure. Yield: about 7 pints. To serve: Add 1 T. butter and thicken with cornstarch or flour to taste. Top with bread cubes that are toasted in butter.

TOMATO SOUP
Mrs. Isaac Plank

14 qts. tomatoes (cooked   7 medium onions
till soft)   Parsley flakes
15 sticks celery

1¾ c. flour   2 c. sugar
Scant ½ c. salt   14 T. melted butter
Pepper to taste

Cook tomatoes till soft - put through sieve. Cook onions, celery and parsley flakes together till soft - put through blender. Make a paste with flour, sugar, salt, pepper, and butter - with enough water for paste. Add to tomatoes. Cook for 30 min. If too thick, add boiling water.

For serving, mix ½ soup and ½ milk.

VEGETABLE SOUP TO CAN
Sadie A. Yoder

2 qts. peas   1 qt. onions
2 qts. corn   6 qts. tomatoes
2 qts. green beans   2 qts. cabbage
2 qts. lima beans   1½ qts. water
2 qts. potatoes   1 t. chili powder
2 qts. carrots   1 t. salt (per qt.)
2 qts. celery   1 c. sugar

Heat and put in cans. Boil 3 hrs. in cold packer or 30 min. in pressure cooker with 10 lbs. pressure. Yields 20 qts.

VEGETABLE SOUP

Katie Hershberger

1 bu. okra
8 qts. onions
3 bu. tomatoes
30 qts. corn
7 qts. lima beans
5 stalks celery

2 lbs. carrots
10 lbs. potatoes
12 qts. butter beans
3 qts. string beans
1 box bay leaves
2 boxes salt and some pepper
1 pt. sugar

Cook each vegetable by itself, then mix in a big tub or cooker of some kind. This makes 114 qts. of soup. If using boiling water bath, cook 3 hrs. (qts.). If pressure cooked, 40 min. for qts. I like it best frozen.

HOW TO COOK A HUSBAND

A good many husbands are utterly spoiled by mismanagement in cooking and so are not tender and good. Some women keep them constantly in hot water; others let them freeze by their carelessness and indifference. Some keep them in a stew with irritating ways and words. Some wives keep them pickled, while others waste them shamefully. It cannot be supposed that any husband will be tender and good when so managed, but they are really delicious when prepared properly.

In selecting a husband, you should not be guided by the silvery appearance as in buying a mackerel; nor by the golden tint as if you wanted salmon. Do not go to the market for hi as the best ones are brought to the door. Be sure to select him yourself as tastes differ. It is far better to have none unless you will patiently learn how to cook him.

Of course, a preserving kettle of the finest porcelain is best, but if you have nothing better than an earthenware pipkin, it will do - with care. Like crabs and lobsters, husbands are cooked alive. They sometimes fly out of the kettle and so become burned and crusty on the edges, so it is wise to secure him in the kettle with a strong silken cord called Comfort, as the one called Duty is apt to be weak. Make a clear, steady flame of love, warmth and cheerfulness. Set him as near this as seems to agree with him.

If he sputters, do not be anxious, for some husbands do this until they are quite done. Add a little sugar in the form of what confectioners call kisses, but use no pepper or vinegar on any account. Season to taste with spices, good humor and gaiety preferred, but seasoning must always be used with great discretion and caution. Avoid sharpness in testing him for tenderness. Stir him gently, lest he lie too flat and close to the kettle and becomes useless. You cannot fail to know when he is done. If so treated, you will find him very digestible, agreeing with you perfectly; and he will keep as long as you choose unless you become careless and allow the home first to grow cold. Thus prepared, he will serve a lifetime of happiness.

42

ANGEL FOOD CAKE

Edna Yoder

1½ c. sugar
1¼ c. cake flour
2 c. egg whites

¼ t. salt
1 t. vanilla
1¼ t. cream of tartar

Sift together 3 times 1½ c. sugar, cake flour. Then beat to soft peaks the egg whites, salt, vanilla and cream of tartar. Gradually add ⅓ c. sugar t'll real stiff. Fold in sifted flour and sugar mixture. Rinse out tube pan. Put batter in tube pan and bake 375° for 40 min.

CHIFFON CAKE

Mrs. Chris L. Miller

1⅛ c. sifted cake flour
¾ c. sugar
1½ t. baking powder
½ t. salt
¼ c. salad oil

⅜ c. water
2 egg yolks
1 t. flavoring
½ c. egg whites
¼ t. cream of tartar

Mix and sift first 4 ingredients. Make a well, and add salad oil, water, egg yolks and flavoring. Beat until smooth. Add cream of tartar to egg whites. Beat until egg whites form very stiff peaks. Gently fold first mixture into egg whites until well-blended. Fold, do not stir. Bake in ungreased 9" tube pan in moderate over 325° for 1 hr., or until cake springs back when pressed with finger. Invert pan on rack until cold. To remove from pan, loosen from side and tube with spatula.

TO MAKE A CAKE...

Light oven; get out utensils and ingredients. Remove blocks and toy autos from table.
Grease pan, crack nuts.
Measure 2 cups of flour; remove Johnny's hands from flour; wash flour off him. Remeasure flour.
Put flour, baking powder and salt in sifter. Get dustpan and brush up pieces of bowl Johnny knocked on floor. Get another bowl. Answer doorbell.
Return to kitchen. Remove Johnny's hands from bowl. Wash Johnny. Answer phone.
Return. Remove ¼" salt from greased pan. Look for Johnny. Grease another pan. Answer phone.
Return to kitchen and find Johnny. Remove his hands from bowl. Take up greased pan and find layer of nutshells in it. Head for Johnny who flees, knocking bowl off table.
Wash kitchen floor, table, walls, dishes. Call baker. Lie down.

COCOA CHIFFON CAKE
Mrs. Eli (Leona) Hostetler

1/2 c. baking cocoa	1 1/2 c. sugar
3/4 c. boiling water	1 1/2 t. baking soda
8 eggs, separated	1 t. salt
1/2 t. cream of tartar	1/2 c. salad oil
1 3/4 c. sifted cake flour	2 t. vanilla

Mix cocoa with boiling water. Beat egg whites with cream of tartar until very stiff peaks form. Sift together dry ingredients into a mixing bowl. Make a well in the center. Add oil, egg yolks, cocoa mixture and vanilla; beat well. Fold in egg whites. Pour into 10" tube pan. Cut through batter with spatula. Bake 325° for 55 min., then 350° for 10 min. Invert to cool. Frost with your favorite chocolate frosting.

If you wish, decorate edges with chocolate glaze made by melting together 2 squares unsweetened chocolate and 2 t. butter over low heat. Cool slightly. Spoon along edge of frosted cake, allowing chocolate to drip down sides.

MAPLE CHIFFON CAKE
Mrs. Sol Yoder

1 1/2 c. all-purpose flour	7 egg yolks, beaten
1 1/2 c. sugar	3/4 c. cold water
3 t. baking powder	1 t. maple extract
1 t. salt	1 c. egg whites
1/2 c. salad oil	1/2 t. cream of tartar

Blend flour, sugar, baking powder, salt thoroughly. Make a hole and add in order, oil, egg yolks, cold water, and maple flavoring. Beat with electric mixer until smooth. Measure egg whites into large mixing bowl and add cream of tartar. Beat until very stiff peaks are formed. Pour egg yolk mixture over beaten egg whites, folding in gently until blended. Pour into ungreased tube pan. Bake in slow oven at 325° for 55 min., then turn oven to 350° for 15 min. Turn pan upside-down until cold before removing from pan.

When painting woodwork, cover door knobs,
and other hardware with vaseline.
If paint splashes where it shouldn't,
it can be wiped off easily.

SPICE CHIFFON CAKE

Becky Plank

2 c. sifted flour
1 1/2 c. sugar
3 t. baking powder
1 t. salt
1 t. cinnamon
1/2 t. nutmeg
1/2 t. allspice

1/2 t. cloves
1 c. egg whites
1 t. cream of tartar
1/2 c. Wesson oil
All egg yolks
3/4 c. cold water
2 t. vanilla

Sift all dry ingredients together 3 times. Set aside. Whip egg whites and cream of tartar till very stiff. Mix oil, water, egg yolks, and vanilla. Add to flour mixture, mix well. Fold in egg whites. Pour into 10" tube pan and bake 325° for 55 min., then 350° for 15 min. Turn upside-down to cool.

1-2-3-4 CAKE

Ruth Yoder

1 c. Crisco
2 c. sugar
3 c. flour
1/4 t. salt

3 t. baking powder
4 eggs
1 c. water
Add coconut or nuts, if desired

Cream Crisco and sugar. Mix dry ingredients and add alternately with eggs and water. Add coconut or nuts, if desired. Put in loaf pan and bake 325° for 40 min. Do not overbake!

COCONUT CAKE ICING:
2 c. sugar
3/4 c. milk

1 T. butter

Boil to soft ball stage; cool; add 1 c. coconut; spread on cake.

When cream will not whip,
add the white of an egg to your cream - chill it, then whip it.

$100 CAKE

Elsie N. Yoder

4 oz. chocolate square
1 stick butter
2 c. sugar
2 eggs
2 c. flour
2 t. baking powder
1/2 t. salt
1 1/2 c. milk
1 c. nuts
2 t. vanilla

ICING:
1 stick butter
2 oz. chocolate square
1 1/2 c. powdered sugar
1 pinch salt
1 t. lemon juice
1 t. vanilla
1 c. nuts

Sift and mix salt, flour, baking powder. Cream butter and sugar well. Add eggs, 1 at a time, and beat well. Add milk, melted chocolate, nuts and vanilla. Pour in tube pan and bake 350° for 1 hr. Cool. Melt chocolate squares for icing. Beat butter, add rest of ingredients and mix well.

APPLE CAKE

Ruth Yoder, Verna Mae Wingard,
and Mrs. Leslie Yoder

4 c. apples (grated coarsely)
2 c. sugar
2 eggs
1/2 c. oil
2 t. vanilla

2 c. flour
2 t. soda
2 t. cinnamon
1 t. salt
1 c. chopped nuts

Mix sugar with apples. Set aside. Beat eggs slightly, then beat in oil, vanilla, and apples. Mix and sift dry ingredients and stir into apple mixture. Add nuts, and pour into greased loaf pan. Serve with Cinnamon Sauce, and top with whipped cream or ice cream. Bake at 350° for 30-35 min.

CINNAMON SAUCE:
2 c. brown sugar
1 t. cinnamon

1 1/2 c. water
1/4 c. clear gel or cornstarch

Mix and cook until thick and clear; remove from heat and add 2 T. butter.

Apple Cake is very good with caramel icing, also.

APPLE CAKE
Kathryn Yoder

3 c. flour
2 c. sugar
1 t. soda
1 t. cinnamon
1 t. salt
3 eggs

1⅓ c. salad oil
2 t. vanilla
1 c. raisins
1 c. nuts
3 c. chopped apples

Combine first 7 ingredients and mix well. Add rest of ingredients and pour in greased and floured 13x9x2" cake pan and bake 325° for 1 hr.

DRUSILLA'S DELICIOUS APPLE CAKE
Ruth Yoder

1½ c. flour
1 c. sugar
1 t. soda
½ t. baking powder
¼ t. salt

½ c. shortening
1 egg
2 c. finely-chopped apples
½ c. milk
1 T. vanilla

Mix first 7 ingredients together and mix well. Add milk, apples and vanilla. Put crumbs on top of cake dough and bake in loaf cake pan 350° for 30 min.

CRUMB TOPPING:
½ c. brown sugar
2 T. soft butter

½ c. chopped nuts
1 T. flour

Put crumbs on top of cake dough and bake.

POP'S APPLE CAKE
Mrs. Allen E. Yoder

2 c. sugar
3 c. flour
2 t. soda
2 t. salt
2 t. cinnamon
1⅓ c. oil

2 eggs
2 t. vanilla
4 c. peeled & chopped apples
½ c. raisins
½ c. nuts

Combine sugar, flour, soda, salt and cinnamon in bowl. Add oil, eggs, and vanilla; mix well. Stir in apples, raisins and nuts. Pour in 13x9" pan and bake 325° for 1 hr. A cream cheese frosting makes it delicious!

BANANA CAKE
Lila Yoder

1⅓ c. sugar
½ c. oleo
2 eggs
1 c. mashed ripe bananas
2 t. baking powder

½ c. buttermilk
½ c. chopped nuts, if desired
1 t. soda
¾ t. salt
1 t. vanilla
2 c. flour

Cream sugar, oleo and eggs. Add dry ingredients alternately with mashed bananas and buttermilk. Pour into greased pan and bake 350° 25-30 min. 2-9" pans or 9x13" pan.

BANANA CAKE
Mrs. Isaac Plank, Elsie N. Yoder

2 c. brown sugar
½ c. butter
1 c. mashed bananas
1 t. soda

2 eggs
¾ c. sour milk
2 c. flour
1 t. baking powder

Beat eggs, butter, brown sugar and bananas - add flour, soda and baking powder along with milk. Pour in 9x12" pan and bake 350° for 30 min. or until done.

BANANA CAKE
Vernie Weaver, Ruby Swartzentruber

1½ c. sugar
¾ c. sour milk
Pinch of salt
1 c. mashed bananas
1 t. soda

½ c. shortening
1 t. baking powder
1 egg
2 c. flour
1 t. vanilla

Cream sugar and shortening. Add egg. Sift flour, baking powder, salt and soda. Add alternately with milk. Add bananas and vanilla. Pour into 2-9" pans or 1-9x13" pan. Bake 350° for 30 min.

Blessed is the person who is too busy in the daytime and too tired at night.

FIESTA BANANA CAKE

Linda Kauffman

2 c. cake flour
1 t. soda
1 t. baking powder
3/4 t. salt
1 1/3 c. sugar
1/2 c. butter or shortening

1/2 c. sour milk or buttermilk
1 t. vanilla
1 c. banana pulp
1/2 c. chopped nuts
2 eggs, unbeaten

Mix dry ingredients with shortening. Add 1/4 c. of the milk, then the bananas. Beat 2 min. Add eggs, vanilla, nuts and remaining milk. Beat 1 min. longer. Bake at 350° for 25 min. in 9" layers or longer in 9x13x2" loaf pan.

BANANA SPLIT CAKE

JoAnn Inhulsen

1 pkg. yellow cake mix or
   favorite yellow cake
1-8 oz. pkg. cream cheese
2-3 oz. pkgs. instant banana
   pudding

2 c. milk
1-20 oz. can pineapple pie filling
1 medium-size Cool Whip

Bake in rectangular cake pan 350° approximately 30 min. Bake cake as diected on box.

Blend together cream cheese, banana pudding and milk. Spread on cake that has been split, making 2 layers. Spread pineapple pie filling on top of cream cheese mixture. Replace top layer of cake and ice with Cool Whip. Place in freezer until about 1 hr. before serving. Keep refrigerated.

"A LOVE CAKE FOR MOTHER"

1 can of "obedience"
Several lbs. of "affection"
1 pt. of "neatness"
Some holiday, birthday, and everyday "surprises"
1 can of "running errands" (willing brand)
1 box powdered "get up when I should"
1 bottle of "keep sunny all day long"
1 can of "pure thoughtfulness"

Mix well, bake in a hearty warm oven and serve to "mother" every-day. She ought to have it in big slices.

BLUE RIBBON BANANA CAKE   Ruth Yoder

3/4 c. shortening
1 1/2 c. sugar
2 eggs
1 c. mashed bananas
2 c. sifted flour
1 t. baking soda
1 t. baking powder

1/2 t. salt
1/2 c. buttermilk
1 t. vanilla
1/2 c. chopped pecans
1 c. flaked coconut
Creamy Nut Filling (recipe follows)

Cream together shortening and sugar in mixing bowl unti llight and fluffy at medium speed of electric mixer. Add eggs; beat 2 more min. Add bananas, beat 2 more min. Sift together flour, soda, baking powder, and salt. Add dry ingredients alternately with buttermilk to creamed mixture, beating well after each addition. Add vanilla; beat 2 min. Stir in pecans. Turn into 2 greased and floured 9" round cake pans. Sprinkle 1/2 c. coconut on each layer. Bake in 375° 25-30 min., or until cake tests done. Remove from pans, cool on racks.

CREAMY NUT FILLING:
1/2 c. sugar
2 T. flour
1/2 c. light cream

2 T. butter
1/2 c. chopped pecans
1 t. vanilla

Combine sugar, flour, light cream and butter in saucepan. Cook, stirring constantly, until thickened. Stir in pecans, salt and vanilla; cool. Spread Creamy Nut Filling between layers. Frost cake with white frosting.

Wisdom—knowing what to do.
Skill—knowing how to do it.
Virtue—doing it.

BOSTON CREAM CAKE

Mrs. Daniel Swartzentruber

1½ c. flour
1 c. sugar
2 eggs
⅓ c. shortening
2 t. baking powder
½ t. salt
1 t. vanilla
⅔ c. milk
1 lg. box vanilla pudding
  (not instant)

RICHMOND CHOCOLATE ICING:
¾ c. sugar
1 T. cocoa
Pinch of salt
½ c. boiling water
2 T. butter
1 t. vanilla

Cream shortening and sugar together. Add eggs and beat well. Sift flour, baking powder, and salt. Add slowly to rest of mixture. Add vanilla and milk. Pour into 13x9x2" pan and bake 350° 22-23 min. Cut cake in half lengthwise. Prepare pudding as directed on box. Cool and spread on bottom layer of cake. Place other layer on top and frost with icing.

RICHMOND CHOCOLATE ICING: Mix sugar, salt and cocoa together. Dissolve cornstarch in a small amount of water and add to dry ingredients. Add water and cool. If too thick, add more water. Remove from heat and add butter and vanilla. Spread on cake immediately.

BUTTER GOLDEN CAKE OR CHESS CAKE

Mrs. Stanley Yoder,
Katie Hershberger

1 box butter recipe cake mix
1 stick butter or margarine
  (melted)
1 egg

1-8 oz. pkg. cream cheese
3 eggs
1 box confectioners' sugar
1 t. vanilla

Combine cake mix, melted butter and 1 egg. Mix thoroughly. (Will be very thick.) Press into a lightly-greased 13x9x2" baking pan; set aside. Combine cream cheese, 3 eggs, confectioners' sugar, and vanilla. Beat with electric mixer until smooth and pour over crust in baking pan. Bake 350° 40-45 min. Cool completely and cut into squares. The cake will fall as it cools, making thin, chewy squares similar to a Chess Pie.

It's better to discipline your appetites than to be defeated by them.

BUTTERMILK CAKE
Mrs. William N. Yoder

2½ c. flour
1½ t. baking powder
½ t. soda
½ t. salt
1⅔ c. sugar

¾ c. shortening
1 c. buttermilk
1 T. vanilla
4 eggs, unbeaten

Sift the first 5 ingredients in mixing bowl. Add shortening and 1/2 c. of the buttermilk; mix well. Then add one egg at a time; beat well after each one. Then add rest of buttermilk and vanilla. Bake 350° 30-35 min. 3-9" layer pans.

CAKE THAT DOESN'T LAST
Alma Yoder, Lorene Plank

3 c. flour
2 c. sugar
3 eggs, beaten
1½ c. cooking oil
1-8 oz. can crushed pineapple
1 c. nuts

1 t. baking soda
1 t. salt
1 t. cinnamon
1 t. vanilla
2 c. mashed bananas

Mix dry ingredients in a large bowl. Make a well in the center. Add eggs, pineapple, nuts, oil, vanilla and bananas. Stir, do not beat (will take only a few stirs to mix). Pour into a greased and floured tube pan. Bake 350° for 75 min.

CARAMEL CAKE
Esther R. Yoder

1 c. butter or margarine
2 c. sugar
3 c. Swans Down cake flour or
   all-purpose flour
3 t. baking powder

½ t. salt
1¼ c. milk
4 eggs
1 t. almond & 1 t. vanilla flavoring
For extra-fine texture, add 1 more
   egg.

Cream butter and sugar; add eggs, one at a time. Blend in flour and baking powder. Add salt and milk. Beat mixture for 2 min., then pour into 3-8" greased and floured pans. Bake 350° 25-30 min.
CARAMEL ICING: 3½ c. brown sugar, ¾ c. of milk (1 small can of evaporated milk). Melt all ingredients together in a saucepan till sugar crystals are dissolved. Cool till icing is just a little warm. Put on cake.

CARROT CAKE
Mrs. Daniel Yoder

1 t. soda
2 t. cinnamon
2¼ c. flour
2 t. baking powder
1 t. salt
1½ c. oil

2 c. sugar
5 eggs
1 c. pineapple
2 c. grated carrots
2 t. vanilla
½ c. nuts

Beat oil and sugar. Add eggs, one at a time, beat well. Sift together dry ingredients and add gradually. Mix well and add vanilla, carrots, pineapple and nuts. Bake in tube or layer pans 350° for 50 min. Frost with cream cheese frosting.

CARTER CAKE
Delores Hostetler

½ c. butter
1 c. dry-roasted peanuts or
   pecans (chopped)
1 c. flour
1-8 oz. pkg. cream cheese
1 c. confectioners' sugar
1 c. smooth peanut butter

1-8 oz. container whipped topping
1 sm. box instant vanilla pudding
1 sm. box instant choc. pudding
2½ c. milk
⅔ c. dry-roasted peanuts or
   pecans (chopped)

Cream butter until softened; mix in 1 c. chopped peanuts or pecans. Add flour. Pat mixture in 9x13" pan and bake 350° for 20 min. Then cool. Combine cream cheese, confectioners' sugar, peanut butter, and 1 c. whipped topping. Spread evenly over cooled crust. Combine vanilla and chocolate instant puddings with milk. Beat with mixer till combined. Spread evenly over cream cheese layer. Spread remaining whipped topping on top. Sprinkle with ⅔ c. chopped peanuts or pecans.

GOURMET CHEESECAKE
Ruth Yoder

1 box zwieback, crushed
3 T. sugar
3 T. butter, melted
2 t. cinnamon

6 eggs
3-8 oz. pkgs. cream cheese
½ c. flour
1½ c. sour cream
1½ T. lemon juice
1 t. vanilla

Grease springform pan. Mix zwieback with sugar, butter and cinnamon; mix well and press in bottom and side of springform pan. Beat egg whites till frothy, add ¾ c. sugar gradually, beat until stiff peaks form. Combine egg yolks, ¾ c. sugar, cream cheese, flour, sour cream, lemon juice and vanilla; beat till smooth. Fold in egg whites into cream cheese mixture. Pour into pan and top with remaining zwieback crumbs. Bake at 350° for 1 hour. Let cool in oven 1 more hr.

MARTHA'S CHEESECAKE

Mrs. Levi Kauffman

1 pt. whipped cream	2 pkgs. gelatine
2-8 oz. bars cream cheese	Sugar, lemon and vanilla to taste

Dissolve gelatine in 1/2 c. boiling water. Mix all ingredients together and put on top of graham cracker crust in a springform pan. Chill until set.

GRAHAM CRACKER CRUST: 2 c. crumbs, 1/4 c. sugar, 1/3 c. buttter. Mix and press in bottom of springform pan. Bake the crust at 375° for 8 min.

CHOCOLATE CAKE

Verda Overholt, Lorene Plank

1/2 c. shortening	1/4 t. salt
1 3/4 c. sugar	1 1/4 t. soda
2 eggs	1/2 c. sour milk or buttermilk
1/2 c. cocoa	1 c. boiling water
2 1/2 c. cake flour	1 t. vanilla

Cream shortening and add sugar gradually. Beat until fluffy. Add eggs and continue to beat. Add vanilla. Sift flour; measure and sift again with cocoa and salt. Add alternately with sour milk. Add soda to boiling water; when dissolved, add all at once to mixture. Stir only enough to blend ingredients well. This makes a very thin batter. Bake in loaf pan or 2-8" layer pans, at 350° for 25-30 min.

CHOCOLATE CHIP CAKE

Mrs. Nelson Yoder

1 box yellow cake mix	4 eggs
1-3 oz. box instant vanilla	1/2 c. oil
pudding	6 oz. chocolate chips
1 c. commercial sour cream	

Beat eggs. Add remaining ingredients and bake in a tube pan. 350° for 1 hr. Let cool in pan.

Confession is good for the soul,
though it may be hard for the flesh and the reputation.

CHOCOLATE HAND-ME-DOWN CAKE   Irene Yoder

³/₄ c. margarine   1³/₄ c. sugar
2 eggs   1 t. vanilla
2 c. flour   1¹/₄ t. soda
³/₄ c. cocoa   ¹/₂ t. salt
1¹/₃ c. water

Cream margarine and sugar, add eggs and vanilla. Add flour, soda, cocoa, and salt. Gradually add water. Bake 350° for 40 min. 2-8" layer pans.

FILLING FOR TOP AND MIDDLE OF CAKE:
1 egg white, unbeaten   2 c. powdered sugar
2 T. milk   1 t. vanilla
¹/₂ c. shortening

Mix egg white, milk and vanilla. Beat in powdered sugar and spread on cake layers. Put chocolate icing around outside edge of cake.

CHOCOLATE LOVERS FAVORITE CAKE   Mary Lois Yoder

1 c. flour   4 eggs
1 t. baking powder   1-16 oz. can Hershey's
1 stick butter   chocolate syrup
1 c. sugar   1 t. vanilla
                                Pinch of salt

FUDGE ICING:
1 c. sugar   ¹/₂ c. chocolate chips
1 stick butter (not margarine) ¹/₃ c. evaporated milk
                                ¹/₂ t. vanilla

Sift flour, baking powder and salt together. In a large bowl, cream butter, adding sugar gradually. Add eggs, one at a time. Alternate adding dry ingredients and chocolate syrup. Beat well. Add vanilla, pour into greased 13x9x2" pan. Bake 350° for 30 min.

FUDGE ICING: Put all ingredients except vanilla in a heavy sauce-pan, stirring constantly, until mixture comes to a boil. Boil 3 min. Remove from heat and add vanilla. Beat icing with a spoon until thick, cool a little, then spread icing on cake. Cut into squares when cool.

CHOCOLATE WACKY CAKE

Ruby Swartzentruber,
Mary Yoder

3 c. flour
2 c. sugar
3 T. cocoa
2 t. soda
1/2 t. salt

ADD:
3/4 c. cooking oil
2 T. vinegar
1 T. vanilla
2 c. cold water

Put all ingredients in bowl before mixing. A very moist cake. Bake 350° for 45 min.

COCA-COLA CAKE

Lena Swartzentruber,
Mrs. Paul E. Yoder

CAKE:
2 T. cocoa
1 1/2 c. sugar
1 c. butter
2 eggs
1 c. cola

2 c. flour
1 t. vanilla
1/2 c. buttermilk
1 t. soda
1 c. sm. marshmallows

FROSTING:
2 T. butter
3 T. cocoa

4 T. cola
2 1/2 c. powdered sugar

Cream butter and sugar, add eggs and beat. Bring cola and cocoa to a boil and add to butter mixture. Add vanilla, buttermilk, flour, soda, and last add marshmallows. Pour in 13x9" pan and bake 350° 25-30 min. Ice cake while a little warm.

FROSTING: Bring butter, cola and cocoa to a boil. Remove from heat, add sugar and beat. Spread on cake while warm.

The smallest pleasure is big enough to share.

COCO LIGHT CAKE

Mrs. Rufus L. Yoder
Mrs. Lloyd Swartzentruber,
Mrs. Salome K. Yoder

2 c. sifted flour
2 c. sugar
1 t. salt
2/3 c. cocoa
1/2 c. Crisco
3/4 c. milk

1 1/2 t. soda
1/2 t. baking powder
1/2 c. milk
3 eggs (unbeaten)
1 t. vanilla

DIVINITY ICING:
1 1/2 c. white Karo syrup
3 eggs whites

1 t. vanilla
3/4 c. chopped pecans

Measure flour, sugar, salt, cocoa, Crisco, 3/4 c. milk into mixing bowl. Mix well. Add soda and baking powder. Mix. Add 1/2 c. milk, 3 eggs (unbeaten), and vanilla. Bake 350° 30 min. 3-9" pans.

ICING: Boil syrup until a thread of syrup cracks in cold water. Beat egg whites until stiff. Pour hot syrup slowly over egg whites, beating constantly until icing is the consistency to spread. Stir in nuts.

DELICIOUS MOIST CHOCOLATE CAKE   Mrs. Ernest W. Yoder

2 c. sugar
2 c. flour
1/2 c. margarine
1/2 c. Crisco
4 T. cocoa

1 c. water
1/2 c. buttermilk
2 eggs, slightly beaten
1 t. soda
1 t. vanilla

FROSTING:
1/2 c. margarine
6 T. milk
4 t. cocoa

1 box powdered sugar
1 t. vanilla
1 c. pecans

Sift sugar and flour together. Melt margarine and Crisco; add cocoa and water. Bring to rapid boil. Then add to sugar mixture. Mix well, add buttermilk, eggs, soda, vanilla and mix well. Bake 400° for 20 min. 16x11" cake pan.

FROSTING: Melt margarine, milk and cocoa. Bring to a boil and remove from heat. Stir powdered sugar into it. Add vanilla and pecans. Put Frosting on cake right after coming out of oven. Frosting may seem runny, but as cake cools, frosting will harden.

GERMAN CHOCOLATE CAKE   Ruth Yoder

1-4 oz. German sweet chocolate 4 eggs (separated)
1/2 c. boiling water   1 t. vanilla
2 c. sugar   1 t. baking soda
1 c. butter or margarine   1/2 t. salt
2 1/4 c. sifted all-purpose flour   1 c. buttermilk
  or use 2 1/2 c. sifted Swans
  Down cake flour

Melt chocolate in boiling water. Cool. Cream butter and sugar until
fluffy. Add egg yolks, 1 at a time, beating well after each. Blend in
vanilla and chocolate. Sift flour with soda and salt. Add alternately
with buttermilk to chocolate mixture, beating after each addition until
smooth. Fold in stiffly-beaten egg whites. Line bottom of pans with
wax paper. Bake 350° 30-35 min. 3-9" layer pans. Cool. Frost tops
only.
COCONUT-PECAN FROSTING: Combine 1 c. evaporated milk, 1 c.
sugar, 3 slightly-beaten egg yolks, 1/2 c. butter or margarine and
1 t. vanilla. Cook and stir over medium heat until thickened, about
12 min. Add 1 1/3 c. flaked coconut and 1 c. chopped pecans. Cool
until thick enough to spread, beating occasionally. Makes 2 1/2 cups.

GEORGIA PEANUT BUTTER FUDGE CAKE   Ruth Yoder

1 c. butter   2 c. all-purpose flour
4 T. cocoa   1 t. baking soda
1 c. water   2 eggs, beaten
1 c. buttermilk   1 t. vanilla
2 c. sugar   2 c. crunchy peanut butter

FROSTING:
1/2 c. butter   1 box powdered sugar
4 T. cocoa   1 t. vanilla
6 T. buttermilk

In saucepan, combine first 4 ingredients, bring to a boil. Set aside.
Sift sugar, flour and soda into large mixing bowl; pour cocoa mixture
over sifted ingredients; mix well. Stir in eggs and vanilla. Pour into
a well-greased 9x13" pan. Bake 350° 25-30 min. Cool in pan, warm
peanut butter to spreading consistency and spread on cold cake.
Cover with Frosting.
FROSTING: In saucepan, combine cocoa, butter and buttermilk.
Bring to a boil. Place powdered sugar and vanilla in large mixing
bowl, then add cocoa mixture. Spread over cake.

FUDGE CAKE

Mrs. Stanley Yoder

³/₄ c. butter or margarine
2¹/₄ c. sugar
1¹/₂ t. vanilla
3 eggs
3-1 oz. sqs. unsweetened
  chocolate or 3 t. cocoa

3 c. sifted flour
1¹/₂ t. soda
³/₄ t. salt
1¹/₂ c. ice water

Cream butter, sugar, and vanilla. Add eggs, beating until light and fluffy. Add melted chocolate or cocoa, and blend well. Sift together dry ingredients. Add alternately with water to chocolate mixture. Bake in 3-9" layer pans. 325° to 350° 30-35 min.

FROSTING FOR FUDGE CAKE:
1 lg. can evaporated milk
1 c. sugar
1 stick margarine

3 egg yolks
1¹/₃ c. flaked coconut
1¹/₄ c. chopped pecans
1 t. vanilla

Melt margarine in saucepan. Add sugar and 1 c. milk. Heat to almost boiling point, then add remaining milk to which beaten egg yolks have been added. Bring to a full bubbling boil. Remove from heat and add coconut, chopped pecans, and vanilla. Cool to spreading consistency.

PAULINE'S COCONUT CAKE

Ruth Yoder

³/₄ c. shortening
1¹/₂ c. sugar
2¹/₄ c. flour
1 t. salt

3 t. baking powder
1 c. milk
5 egg whites

ICING:
³/₄ c. shortening
2 or 3 unbeaten egg whites

3 T. milk

Cream sugar and shortening. Sift dry ingredients and add alternately with milk and stiffly-beaten egg whites. Bake at 350° for 20 min. 3-8" pans.

ICING: Mix and add powdered sugar until Icing is thick enough. Add 1 t. vanilla and put coconut all over cake.

CREAMY COCONUT CAKE

Elsie Yoder

1/2 c. shortening
1/2 c. butter (softened)
2 c. sugar
5 eggs, separated
1 t. soda
1 t. salt
1 c. buttermilk
2 c. flour
1 t. vanilla

2/3 c. flaked coconut
Pinch of cream of tartar
COCONUT PECAN FROSTING:
1-8 oz. cream cheese, softened
1/2 c. butter or margarine,
    softened
1-16 oz. pkg. powdered sugar
1 t. vanilla
Dash of salt
1/2 c. flaked coconut
1/2 c. chopped pecans

Cream shortening, butter, sugar until light and fluffy. Add egg yolks, one at a time, beating well after each addition. Combine flour, soda, and salt. Add to creamed mixture alternately with buttermilk, beginning and ending with flour. Beat well after each addition. Add vanilla and coconut. Beat egg whites, add cream of tartar and continue beating until egg whites are stiff, but not dry. Fold in batter. Pour in 3-9" pans. Bake 350° for 30 min.
COCONUT PECAN FROSTING: Cream together cream cheese and butter; stir in powdered sugar, vanilla and salt. Fold in coconut and pecans.

COFFEECAKE

Sadie A. Yoder

1/2 c. shortening
2 eggs
1 t. soda
1 t. salt

2 c. brown sugar
2 1/8 c. flour
1 t. cinnamon
1 1/2 c. buttermilk

TOPPING:
3/4 c. flour
1 c. brown sugar

2 T. shortening

Cream together shortening and sugar. Add eggs. Sift together salt, flour, soda and cinnamon. Add buttermilk alternately with dry ingredients.

FOR TOPPING: Make fine crumbs and sprinkle over batter, bake until done; 35-45 min. at 350°.

*Middle age is when you have all the answers
and nobody asks you the questions.*

CRUMB COFFEECAKE

Elsie N. Yoder

2 c. sifted flour
1 t. baking powder
1 t. soda
1 t. salt
1/3 c. butter
1 c. sugar
2 eggs, beaten
1 c. sour cream

1 1/2 t. vanilla
TOPPING:
1/3 c. brown sugar
1 t. cinnamon
1/4 c. sugar
1 c. finely-chopped pecans
Combine all ingredients and mix well.

Sift flour with baking powder, soda, and salt. Cream butter with sugar until fluffy and light. Add eggs and beat well. Alternate adding the dry ingredients with the sour cream. Beat until smooth. Add vanilla. Pour half batter into buttered and lightly floured 9x9" pan. Cover with half of the Topping. Pour in remaining batter and sprinkle the remaining Topping over all. Bake at 325° for 45 min.

SOUR CREAM COFFEECAKE

Verna Mae Wingard

2 sticks oleo
6 eggs (separated)
3 c. sugar
3 c. flour

1/4 t. soda
1 c. sour cream
1 t. almond or maple flavoring
1/4 t. salt

CRUMB MIXTURE:
1 c. nuts
1 1/2 t. sugar

2 1/2 t. cinnamon

Cream oleo and sugar. Add egg yolks and beat well. Mix flour, salt and soda and add to creamed mixture. Add sour cream and flavoring. Beat egg whites stiff and fold in. Alternate layers of batter and crumb mixture in greased tube pan and bake 350° 45-60 min. CRUMB MIXTURE: Mix well.

The true measure of God's love is that
He loves without measure.

SOUR CREAM COFFEECAKE

Mary Lois Yoder,
Mrs. Paul E. Yoder

2 sticks butter
1¼ c. sugar
1 c. sour cream
2 eggs

2 c. flour
1 t. baking powder
¼ t. salt
½ t. soda
1 t. vanilla

FILLING:
1 c. nuts, chopped
2½ t. cinnamon

1½ t. sugar

Cream butter, sugar, and sour cream. Add eggs and vanilla and beat well. Add dry ingredients. In separate bowl combine Filling ingredients. In tube pan, sprinkle ⅓ of Filling, top with ½ of batter. Alternate layers, ending with batter. Bake 350° for 45 min.

CRUMB CAKE

Mrs. Robert Paul Yoder

2 c. brown sugar
½ c. shortening
2½ c. flour
1 t. cinnamon

¼ c. pecans
1 egg
1 c. buttermilk
1 t. soda

Mix together first 4 ingredients. Take out ½ c. crumbs for top and add ¼ c. pecans. To the rest add egg and buttermilk, in which 1 t. soda has been dissolved. Pour in 8x12" or 2-9" pans. Sprinkle crumbs over top and bake 375° for 30 min.

DESSERT CAKE

Laura Whitt

1 box yellow cake mix (or devil's food cake)

1-13 oz. Cool Whip
2-6 oz. frozen coconut

1-6 oz. sour cream
Small amount of confectioners' sugar to taste

Bake cake according to directions and put in 2-9" pans. Mix together Cool Whip, sour cream and 1 package coconut and sugar. Spread between layers of cake. Sprinkle remaining package of coconut on layers, on top and side of cake.

EASY FRUITCAKE

Linda Kauffman, Ruth Yoder

5 lg. eggs
2 sticks butter
1 c. sugar
1¾ c. flour
½ t. baking powder

1 lb. candied cherries
1 lb. candied pineapple
4 c. coarsely-chopped pecans
1 T. vanilla
1 T. lemon extract

Cream together butter and sugar. Add eggs and blend well. Chop the fruit with about half the flour and baking powder mixture. Add nuts and flavorings and mix all together. Pour into large bundt pan or 2 to 3 bread pans, as preferred. Place in cool oven, then bake at 250° for 2 hrs.

HAPPINESS CAKE

Linda Yoder

1 c. good thoughts
1 c. consideration for others
2 c. well-beaten faults

1 c. kind deeds
2 c. sacrifice
3 c. forgiveness

Mix thoroughly, add tears of joy, sorrow, and sympathy. Flavor with love and kindly service. Fold in 4 c. of prayer and faith. Blend well. Fold into daily life. Bake well with the warmth of human kindness and serve with a smile. It will satisfy the hunger of starved souls.

ADVICE TO THE HOUSEWIFE

Well mix and bake the dainty cake,
And beat the frosting light;
The sweetest plan to please a man
is through his appetite.

HO-HO CAKE
Mrs. Leslie Yoder

3 c. flour
2 c. sugar
2/3 c. cocoa
1 1/2 t. salt
2 t. vanilla

2 eggs
2 t. soda
1 c. boiling water
1 c. sour milk
1 c. vegetable oil

Mix all ingredients together and put in 3-9" pans. Bake 350° for 30 min. Cool, then put Filling on top.

FILLING:
1/2 c. Crisco
1/2 c. oleo
1 t. vanilla

1 c. white sugar
2 egg whites
1/2 c. hot milk

Cream shortening and sugar, add egg whites and vanilla. Beat well. Add hot milk, a little at a time. Beat till creamy.

FROSTING:
1 stick oleo
2 T. cocoa

2 t. vanilla

Add enough powdered sugar to make a thin frosting. Drizzle over top of the Filling.

HUMMINGBIRD CAKE
Mrs. Bertha Yoder, Delores Hostetler

3 c. flour
2 c. sugar
1 t. salt
1 t. soda
1 t. cinnamon
1 1/2 t. vanilla

1 1/2 c. oil
3 eggs, beaten
1 1/2 c. pineapple (crushed and
    undrained)
1 1/2 c. bananas
1 c. nuts
1/2 c. coconut (optional)

With large spoon, mix dry ingredients. Mix eggs and oil and stir into dry ingredients. Add vanilla, pineapple, bananas and nuts. Makes a 3-layer cake, 9" pans. Bake 350° for 30 min. and cool. Frost with cream cheese icing.

ITALIAN CREAM CAKE
Linda Weaver, Mrs. William N. Yoder
(Yoder's Bakery recipe), Mrs. Noah Yoder

1 stick margarine
1/2 c. vegetable shortening
2 c sugar
5 egg yolks
2 c. flour
1 t. soda

1 c. buttermilk
1 t. vanilla
1 sm. can Angel flake coconut
1 c. chopped nuts
5 egg whites (stiffly beaten)

Cream margarine and shortening. Add sugar and beat until mixture is smooth. Add egg yolks and beat well. Combine flour and soda. Add to creamed mixture, alternately with buttermilk. Stir in vanilla. Add coconut and nuts. Fold in egg whites. Pour in 3-9" layer pans or large loaf pan. Bake 350° for 30 min. Frost with cream cheese icing.

ITALIAN CREAM CAKE II
Mary Lois Yoder

1 box yellow cake mix
1-3 oz. box instant vanilla
  pudding
1/4 c. Crisco oil
1 c. water
1 c. coconut
1 c. pecans
4 eggs
1 t. vanilla

CREAM CHEESE FROSTING:
8 oz. cream cheese
1/2 stick margarine
1 box powdered sugar
1 t. vanilla
Pecans

CAKE: Blend all ingredients, except coconut and pecans. Blend for 2 or 3 min., than add coconut and pecans. Makes 3-9" layers or oblong pan. Bake at 350° for 25-30 min, or until done.
FROSTING: Beat cream cheese and margarine until smooth. Add sugar and mix well. Spread on cake. Sprinkle with pecans.

MAYONNAISE CAKE
Mrs. Norman Yoder, Mrs. Noah Yoder

2 c. flour
1 c. sugar
2 t. soda
1/2 t. salt

1/2 c. cocoa
3/4 c. mayonnaise
1 c. cold water
2 t. vanilla

Mix flour, sugar, soda, salt and cocoa together in large bowl. Add mayonnaise, cold water and vanilla. Beat well until it is all blended. Bake in 2 greased and floured 9" cake pans or loaf pan at 350° for 30-40 min.

MILKY WAY CAKE

Verda Overholt

MELT IN A DOUBLE BOILER:
1 stick oleo
4 Milky Way candy bars
CREAM:
1 stick oleo
2 c. sugar

THEN ADD:
4 eggs
2¹/₂ c. flour
¹/₂ t. soda
1 c. buttermilk
Add the butter and Milky Way
   mixture - mix well - pour in pan

Bake 350° 30-35 min. 2-8" pans or oblong pan.

FROSTING:
Melt in double boiler:
1 stick oleo
1¹/₂ Milky Way bars

Then add:
2 T. milk
2 c. powdered sugar

OATMEAL CAKE

Ruth Yoder

1 c. rolied oats
1¹/₄ c. boiling water
1 c. sugar
1 c. brown sugar
¹/₂ c. butter
2 eggs

1¹/₃ c. flour (sifted)
1 t. soda
¹/₂ t. salt
¹/₂ t. cinnamon
¹/₂ c. chopped pecans
1 t.vanilla

TOPPING:
6 T. butter
1 c. brown sugar

¹/₄ c. canned milk
¹/₂ c. coconut
¹/₂ c. chopped pecans

Stir oats in boiling water, remove from heat, cover, let set 20 min.
Cream brown and white sugar, butter and eggs. Add dry ingredients,
oatmeal and vanilla.
TOPPING: Mix Topping real well, put on top of unbaked cake and
bake 350° 35-40 min. 9x13" loaf pan.

Swallow your pride occasionally, it's non-fattening.

OATMEAL CAKE
Mrs. Daniel Yoder, Mrs. Milton Yoder
Mrs. Rufas L. Yoder, Mrs. Melvin (Katherine) Yoder

1 c. rolled oats
1¼ c. boiling water
1 c. sugar
1 c. brown sugar
½ c. margarine
2 eggs

1⅓ c. flour, unsifted
1 t. soda
½ t. salt
½ t. cinnamon
½ c. broken nutmeats
1 t. vanilla

Stir oats in water, remove from heat, cover; let stand 20 min. Cream sugar, brown sugar, margarine, and eggs. Add sifted dry ingredients and nutmeats. Add vanilla and bake 350° 30-40 min. in oblong pan.

TOPPING:
6 T. oleo
1 c. brown sugar
¼ c. canned milk

½ c. coconut
½ c. broken nutmeats

Cook over low heat until it bubbles. Spread on baked cake. Return to oven until it boils again.

OUR FAVORITE CAKE
Esther Ruth Yoder

1 box yellow cake mix
¾ c. oil
1-3 oz. box instant lemon
  pudding
¾ c. water

4 eggs
1 t. vanilla
1 T. butter flavoring

GLAZE:
1 c. powdered sugar
2½ T. butter flavoring

Juice of 1 lemon

Combine cake mix, oil, pudding, and water; mix well. Add eggs and flavoring to cake; mix well. Grease tube pan and pour in ¼ c. nuts, then pour ½ of batter on top, next sprinkle on sugar mix made of ¼ c. sugar, ½ c. nuts, 2 t. cinnamon and pour in remaining batter. Bake 300° for 1 hr. Glaze while warm.

PINEAPPLE CAKE
Naomi Yoder

³/₄ c. shortening
1²/₃ c. sugar
4 eggs
1 t. vanilla
1 c. buttermilk

2¹/₂ c. flour
1¹/₂ t. baking powder
¹/₂ t. salt
¹/₂ t. soda

Cream shortening and sugar together. Add eggs and beat well. Add sifted dry ingredients, alternately with buttermilk and vanilla. Beat well. Bake 350° for 35 min. 3-8" pans.

"ICING" FOR BETWEEN LAYERS:
1¹/₂ c. crushed pineapple
   (undrained)
1¹/₂ c. sugar
3 eggs (beaten)

3 T. cornstarch
¹/₂ c. water

Beat eggs in a saucepan. Add sugar and pineapple. Mix cornstarch with water till dissolved. Heat first 3 ingredients to a boiling point. Add water and cornstarch and cook and stir over low heat till thick. **Cool** and spread between layers of cake.

Ice sides with cream cheese icing or your favorite white icing.

PINEAPPLE CRUNCH CAKE
Mrs. Stanley Yoder

1-20 oz. can crushed pineapple
²/₃ c. shortening
1 c. sugar
2 t. vanilla
2 eggs
2¹/₂ c. sifted flour

3 t. baking powder
¹/₂ t. salt

²/₃ c. brown sugar
²/₃ c. chopped pecans
6 T. butter or margarine, melted

Drain pineapple thoroughly, reserving 1 c. syrup. Thoroughly cream shortening, sugar and vanilla. Add eggs and beat well. Sift together dry ingredients. Add to creamed mixture alternately with reserved syrup, beating after each addition. Spread half of the batter evenly in greased 9x13" cake pan. Spoon pineapple over batter. Cover with remaining batter. Combine brown sugar, chopped pecans and butter. Sprinkle over batter. Bake 350° 35-40 min. Cut in wedges. Serve warm with ice cream.

Cover cake with foil; next day reheat briefly at 350°. Twice - good!

PINEAPPLE UPSIDE-DOWN CAKE   Mrs. Raymond Weaver

1/2 c. butter
1 c. brown sugar
Sliced pineapple circles

3 eggs
1 c. sugar
5 T. pineapple juice
1 c. flour
1 t. baking powder

Melt butter, then add brown sugar and heat; spread evenly in oblong pan. Place pineapple over butter and sugar mixture, covering bottom of pan, then place 1/2 circles all around side. Beat egg yolks. Add sugar and pineapple juice. Sift flour and baking powder. Fold in stiffly-beaten egg whites. Pour batter over pineapple mixture in 9x13" baking pan. Bake 350° 45 min. to 1 hr.

PISTACHIO CREAM CAKE   Mrs. Alva Yoder, Elsie N. Yoder

9 eggs
1 c. + 2 T. sugar
1/4 c. orange juice and rind of
    1 orange

1 c. + 2 T. flour
1/2 t. salt
1 t. cream of tartar

Beat egg yolks well. Add 1/3 c. sugar. Mix well. Add orange juice, rind and flour and rest of sugar. Add salt and cream of tartar to egg whites. Whip until sfiff. Fold into yolk mixture and pour into 10" tube pan. Bake 300° for 1 hr.
ICING: Combine 1 c. sugar, juice and rind of 1 orange, 1/4 c. flour, 1 egg, 1/4 t. salt in top of double boiler. Cook until thick. Fold in 1 c. cream, whipped. Spread over top and sides of cake.

POLKA DOT CAKE   Vernie Brenneman

1 1/4 c. chopped dates
1 c. hot water
3/4 c. shortening
1 c. sugar
2 eggs
1/2 c. nuts

2 c. flour
1 t. soda
1/2 t. salt
1 t. vanilla
1-6 oz. pkg. chips - butterscotch
    or chocolate

Mix dates and hot water; cool. Cream shortening and sugar. Add eggs. Beat until fluffy. Sift dry ingredients. Add to creamed mixture alternately with dates. Mix well after each addition. Stir in vanilla and a few chips and nuts. Spread in greased pan. Sprinkle remaining chips and nuts on batter and bake 350° for 40 min. 9x13" pan. Chips and nuts are frosting.

POUND CAKE   Mrs. William N. Yoder (Yoder's Bakery recipe)

1 c. butter
2 c. sugar
4 eggs, unbeaten
1 t. vanilla
1 t. lemon extract

3 c. flour
1/2 t. soda
1/2 t. baking powder
3/4 t. salt
1 c. buttermilk

Cream butter and sugar thoroughly. Add eggs, one at a time. Beat at medium speed 2 1/2 min. Add flavorings. Sift dry ingredients together and add to ceamed mixture alternately with buttermilk. Beat 3 1/2 min. at medium speed. Do not overbeat or cake will fall. Bake in tube pan 325° for 1 hr. and 10 min.

APPLE POUND CAKE   Mrs. Stanley Yoder

1 1/2 c. corn oil
2 c. sugar
3 eggs
2 t. vanilla
3 c. all-purpose flour
1 t. soda

1 t. salt
1/2 t. ground cinnamon
1/2 t. ground nutmeg
2 c. finely-chopped apples
1 c. chopped nuts
1/2 c. raisins
Apple Cider Glaze (optional)

Beat oil, sugar, eggs, and vanilla until well blended. Sift dry ingredients and add to sugar mixture, beating well. Stir in apples, nuts, and raisins. Spoon batter into a greased and floured 10" tube pan or bundt pan. Bake 325° for 1 hr. and 15 min. Let cake cool 10 min. before removing from pan. If desired, prick top of cake with a fork and drizzle on Apple Cider Glaze.

APPLE CIDER GLAZE:
1/2 c. apple cider or juice
1/4 c. firmly-packed brown sugar

3 T. margarine
1 c. powdered sugar
(more or less)

Combine apple juice, margarine, and brown sugar in small saucepan. Bring to a boil, stirring until sugar is dissolved. Remove from heat and add powdered sugar, beating until spreading consistency. Drizzle on cake while warm.

BUTTERMILK POUND CAKE

Mrs. Norman Yoder

1$\frac{1}{2}$ c. butter (3 sticks)
2$\frac{1}{2}$ c. sugar
3$\frac{1}{2}$ c. flour
$\frac{1}{2}$ t. soda
$\frac{1}{2}$ t. salt

4 eggs
1 c. buttermilk
1 t. vanilla
$\frac{1}{4}$ t. lemon

Cream butter and sugar. sift dry ingredients together. Add eggs, flour mixture and buttermilk alternately. Beat well after each addition. Bake in tube pan 325° for 1 hr. and 15-30 min.

CHOCOLATE POUND CAKE

Mrs. Harley Yoder

$\frac{1}{2}$ lb. butter
$\frac{1}{2}$ c. shortening
3 c. sugar
5 eggs
3 c. flour (all-purpose)

2 t. baking powder
$\frac{1}{2}$ c. cocoa
$\frac{1}{2}$ t. salt
1$\frac{1}{4}$ c. milk
1 T. vanilla

Cream butter, shortening and sugar. Add one egg at a time. Beat until creamy. Add flour and baking powder, cocoa, and salt alternately with milk. Mix well. Add vanilla. Bake in greased tube pan 325° for 1$\frac{1}{2}$ hrs.

GRANNY JOINER'S POUND CAKE

Mrs. Floyd E. Yoder,
Ms. Raymond Weaver, Vernie Weaver,
Sara Marie Yoder, Mrs. Milton Yoder,
and Katie Hershberger

1 stick margarine
$\frac{1}{2}$ c. Crisco
2 c. sugar
6 eggs

2 c. flour
$\frac{1}{4}$ t. salt
1 T. vanilla or 1 T. lemon flavoring
$\frac{1}{3}$ c. oil

Cream 1 stick margarine and $\frac{1}{2}$ c. Crisco. Add 2 c. sugar and cream again. Add 3 eggs - beat real well. Add 1 c. flour, beat again. Add 3 eggs, beat real well. Add 1 c. flour, beat again. Flavor with $\frac{1}{4}$ t. salt, 1 T. vanilla. Fold in $\frac{1}{3}$ c. cooking oil at the last. Bake in tube pan 325° for 1 hr.

Start in a cool oven!

LEMON POUND CAKE

Dorothy Yoder

1/2 c. butter
1/2 c. solid shortening
2 c. sugar
3 eggs
2 c. all-purpose flour

1/2 t. soda
1/4 t. salt
1 c. buttermilk
1 T. lemon juice
1 T. lemon rind

Cream shortening, butter and sugar. Add eggs. Sift flour, soda and salt together. Add alternately with buttermilk. Add lemon juice and rind. Bake in floured tube pan 325° for 1 hr.
ICING: Soften 1 stick or margarine with 1 box of confectioners' sugar. Add the juice and rind of 2 lemons. Beat well and put on cooled cake.

LEMON POUND CAKE

Lila Yoder

2 1/2 c. sugar
1 c. shortening (half oleo)
4 eggs
1/2 t. soda

1 t. salt
1 t. vanilla & lemon flavor
3 1/2 c. flour
1 c. buttermilk

Cream shortening and sugar; add eggs and beat well. Add rest of ingredients. Bake in bundt pan 350° for 1 hr. and 15 min. After cake comes out of oven, pour lemon sauce over cake still in pan. Pour slowly over and around edges.
SAUCE: 1 c. sugar, 1/2 c. hot water, juice and rind of 1 large lemon. Boil a few min. After cake sets a few min., remove from pan.

SOUR CREAM POUND CAKE

Becky Plank

3 c. flour
3 c. sugar
1 c. sour cream
1 t. vanilla

6 eggs, separated
1/4 t. soda
2 sticks margarine or 1 c.
1/4 t. salt

Cream sugar and margarine. Add egg yolks, one at a time, beat well after each addition. Mix flour, salt and soda. Add alternately with sour cream to egg mixture. Add vanilla. Fold in whipped egg whites. Pour into ungreased tube pan and bake 350° for 1 1/4 hrs.

Baking time may have to be increased 10 min. if cake tests undone.

SOUR CREAM POUND CAKE

Mary M. Yoder

3 c. sifted flour
1/2 t. soda
3 sticks soft margarine
2 c. sugar
1/4 t. salt

6 eggs
1 c. sour cream
1 t. lemon extract
1 t. vanilla

Sift flour with soda and salt; set aside. Cream margarine and slowly add sugar, beating well. Add eggs, one at a time, beating well after each addition. Stir in sour cream. Add flour mixture, 1/2 c. at a time, beating constantly. Add lemon and vanilla flavoring. Pour batter into greased tube pan. Bake in tube pan 350° for 1 hr. and 15 min. Cool in pan 5 min. before removing.

PUDDING CAKE WITH JELLO

Alta Kauffman

2-3 oz. boxes strawberry jello
1 3/4 c. boiling water

1 box cake mix, fixed like
   directions on box. Bake.

Pour hot jello mixture over warm cake that has been punched with a fork. Prepare 2 boxes instant pudding (your choice) like directions on box and spread on cake. Top with whipped cream.

PUMPKIN CAKE

Mrs. Floyd E. Yoder

4 eggs
2 c. sugar
1 c. oil
2 c. flour

1/2 t. salt
2 t. cinnamon
2 t. soda
2 c. unseasoned pumpkin

Beat eggs, add sugar and oil. Mix dry ingredients and add to egg mixture. add pumpkin, blend well. Pour into greased and floured tube pan. Bake 350° for 1 hr. and remove from pan. Frost with following recipe.

CREAM CHEESE ICING:
1-3 oz. pkg. cream cheese
1 stick softened margarine

1 box powdered sugar
1 t. vanilla

Mix and add milk till the right consistency.

MOIST PUMPKIN CAKE

Irene Yoder

1 c. white sugar
2 eggs
1/2 t. salt
1/2 c. milk
2 heaping t. baking powder
1 t. nutmeg

1/2 c. butter
2 t. vanilla
3/4 c. pumpkin (canned or fresh)
2 c. flour
1/2 t. baking soda
1/4 t. pumpkin pie spice

Cream butter and sugar. Add eggs and beat well. Sift dry ingredients together with milk, pumpkin, and vanilla. Beat well. Bake in 9x9" pan at 350° for 30-35 min. Serve plain or with butter cream icing.

RED VELVET CAKE

Mrs. Louis Yoder

1 1/2 c. sugar
2 eggs
2 1/2 c. cake flour
1 1/2 c. oil
1 c. buttermilk

1 t. vanilla
1 t. soda
1 t. vinegar
1 oz. red food coloring
1 t. cocoa

Beat eggs and sugar till fluffy. Combine dry ingredients. Add oil and vinegar to sugar and egg mixture. Add dry ingredients alternately with buttermilk. Mix well and bake in 3-8" layer pans at 350° for 25 min. Use cream cheese icing.

SEVEN-UP CAKE

Ruth Yoder

1 box lemon supreme cake mix
4 large eggs
3/4 c. cooking oil

1-3 oz. box vanilla pudding mix
1-10 oz. bottle 7-Up

Mix all ingredients and bake in 4 layer pans at 325° for 45 min.

FROSTING:
1 lg. can crushed pineapple
2 egg yolks (beaten)
2 c. sugar

3 T. flour
1 stick butter
1 c. coconut
1 c. pecans

FROSTING: Mix and cook over low heat first 5 ingredients. Cool. Add coconut and pecans.

SOUTHERN PECAN CAKE
Mrs. Eli Hostetler

3 c. flour
3 t. baking powder
1 t. salt
3/4 c. butter or oleo
1 2/3 c. sugar
3/4 c. milk

1/2 c. water
1 t. vanilla
1/2 t. almond extract
3/4 c. pecans
3 egg whites, beaten

Combine all ingredients together in a mixing bowl. Then fold egg whites in last. Bake in 3-9" layer pans at 350° 40-45 min. Delicious with your favorite caramel icing.

STRAWBERRY PECAN CAKE
Laura Whitt, Ruth Yoder

1 box white cake mix
4 eggs
1/2 c. milk
1 c. strawberries

1 c. cooking oil
1 c. coconut
1-3 oz. box strawberry gelatin
1 c. pecans, chopped

Mix dry gelatin and cake mix together. Add remaining ingredients, adding eggs one at a time. Bake in 3 greased 8" layer pans at 350° 25-30 min.

STRAWBERRY FROSTING:
1 stick butter or
  margarine (1/2 c.)
1/2 c. strawberries, drained
1/2 c. coconut

1 box confectioners' sugar
1/2 c. pecans

Cream sugar and butter. Add remaining ingredients.

SUN-MAID RAISIN NUT CAKE
Mrs. Henry Overholt, Sr.
Mrs. Crist Yoder, Sr.

2/3 c. lard or butter
1 c. brown sugar
1/2 c. syrup (pancake)
2 eggs
1 c. sour milk
1 t. baking soda

1 1/2 t. cinnamon
1/2 t. cloves
2 t. baking powder
2 1/2 c. flour
1 1/2 c. raisins
1/2 c. pecans

Cream butter with brown sugar, then add syrup, beaten eggs and sour milk which baking soda has been dissolved in. Mix and sift flour, baking powder, cinnamon, and cloves. Add dry mixture to first mixture. Add raisins and chopped pecans. Bake in 3 layer pans or small loaf pan 350° for 25 min.

TEXAS SHEET CAKE

Mrs. Crist Yoder, Jr.,
Mrs. Sol Yoder, Mrs. Louis Yoder

2 sticks or 1 c. butter
1 c. water
4 T. cocoa
2 c. sugar
2 c. flour
½ t. salt
1 t. soda
2 eggs

1 t. vanilla
½ c. sour cream
FROSTING:
1 stick butter
3 T. cocoa
⅓ c. milk
2 to 3 c. confectioners' sugar
1 c. pecans
1 t. vanilla

Melt butter and add cocoa and water; bring to a boil, then add sugar, flour, salt, soda, eggs, vanilla, and sour cream; beat together and bake at 350° till done. While cake is still warm, put on Frosting. FROSTING: Melt butter, cocoa and milk; bring to a boil and add nuts and vanilla. Add confectioners' sugar to spreading consistency.

TURTLE CAKE

Ruth Yoder

1 pkg. German chocolate
   cake mix
14 oz. pkg. caramels
6 oz. chopped pecans

¼ lb. butter or oleo
7 oz. Eagle Brand milk
6 oz. semi-sweet chocolate chips

Mix cake as on package. Bake half the mix in greased and floured 13x9" pan at 350° for 15 min. In top of double boiler, melt together butter, caramels and milk. Remove top of double boiler from heat. Cool mixture slightly and pour over baked half of cake. Pour over the rmaining cake batter. Sprinkle with pecans and the chocolate chips. Bake at 350° for 25 min.

VIRGINIA CHOCOLATE SHEET CAKE

Mari Yoder

2 c. sifted flour
2 c. sugar (sifted with flour)
1 stick oleo or ½ c. butter
4 T. cocoa
1 c. water

½ c. Crisco
½ c. buttermilk or sour milk
1 t. soda
2 eggs, beaten
1 t. vanilla

Bring oleo and Crisco, cocoa and water to rapid boil; pour over flour and sugar mixture; beat well. Add buttermilk or sour milk and soda, then eggs and vanilla. Pour in greased 9x13" pan. Bake 350° for 45 min.

YELLOW CRISCO LAYER CAKE

Mrs. Salome K. Yoder

Measure 2 c. sifted flour, 1⅓ c. sugar, ½ c. Crisco and ⅔ c. milk into mixing bowl. Beat vigorously 2 min. Add 3 t. double-action baking powder, 1 t. salt, and 1 t. vanilla. Add 2 unbeaten eggs and ⅓ c. milk. Beat 2 min. Nuts may be added, if desired. Bake 375° 25-30 min. 9x1½" pan.

YUM-YUM CAKE

Esther Ruth Yoder

1 box Duncan Hines yellow
  cake mix
1-11 oz. mandarin oranges
  (undrained)
½ C. Crisco or oil
4 eggs

ICING:
1-2 oz. crushed pineapple
  (drained)
1-9 oz. Cool Whip
1 c. coconut
Mix, then add 1 lg. box instant
  vanilla pudding.

Mix above ingredients together and mix 2 min. at medium speed. Bake in 3-9" or 10" pans at 350° for 25 min. Cool and frost with Icing.

ZUCCHINI CAKE

Bertha G. Yoder

4 eggs
2¼ c. sugar
1 c. cooking oil
2 c. grated zucchini
3½ c. flour
1 t. salt

1¾ t. soda
3 t. cinnamon
¾ t. baking powder
1½ c. pecans
1 c. raisins
2 t. vanilla

Blend together eggs, sugar, oil, zucchini, and vanilla. Then add flour, salt, soda, cinnamon, and baking powder and mix well. Add chopped pecans and raisins, blend well. Pour into a greased tube or bundt pan and bake 325° for 1 hr. and 15 min.

GLAZE TOPPING (if desired): ½ c. powdered sugar, 1 t. lemon flavoring, and 1 t. milk.

ZUCCHINI CAKE

Mrs. Raymond Weaver

4 eggs
3 c. sugar
1½ c. oil
3 c. peeled & grated squash
3 c. flour

2 t. baking powder
2 t. soda
1 t. salt
1½ t. cinnamon
1½ c. pecans

Mix grated squash, sugar, oil and eggs. Combine dry ingredients. Mix together and beat until smooth. Pour into greased 10x14" pan. Bake 350° for 1½ hrs. Serve with whipped cream or ice cream.

MAGIC CUPCAKES

Alta Kauffman

Use your favorite chocolate cupcake recipe!

FILLING:
1-8 oz. pkg. cream cheese
½ c. sugar
1 egg

1 c. chocolate chips
½ c. chopped nuts
Pinch of salt

Mix cream cheese, sugar and egg till creamy. Add remaining ingredients. Fill muffin pans ½ full and drop a heaping teaspoonful of the Filling and bake at 375° for 15-20 min. Makes approximately 24.

RAISIN CUPCAKES

Mrs. Henry Overholt, Sr.

¼ c. butter
¾ c. sugar
1 c. raisins
1 egg

½ c. milk
1¾ c. flour
3 t. baking powder
1 t. lemon extract

Cream butter and sugar. Add egg and lemon extract. Add flour, baking powder, milk and raisins. Fill paper cups in muffin pans ⅔ full. Bake 375° 15-20 min.

For black icing for party cupcakes, add blue food coloring to your favorite chocolate icing.

CARAMEL FROSTING — Mrs. Melvin (Katherine) Yoder

1 c. brown sugar
1/3 c. evaporated milk or cream
1 T. butter
1 t. vanilla
Powdered sugar

Heat together these ingredients until it comes to a boil—all except vanilla and powdered sugar. Remove from heat. Add powdered sugar and vanilla and beat well.

CARAMEL FROSTING — Ellen R. Brenneman

1 stick margarine
3/4 c. brown sugar
Pinch of salt
1/4 c. cream
1 box powdered sugar
1 t. maple flavoring

Melt butter and add brown sugar and cream; mix thoroughly. Add powdered sugar, maple flavoring, and salt. Mix well.

CARAMEL ICING — Mrs. Raymond Weaver

1/2 c. butter
1/2 c. milk
3 c. powdered sugar
1 c. brown sugar
1 t. vanilla

Melt butter and add sugar, cook 1 min. Add milk and bring to a boil. Add vanilla. Let cool and add powdered sugar till thick enough to spread.

QUICK CARAMEL FROSTING — Linda Kauffman

1 c. brown sugar
1/2 c. butter
1/4 c. milk or cream
2 c. powdered sugar

Stir together sugar, butter and milk in heavy saucepan. Boil for 2 min. Add the powdered sugar and beat well. Spread on cake while still hot.

NOTE: Caramel icing will turn out much better if sugar is completely dissolved in butter before adding other ingredients.

Lumpy brown sugar? Heat your oven to 350°. Place sugar in pan or baking dish and put in oven. In a matter of minutes it will be soft as when fresh. Watch that it doesn't melt - break up with a fork as it softens.

CHOCOLATE RICHMOND FROSTING

Lela Brenneman,
Esther Ruth Yoder

3/4 c. sugar
Pinch of salt
1 1/2 T. cocoa
3/4 c. hot water

2 1/4 T. cornstarch
2 T. butter
3/4 t. vanilla

Stir together sugar, salt, cornstarch, cocoa, hot water. Cook till thickened. Remove from heat. Add butter, vanilla. Spread on cake while hot.

CHOCOLATE FROSTING

Sara Marie Yoder

1/4 c. Crisco, margarine or
    butter
1/2 c. cocoa
1/4 t. salt

1/2 c. milk
1 1/2 t. vanilla
3 1/2 c. confectioners' sugar

Combine melted Crisco, cocoa and salt. Add milk and vanilla. Add sugar in 3 parts.

CHOCOLATE ICING

Becky Plank, Irene Yoder

2 T. cocoa
2 1/2 T. cornstarch
3/4 c. sugar

3/4 c. boiling water
3/4 t. vanilla
2 T. butter

Mix cocoa, cornstarch, and sugar very well. Add water, a little at a time, till smooth. Cook till thick, stirring constantly. It gets lumpy but continued, rapid stirring makes it smooth. Add vanilla and butter. Spread while warm. Makes enough to frost a 13x9" cake.

CREAM CHEESE FROSTING

Mrs. Bertha Yoder, Linda Weaver,
and Mrs. Noah Yoder

8 oz. cream cheese (softened)
1 t. vanilla

1/2 c. butter (softened)
1 lb. powdered sugar
1 c. chopped nuts

Cream butter and cream cheese. Add rest of ingredients and beat until creamy and smooth. Add nuts and spread on cake.

CREAMY FROSTING

Beulah Yoder, JoAnn Inhulsen,
and Linda Kauffman

2 T. flour
3/4 c. milk
1/2 c. Crisco

1/2 c. oleo
1 c. sugar
1 t. vanilla

Cook flour and milk until thick. Cool. Beat together Crisco, oleo, sugar, and vanilla. Add milk mixture and continue beating until fluffy.

FROSTING

Mrs. Eli Hostetler

Boil together: 4 T. white sugar, 4 T. water about 5 min. or until syrupy. Mix thoroughly 1/2 c. Crisco and 1/2 c. oleo. Add 1 egg and 1/2 t. vanilla. Next add the syrup. Then stir in 2 to 4 c. powdered sugar.

This is a very fluffy icing and will not get hard or sticky.

DECORATING ICING

Irene Yoder

1/2 c. Crisco
1 egg white
1 oz. water

1 t. vanilla
1 box powdered sugar

Beat Crisco, egg white, water, and vanilla real well. Add powdered sugar and beat till well blended.

ROYAL ICING

Irene Yoder

1 box powdered sugar
1/3 c. egg whites
(room temperature)

1/4 t. cream of tartar

Put egg whites and cream of tartar in bowl, and start beating. Add powdered sugar right away, beat 7 to 10 min. You may need to use more powdered sugar in icing for roses.

Notes

CASSEROLES

BREAKFAST DISH
Mrs. Lloyd Swartzentruber, Mary M. Yoder

6 slices bread
2 c. milk
1 t. dry mustard
1 lb. sausage, bacon or ham

6 eggs, beaten
1 t. salt
1 c. shredded Cheddar cheese

Break bread in small pieces. Fry sausage or bacon. Ham doesn't need to be fried. Mix well and put in casserole and bake. This may be made in the evening and refrigerated overnight and baked the next morning. Serves 8. Bake at 350° for 45 min.

Delicious served with tomato gravy.

CHEESE SOUFFLE
Anna Yoder

8 slices bread
1 lb. cheese, grated
6 eggs, beaten
¼ c. margarine
Cubed ham, bacon or mushrooms

2 c. milk
1 T. onion salt
Salt
Pepper

Cube bread, put in bottom of casserole. Combine cheese, margarine and meat. Sprinkle over bread cubes. Mix eggs, milk and seasoning. Add over top of the other ingredients. Refrigerate overnight. Bake 325° for 45 min. Serves 8 to 10.

COMPANY EGG OMELET
Lena Yoder

6 slices cubed white bread
  (remove crusts)
2 c. milk
6 eggs
1 t. salt
1 t. dry mustard

1 c. cheese, shredded
1 lb. bacon or sausage
¼ c. mushrooms
¼ c. peppers
Bits of tomato for color
Garnish with parsley

Combine ingredients in order as listed. Bake 350° for 45 min. Serves 10.

This recipe can be mixed the night before.

SAUSAGE EGG CASSEROLE   Mrs. Alva Yoder

1 lb. lean ground sausage   2¹/₂ c. milk
6 eggs, whipped   2 c. grated cheese
³/₄ t. dry mustard   8 slices bread

Place cubed bread in bottom of pan. Brown sausage and drain, then
spread over bread. Whip eggs and add dry mustard and milk. Mix
well and pour over bread and sausage. Sprinkle cheese on top.
Refrigerate overnight. Next morning, mix 1 can mushroom soup and
¹/₂ can milk; pour over top of casserole and bake in 8x13" pan at
350° for 45 min. Serves 8 to 10.

SAUSAGE AND CHEESE OMELET   Ruth Yoder

6 pieces bread, cubed   1 T. salt
3 c. milk   ¹/₂ lb. sausage, fried
6 eggs   5 slices cheese
1 t. seasoning salt

Beat eggs. Add milk, salt and bread. Put half of mixture in pan. Then
spread sausage, then cheese over top of this. Pour remaining egg
mixture on top of cheese. Bake in 9x13" pan at 350° for 30 min. Serves
8.

10-MINUTE OMELET   Mari Yoder

4 eggs   ¹/₄ t. salt
¹/₈ t. pepper   1 T. flour
1 T. softened butter   1 T. water

Beat egg whites with salt till stiff, but not dry. Beat together other
ingredients till fluffy. Then fold in egg whites. Pour in well-greased
skillet (hot enough to sizzle water). Cover tightly, cook low for 8 to
10 min. - until surface is dry when touched. Fold. (Can be filled, if
desired, with cheese, ham or bacon before folding.) Serves 1 or 2.

OMELETTE

Mrs. Loretta Brenneman

10 slices buttered bread	MIX TOGETHER:
1 lb. chopped ham (bacon or	6 eggs
grated cheese)	3 c. milk

Put items in baking dish as they are listed, having the milk and eggs mixed together. Leave set overnight in refrigerator. Bake in 9x13" pan at 350° for 1 hr. Serves 6 to 10.

Bread can be put in dish in layers. This is a handy breakfast for company.

CREAMED EGGS

Barbara Jean Hershberger,
Linda Kauffman

6 eggs	1¹/₂ t. salt
6 T. butter or margarine	3 c. milk
6 T. flour	Dash of pepper
	Optional: 1 pkg. dried beef,
	cut in strips

Hard boil eggs. Peel. Melt butter in heavy saucepan. Add flour and seasoning. Sir until well blended. Slowly add milk, stirring constantly. Cook until smooth. Chop eggs and dried beef and add to sauce. Serve on toast. Serves 6 to 8.

EGG DUTCH

Naomi Yoder

| 4 eggs | 1 rounded T. flour |
| 1¹/₂ c. milk | Salt to taste |

Mix all ingredients. Fry till golden brown, turning occasionally till thick. Serves 2 to 3.

This is a good breakfast. Serve with tomato gravy.

*Add a little vinegar to the water
when an egg cracks during boiling.*

SCRAMBLED EGGS & BACON

Mrs. Ernest W. Yoder

1/4 lb. bacon
8 eggs
1 c. milk

3/4 t. salt
1/8 c. butter, melted

Fry bacon; drain and crumble. Put eggs in a bowl. Beat lightly. Add milk, salt and butter. Add crumbled bacon last. Grease pan. Bake in 12x9" pan at 425° till knife comes out clean. Serves 10 to 12.

BEEF AND PEPPER SPAGHETTI

Anna Yoder

6 beef cubed steaks
1 lg. green pepper
2 T. cooking oil
1 c. sliced fresh mushrooms
1/2 t. dried basil, crushed

1 clove garlic, minced
1-16 oz. jar spaghetti sauce
Hot cooked spaghetti
3/4 c. shredded mozzarella
cheese (3 oz.)

Cut beef and green pepper into 1/2" wide strips. Heat wok over high heat. Add cooking oil. Stir-fry the meat, half at a time, till browned. Remove meat from wok. Stir-fry green pepper, mushrooms, basil and garlic for 3 to 5 min. or till vegetables are tender. Stir in spaghetti sauce and meat. Reduce heat, cover and simmer for 10-15 min., stirring often. Serve over hot cooked spaghetti. Sprinkle with cheese. Skillet may be used instead of wok. Serves 6.

GRANDMA'S GOULASH

Mrs. Fannie Byler

1 qt. meat chunks
(pork is best)
3/4 c. onion
1 qt. tomato chunks or juice
8 oz. tomato sauce
1/2 c. sugar

1 1/2 oz. Italian spaghetti sauce
mix
1 t. salt
1 t. pepper
Approximately 1 lb. spaghetti
(broken up)
3 qts. water

Add onions to the meat and brown. Add other ingredients except spaghetti and sauce mix - you add this after the mixture comes to a boil - 1/2 hr.

HUNGARIAN GOULASH

Mary Plank

2 lbs. round steak, cut in
  1/2" pieces
1 c. chopped onion
1 clove garlic, minced
2 T. flour
1 t. salt
1/2 t. pepper

1 T. paprika
1/4 t. dried thyme, crushed
1 bay leaf
1-1 lb. 12 oz. can tomatoes
1 c. sour cream

Put steak cubes, onion, garlic in crock pot. Stir in flour and mix to coat steak cubes. Add all remaining ingredients except sour cream. Stir well, cover and cook on low for 7 to 10 hrs. Add sour cream 30 min. before serving and stir in thoroughly. (High: 5 to 6 hrs., stirring occasionally.) Serve over hot buttered noodles.

ITALIAN DELIGHT

Delores Hostetler

1/2 lb. steak, cut in cubes
  & browned
1/2 lb. noodles, cooked
1 can cream of mushroom soup

1 can cream of chicken soup
1 qt. corn
1/2 lb. Velveeta cheese

TOPPING:
1 c. cracker crumbs

3 T. butter

Mix all ingredients together. Brown cracker crumbs in the butter, spread on top and bake in 2-qt. casserole at 375° for 1 hr.

HASTY TASTY

Vernie Brenneman

1 pt. beef chunks
6 slices bread
3 eggs
1 t. salt
2 c. milk

1 qt. corn
1 c. chopped onion
1 c. grated cheese
2 T. butter

Place meat into baking dish. Beat eggs, milk, and salt. Then add bread, corn, onions, and pour over top of meat. Melt butter; pour over top. Sprinkle cheese over top **after baked.** Bake in 2-qt. casserole at 350° for 30 min. till cheese is melted. Serves 10.

HEARTY BEEF STEW
Mary Plank

2 lbs. stew beef, cut in 1" cubes
5 carrots, cut in 1" pieces
1 lg. onion, cut in chunks
3 stalks celery, sliced
1-1 lb. 12 oz. can tomatoes

1/2 c. quick-cooking tapioca
1 whole clove (or 1/2 t. ground clove)
2 bay leaves
Salt and pepper to taste

Trim all fat from meat. Put all ingredients in crock pot. Mix thoroughly. Cover and cook on low for 12 hrs. (High: 5-6 hrs.)

DRIED BEEF MACARONI CASSEROLE
Mrs. Melvin (Katherine) Yoder

1 c. raw elbow macaroni
1 can cream of mushroom soup
1 pg. dried beef or chopped ham
1 c. milk

2 hard-boiled eggs
1 c. grated cheese
1 t. diced onion

Mix all ingredients together and bake in a 1 1/2 qt. casserole 350° for 1 to 1 1/2 hrs. or until tender.

AMERICAN CHOP SUEY
Mrs. Eli (Leona) Hostetler

1 lb. ground beef
3/4 c. rice, uncooked
1 1/2 c. celery, cut fine
2 sm. onions, chopped

1/4 c. soy sauce
1 can mushroom soup
2 cans water

Put rice in bottom of pan. Brown meat. Do not season. Add all other ingredients to meat and pour over rice. Do not stir. 350° for 1 hr. 9x12" pan.

BAKED CHOP SUEY
Marie King, Mrs. Ernest W. Yoder, Mrs. Milton Yoder, Linda Weaver, and Mrs. Nelson Yoder

1 lb. hamburger
2 t. butter
2 medium onions (chopped)
1 c. celery (chopped)
1 can cream of chicken soup

1 can cream of mushroom soup
1 1/4 c. warm water
1/2 c. Minute rice (uncooked)
1/4 c. soy sauce
Salt and pepper to taste

Brown hamburger in butter. Add remaining ingredients. Mix well. Serve with chow mein noodles. 350° for 1 hr.

BALLARD BISCUITS CASSEROLE   Mrs. Bertha Yoder

1½ lbs. hamburger   1-8 oz. pkg. cream cheese, cubed
1 c. chopped onions   ¼ c. milk
1 can cream of mushroom soup   1 t. salt
1 can cream of chicken soup   ¼ c. catsup
                               Ballard biscuits

Fry hamburger, onions and salt. Add rest of ingredients. Mix well. Pour into loaf pan and bake until bubbly. Remove from oven. Put unbaked Ballard Biscuits on top. Bake at 375° for 15-20 min. or until biscuits are brown.

BEEF CASSEROLE   Beulah Yoder

1 lb. ground beef   2 T. brown sugar
1 t. salt   1 T. minced onion
16 oz. can pork and beans   1 can flaky biscuits
½ c. barbecue sauce   1 c. shredded cheese
¼ c. catsup

Brown ground beef. Heat next 6 ingredients until bubbly. Add to ground beef. Add biscuits and shredded cheese on top 375° 25-30 min. 2-qt. casserole.

CHEESEBURGER PIE   Mrs. Marlene Swartzentruber,
                                        Mrs. Ivan Yoder

1 lb. ground beef   ¾ c. Bisquick baking mix
1½ c. chopped onion   3 eggs
½ t. salt   2 tomatoes, sliced
¼ t. pepper
1½ c. milk

Brown beef and onion; drain. Stir in salt and pepper. Spread in pan. Beat milk, baking mix and eggs until smooth - 1 min. with hand beater. Pour into 10x1½" pan. Bake 400° for 25 min. Top with tomatoes; sprinkle with cheese. Bake until knife inserted in center comes out clean, 5 to 8 min.. Cool 5 min. Makes 6 to 8 servings.

CHEESEBURGER PIE
Marie King

1 lb. hamburger
1½ c. chopped onion
½ t. salt
¼ t. pepper

1 c. shredded cheese
1 c. milk
½ c. Bisquick
3 eggs

Brown hamburger and onions. Drain. Stir in salt and pepper. Place in bottom of 9" greased pan. Sprinkle with cheese. Combine milk, Bisquick and eggs; beat until smooth. Pour over meat and cheese. Bake 350° for 30 min.

EL RANCHO CASSEROLE
Sara Marie Yoder

1 lb. ground beef
1 c. chopped onion
1-8 oz. macaroni (uncooked)
3½ c. tomato juice
½ lb. Velveeta cheese

½ c. water
1½ t. chili powder
1 t. salt
¼ t. pepper
1 pt. corn (optional)

Brown meat. Add onions and cook till tender. Add the rest and simmer 30-35 min.

Tastes like Hamburger Helper.

FAVORITE BARBECUED BEANS
Barbara Jean Hershberger, Mrs. Samuel Nisly, Sara Marie Yoder

1 lb. hamburger
½ c. onion, chopped
Salt and pepper
1-1 lb. 12 oz. can pork
  and beans

½ c. ketchup
1 T. Worcestershire sauce
2 T. vinegar (optional)
¼ t. Tabasco (optional)

Brown beef and onion, pour off fat. Add remaining ingredients and bake 350° for 30 min. Serve with a salad or fresh raw vegetables.

A day hemmed in prayer rarely unravels.

FIVE-DECKER DINNER
Miriam Brenneman

6 slices bacon
3/4 lb. ground beef
Salt
4 to 6 onions, sliced
4 to 6 potatoes, sliced

4 to 6 carrots, sliced
1/4 c. chopped green pepper
1 T. chopped parsley
1/4 c. water

Cut bacon into 1" pieces and line pan bottom. Make ground beef into patties and place on bacon. Sprinkle salt over meat and each subsequent layer. Add onions, potatoes, carrots, and green pepper in order given. Sprinkle parsley over top. Cook over medium heat 3 min., or until bacon begins to sizzle. Add water, cover and turn heat to low. Cook 35-40 min., or until done. 2-qt. casserole. Serves 4 or 5.

GOLDEN MEATBALL CASSEROLE
Mrs. Milton Yoder

1 lb. hamburger
1 egg
2 c. water
2 lg. carrots
1/4 c. onion

1/2 c. fresh bread crumbs
1 t. salt
1 c. rice
1/2 c. chopped green pepper
1/2 c. cheese

Mix hamburger, egg, salt and bread crumbs. Shape into balls and fry in a little oil. Add water, carrots, onion, rice and green pepper. Add cheese and simmer 25 min. Or put in 2-qt. casserole and bake at 350° until vegetables are tender.

GREEN BEAN DISH
Mrs. Sol Yoder

4 lg. potatoes (raw), cut up
1 lb. wieners, cut up or 1 lb.
 browned hamburger
1 qt. canned green beans
1/2 onion

SAUCE:
2 c. milk
1/2 c. flour
1/2 lb. soft cheese
2 t. salt

Place ingredients in 3-qt. casserole. Heat 1 1/2 c. milk, mix flour with the other 1/2 c. milk. Melt cheese in hot milk, then add flour-milk and salt. Pour over potatoes, beans and onions. Bake 300° for 2 hrs. Serves 10-12.

91

HAMBURGER CASSEROLE

Mary M. Yoder

2 lbs. ground beef
1 c. chopped onions
1 pt. peas
1-8 oz. fine noodles, cooked
¾ c. shredded cheese

1 can cream of chicken soup
1 can cream of mushroom soup
1 c. sour cream
3 sprigs chopped parsley
1 T. sugar

Fry ground beef and onions. Add remaining ingredients. Place in 2 qt. casserole and top with buttered bread crumbs and bake 350° for 1 hr.

HAMBURGER CHEESE PIE

Mrs. Eli Hostetler

½ lb. ground beef
¼ c. finely-chopped onion
Cook together.
1-9" unbaked pie shell
½ c. grated cheese

MIX TOGETHER:
2 eggs, well beaten
⅓ c. milk
2 t. cornstarch
¼ t. salt
Pepper
¼ c. mayonnaise

Put meat and onion mixture on pie shell, then arrange cheese on there, then remaining mixture on top. Bake at 350° for 35 min.

HAMBURGER CRUNCH

Mrs. Elmer M. Yoder (Esther)

1 lb. ground beef
1 medium-size onion, chopped
4 T. soy sauce
1 c. sliced celery
½ c. uncooked rice

1-4 oz. can mushrooms with liquid
   (optional)
1 can cream of mushroom soup
1 can cream of chicken soup
Chow mein noodles

Brown meat and onion in large skillet. Combine meat mixture with rest of ingredients except chow mein noodles. Mix thoroughly. Turn into 1½ qt. casserole and bake, uncovered, in a 350° oven for 50 min. Sprinkle top with noodles return to oven and bake 10 min. longer. (Or serve noodles with the casserole.)

HAMBURGER-NOODLE CASSEROLE   Mrs. Henry Overholt, Sr.

1 lb. hamburger
2 T. chopped onion
1½ T. flour
2 t. salt
1 can cream of mushroom soup

1¼ t. pepper
2 c. noodles, cooked
2 c. water
Buttered bread crumbs

Fry hamburger, onion, salt and pepper together. When brown, add flour and blend well. Mix with other ingredients and top with crumbs. Put in 2-qt. pan and bake at 350° for 45 min. Serves 8.

HAMBURGER NOODLES   Verda Overholt

1 pkg. noodles
Salt water
1 lb. hamburger
1 onion

1 can cream of mushroom soup
1 can cream of celery soup
Salt and pepper to taste

Cook noodles in salt water. Drain. Brown hamburger and onion in skillet till lightly browned, add soups. Mix together with noodles. Season with salt and pepper. Pour into 2 qt. casserole and bake at 350° for 30 min.

LAYERED HAMBURGER BAKE   Mary Lois Yoder, Ruth Yoder,
Mrs. Daniel Yoder

4 oz. or 3 c. wide noodles
1 lb. ground beef
2 c. tomato sauce
1 t. sugar
½ t. salt
⅛ t. pepper

1-8 oz. pkg. cream cheese
½ c. sour cream
3 T. milk
2 T. onions
1-10 oz. pkg. broccoli, cooked
    and drained

Cook noodles and drain, brown meat and drain. Mix cooked noodles, hamburger, tomato sauce, sugar, salt, and pepper. Put ½ of mixture in baking pan. Mix together cream cheese, sour cream, milk, and onions. Spread ½ of this mixture over first layer. Place all of broccoli on this and cover with remaining hamburger mixture. Bake at 350° for 40 min., uncover and add remaining cream cheese mixture. Top with grated Cheddar cheese. Bake 10 min. more. Serves 6 to 8.

HAMBURGER-VEGETABLE DISH — Verda Overholt

1 lb. ground beef	6 medium potatoes, boiled & sliced
1 lg. onion, diced	1 can peas, drained
Salt to taste	Pepper to taste
1 can cream of celery soup	1 can cream of mushroom soup

Pat ground beef evenly into baking dish. Spread the boiled potatoes, onions, and peas evenly over the meat. Salt and pepper to taste. Mix cream of celery and cream of mushroom soups together and spread evenly on top. Cover and bake in 9x12" baking dish at 350° for 50 min.

HAMBURGER-VEGETABLE DISH — Mrs. Isaac Plank, Mrs. Simon L. Yoder

2 lbs. hamburger	1 c. chopped onions
8 oz. noodles	1 can cream of chicken soup
2 cans cream of mushroom soup	1 pt. cooked peas
1 c. sour milk	Salt and pepper to taste

Cook hamburger and onions together till the rawness is out of hamburger. Cook noodles till soft and drain. Cook peas till soft. Mix all ingredients together, pour into 2 qt. casserole dish or cake pan and cover with buttered bread crumbs and bake at 350° for 45 min.

HUNGRY JACK CASSEROLE — Mrs. Levi Kauffman

1 lb. hamburger	1 lb. 12 oz. can pork & beans
1 chopped onion	1/2 c. ketchup
2 T. brown sugar or dark Karo	1 T. Worcestershire sauce
Salt to taste	2 T. vinegar
3/4 c. shredded cheese	1 can Hungry Jack biscuits
1/2 c. barbecue sauce	

Fry hamburger and onion together until brown. Then add beans, seasoning and liquids and bake in 2 qt. casserole at 350° for 25 min. Then cut biscuits into half and place them on the cut side around the dish and bake until brown. (Sprinkle cheese on biscuits.) Serves 12.

HOBO SUPPER

Verda Overholt

1 lb. hamburger
1 head cabbage
Salt and pepper

1 box frozen mixed vegetables
1 sm. onion

Divide the hamburger in 4 patties and the vegetables in 4 parts. Take 4 pieces of tin foil and on each piece of foil, place some cabbage leaves, then a few slices of onion, then the hamburger pattie. Salt and pepper to taste, then add mixed vegetables. Bring each of the tin foil edges together to seal at top. Set side-by-side in a roaster and bake at 350° for 1 hr. Serves 4.

AMERICAN LASAGNE

Mrs. Marlene Swartzentruber

1 lb. ground beef
2 cloves garlic, minced
1 T. hot fat
1-6 oz. tomato paste
1-1 lb. 4 oz. can tomatoes
  (2½ c.)
1 t.salt

¾ t. pepper
½ t. oregano
8 oz. wide noodles, cooked
  and drained
8 oz. Swiss cheese, cut up
1-12 oz. carton cottage cheese

Brown beef and garlic in hot fat. Add tomato paste, tomatoes, and seasonings. Cover and simmer 20 min. In oblong baking dish, alternate layers of cooked noodles, Swiss cheese, cottage cheese and meat sauce. Bake at 350° for 20-30 min. Serves 6 to 8.

IMPOSSIBLE LASAGNE PIE

Esther Yoder

1 lb. ground beef
1 t. dried oregano leaves
½ t. dried basil leaves
1-6 oz. can tomato paste
1 c. shredded mozzarella
  cheese
½ c. sm. curd cottage cheese

¼ c. grated Parmesan cheese
1 c. milk
⅔ c. Bisquick baking mix
2 eggs
1 t. salt
¼ t. pepper

Grease pie pan. Cook and stir beef over medium heat until brown; drain. Stir in oregano, basil, tomato paste and ½ c. of the mozzarella cheese. Layer cottage cheese and Parmesan cheese in plate. Spoon beef mixture over top. Beat milk, baking mix, eggs, salt and pepper until smooth, 15 seconds in blender on high or 1 min. with hand beater. Pour into 10x1½" pie pan. Bake at 400° for 30-35 min. until knife inserted between center and edge comes out clean. Sprinkle with remaining cheese. Cook 5 min. Makes 6 to 8 servings.

95

SKILLET LASAGNA   Laura Whitt

10 lasagna noodles   1 medium onion, minced
  (1/2-6 oz. pkg.)   1 lb. ground beef
1-15 oz. container ricotta cheese 1-14 to 15 1/2 oz. jar spaghetti
1/4 t. salt   sauce
1-4 oz. shredded mozzarella   1 egg
  cheese   1/4 t. pepper

Using very hot tap water, prepare lasagna noodles as label directs;
drain. Meanwhile, in 12" skillet over medium-high heat, cook ground
beef and onion until beef is brown and onion is tender, about 10 min.
Stir in 2/3 of spaghetti sauce. Cook until heated through. Spoon half
of mixture into small bowl, set aside. Reduce heat to low and keep
remaining meat mixture simmering in skillet. Combine ricotta cheese,
ege, salt, pepper. Spread half of ricotta mixture evenly on meat
mixture in skillet, top with half of noodles, sprinkle with half of
mozzarella. Repeat layering with remaining meat, ricotta, lasagna
mixture. Then remaining sauce and mozzarella. Cover and cook 5
min. until heated through.

MACARONI & CHEESE   Mary Plank

3 to 4 c. cooked macaroni   2 T. minced onion
SAUCE: 1 egg, beaten
2 c. evaporated milk   2 c. cubed cheese (Cheddar or
1/2 t. paprika   processed)
1 t. salt   2 T. butter

Put all Sauce ingredients in crock pot. Stir well. Cover and cook on
high for 1 hr., stirring occasionally. Add cooked and drained macaroni. Cover and cook on low for 3 to 5 hrs.

MARZELTIA CASSEROLE   Barbara Jean Hershberger

1 lb. hamburger   1 can water
3 medium-size onions   1 pkg. noodles
2 cans tomato soup   1/2 lb. pimento cheese

Fry hamburger and onions until brown. Add tomato soup and water
and boil. Cook noodles and add to the hamburger, soup, and pimento cheese. Put in 3 layers, add cracker crumbs on top. May add
a little more tomato juice and water if so desired. Bake at 350° for 20
min. Serves 8 to 10.

MEXICAN MIX-UP
Mrs. Daniel Swartzentruber

1½ lbs. ground beef
½ c. chopped green pepper
1 lg. clove garlic, minced
2 c. kidney beans, drained
¼ t. salt
½ c. shredded Cheddar cheese

1 c. chopped onion
1 T. chili powder
2 c. beef gravy
⅛ t. pepper
2 c. cooked elbow macaroni

In skillet, brown beef and cook onion and green pepper with chili powder and garlic until vegetables are tender. Add gravy, beans, macaroni, salt and pepper. Pour into 2 qt. casserole and bake at 450° for 15 min. Stir. Top with cheese; bake until cheese melts.

MOCKED TURKEY
Mrs. Raymond Weaver, Mrs. Alva Yoder, Mrs. Noah Yoder

2 lbs. hamburger
2 T. butter
2 cans cream of chicken soup
1 can cream of celery soup

4 c. milk
1 loaf toasted bread
Salt and pepper to taste

Brown hamburger in butter; drain, set aside. Break up toasted bread and soak in milk. Add rest of ingredients and mix well. Pour in baking dish. Bake at 350° for 45 min.

PIZZA CASSEROLE
Kathryn Yoder, Mrs. Ivan Yoder

2 lbs. hamburger
½ green pepper
1 can cream of mushroom soup
1 sm. can pizza sauce
¼ t. garlic powder
1 can mushrooms with liquid

¼ t. oregano
½ c. Parmesan cheese
1-8 oz. pkg. wide noodles
Pepperoni
Mozzarella cheese

Cook noodles and drain. Brown hamburger. Mix all ingredients and top with mozzarella cheese. Put into 2½ qt. casserole dish and bake at 350° for 30 min. Serves 6.

PIZZA CASSEROLE

Barbara Jean Hershberger

1 lb. hamburger
1 onion, chopped
1-16 oz. cans pizza sauce
1-10 oz. pkg. mozzarella
   cheese

1-7 oz. pkg. macaroni (cooked)
4 oz. pepperoni, thinly sliced
1 can mushrooms
Salt and pepper to taste

Brown hamburger, salt, pepper, and chopped onion. Add pizza sauce, macaroni and mushrooms. Top with pepperoni and shredded cheese after putting in large casserole. Bake at 350° for 30 min.

PIZZA LOAF

Mrs. Nelson Yoder

2 lbs. hamburger
1-8 oz. pkg. noodles
1 can cream of mushroom soup

1 sm. jar pizza sauce
Cheese

Brown the hamburger. Mix in the pizza sauce. Cook noodles as directed on bag - then drain. Heat the cream of mushroom soup. Put in layers - 1) noodles; 2) hamburger; 3) cream of mushroom soup. Bake at 350° for 30 min. Put cheese on top. Put in oven till cheese melts.

POOR MAN'S CASSEROLE

Mrs. Nelson Yoder

1 lb. ground beef
1 medium onion, sliced
3 medium potatoes, sliced

1-#303 can garden peas, or
   1 pt. frozen peas
1 can cream of chicken soup
1 carrot, sliced

Brown ground beef in skillet over medium heat. Pour off excess fat. Place a layer of ground beef, layer of potatoes, layer of onion, carrot and peas in 2½ qt. casserole dish. Repeat layers until ingredients are used up. Pour can of chicken soup on top. Bake 375° for 1 to 1½ hrs.

POTATOES IN BEEF JACKETS

Ellen R. Brenneman

12 sm. potatoes
1 lb. hamburger
1 egg
1½ t. salt

¼ t. pepper
2 c. tomato juice
1 lg. onion, chopped
1 green pepper

Cook potatoes in jackets till almost tender and remove skins. Mix hamburger, egg, salt, and pepper. Cover each potato with hamburger, forming a jacket, pressing well. Place balls in greased 13x9" casserole. Pour tomato juice over balls and add chopped onion and pepper. Bake at 350° till done. Serves 6 to 8.

POTATO AND HAMBURGER CASSEROLE

Verda Overholt

4 c. thinly-sliced potatoes
1 medium onion (chopped)
1 t. salt
Several strips of parsley

1 lb. hamburger
½ c. cracker crumbs
¾ c. milk
½ c. ketchup
Small onion and several stems
    of celery (cut fine)
1 t. salt

Put first 4 ingredients in a greased 2-qt. casserole, then mix hamburger and the rest of the ingredients and put on top of the potatoes. Bake at 350° for 1½ hrs.

PREACHER'S SPECIAL

Ellen R. Brenneman

¼ c. butter
1 green pepper, chopped
1 medium onion, chopped
1 to 1½ lbs. hamburger
4 medium potatoes, or more

Salt as desired
1 can cream of asparagus soup
1 can cream of chicken soup
Cheese, grated

Grease pan with butter. Brown hamburger, onion, pepper in skillet. Put a layer of raw potatoes in bottom of pan. Top with a layer of meat and pour asparagus soup over this. Add another layer of potatoes, top with meat layer and pour cream of chicken soup over this. Bake in 9x12' pan at 350° for 1 hr. After baked, top with cheese. Serves 6 to 8.

QUICK SKILLET SUPPER

Mrs. Daniel Yoder

1 lb. ground beef
1 c. chopped onion
1 T. fat
3 c. noodles, uncooked
3 c. tomato juice

1/2 c. sour cream
2 t. salt
1/8 t. celery salt
2 t. Worcestershire sauce
1/2 c. water

Fry beef and onion in hot fat. Place uncooked noodles over top of meat mixture. Combine remaining ingredients and blend well. Pour over noodles, taking care to moisten noodles well. Do not stir; bring to a boil. Turn heat low, cover and simmer for 30 min., or until noodles are tender. Serves 6 to 8.

SOUPER MEAT 'N POTATOES PIE

Linda Kauffman

1 can cream of mushroom soup
1 lb. ground beef
1/4 c. finely-chopped onion
1 egg
1/4 c. bread crumbs

2 T. chopped parsley
1/2 t. salt
1/4 t. pepper
2 c. mashed potatoes
1/4 c. shredded mild cheese

Mix thoroughly 1/2 c. soup, beef, onion, egg, bread crumbs, parsley, and seasonings. Press firmly into 9" pie plate. Bake at 350° for 25 min. Spoon off fat. Frost with potatoes; top with remaining soup and cheese. Bake 10 min. more, or till done. Garnish with cooked bacon strips, if desired. This recipe can be doubled and baked in an oblong casserole dish. Serves 6 to 8.

SPAGHETTI DISH

Sara Marie Yoder

1 lb. hamburger
2 c. tomatoes
1/2 lb. spaghetti
1 medium onion, minced

1 1/2 t. chili powder
1 t. salt
1/2 c. grated cheese
1/4 c. catsup

Cook spaghetti in salt water until tender. Drain. Brown hamburger and onion in a little fat. Add tomatoes, spaghetti and seasoning. Simmer 20 min. on top of stove. Just before serving, add grated cheese. Stir until cheese melts. Serves 6 to 8.

SUPPER CASSEROLE
Mrs. Floyd E. Yoder

1 layer sliced potatoes
1 layer sliced onions
1 layer sliced carrots

1 layer chopped celery
1 layer raw ground beef
Salt to taste
1 can cream of celery soup

Place layers in order given in any size casserole dish. Use 1 can cream of celery soup to a 2-qt. casserole dish. Bake 375° for 1 hr.

SHIPWRECK
Verda Overholt

1 lb. hamburger
1 medium onion

5 medium potatoes, diced
1 can cream of mushroom soup
1/2 can milk

Brown hamburger - partly cook potatoes. Dice onion. Put all in casserole dish and add cream of mushroom soup to which 1/2 can milk has been mixed with. Mix well and bake at 350° for 1 1/2 hrs.

SHIPWRECK
Lorene Plank

1 lb. ground beef
1 c. kidney beans
1/2 c. cooked leftover rice

5 potatoes
1 onion (optional)
1 lg. can tomato sauce

Brown ground beef. Layer in greased casserole dish the browned meat, sliced potatoes (cooked or raw), kidney beans, sliced onion rings (if desired). Repeat with second layer of each, then sprinkle rice over top, then add tomato sauce. Bake 350° for 1 hr. Serves 8 to 10.

Charity begins anywhere and should have no end.

DEEP DISH TACO SQUARES

Mrs. Chris L. Miller

1/2 lb. ground beef
1 medium onion, chopped
1/2 c. dairy sour cream
1/3 c. salad dressing
1/2 c. shredded sharp Cheddar
  cheese
1 c. biscuit mix (little more)
1/4 c. cold water
1 to 2 tomatoes, sliced
1/2 c. green pepper, chopped

Brown beef and onion. Mix sour cream, salad dressing, and cheese. Combine biscuit mix and water and put into pan. Layer in beef and onions. Carefully put tomatoes and green peppers on top. Spoon sour cream mixture over all. Bake in 8x8x2" pan at 350° 30-40 min. Test dough for doneness.

TACO CASSEROLE

Shirley Yoder

1 lb. ground beef
1/2 c. onions, chopped
1/4 c. celery
Taco or pizza sauce
1 t. salt
1/4 t. pepper
1 can kidney beans
1 c. shredded cheese
1 bag taco chips

Brown meat; add onions and celery. Cook till tender. Drain grease. Add beans and sauce and mix well. Place a layer of chips in greased dish. Alternate layers of meat mixture and chips and cheese, ending with chips. Bake at 350° for 10 min.

TACO CRESCENTS

Mrs. Ivan Yoder

1 lb. ground beef
1 pkg. taco seasoning mix
8 oz. can tomato sauce
2 cans crescent rolls
1 c. mozzarella cheese

Brown beef and drain off grease. Stir in seasoning mix and tomato sauce. Stir in cheese. Place rounded T. of mixture on each roll and roll up. Bake at 375° for 15-20 min. or until golden brown.

TATER TOT CASSEROLE

Joyce Yoder

1¹/₂ lbs. hamburger
Salt and pepper
1 medium onion (chopped)

1 qt. drained green beans
1 can Cheddar cheese soup
1 lb. tater tots

Crumble raw hamburger in bottom of casserole. Sprinkle with salt, pepper, and onions. Cover with beans. Spread soup on top of beans. Top with tater tots to make a cover. Bake at 350° for 1 hr.

TATER TOT CASSEROLE

Ruth Yoder

1 lb. hamburger
1 pt. peas
1 can cream of mushroom soup

1 can cream of celery soup
1 lg. bag tater tots
Salt, pepper and garlic salt

Brown hamburger, add salt, pepper and garlic salt. Put into casserole dish. Heat soups and 1 soup can of milk together, pour on top of hamburger mixture. Put peas on top of soup mixture. Top with tater tots. Bake at 350° for 25 min. Put cheese over tater tots the last 5 min.

TEXAS HASH

Mary Plank

2 lbs. ground chuck or beef
2 medium onions, chopped
2 green peppers, chopped
2-1 lb. cans tomatoes

1¹/₂ t. chili powder
2¹/₂ t. salt
2 t. Worcestershire sauce
1 c. raw rice (converted)

Brown beef in skillet and drain off fat. Put all ingredients in crock pot. Stir thoroughly, cover and cook on low 6 to 8 hrs. (High: 4 hrs.) Serves 10.

If you can't forgive others,
you have burned the bridge over which you must pass.

TORTILLA DISH

Bertha Swartzentruber

2 lbs. ground beef
1 onion, chopped
1 lb. longhorn cheese
2 cans tomato sauce (1 cupful)
1 can cream of mushroom soup

1 can cream of chicken soup
1/2 can green chili
   (Old El Paso brand)
2 T. red chili powder
1 pkg. corn tortillas

Line pan with 6 tortillas. Cover with ground beef mixture. Cover with remaining tortillas. Put the cheese on top of this. Bake in 9x13' pan at 350° for 20-25 min. Serves 10.

WIGGLERS

Verda Overholt

3 lbs. hamburger
9 slices bacon
3 onions
3 c. raw potatoes
3 c. celery
3 c. carrots

3 c. peas
2 cans cream of mushroom soup
3 c. uncooked spaghetti
1 qt. tomato juice
1 lb. grated cheese
Salt to taste

Fry bacon and crumble in pieces, fry hamburger and onions together in some drippings from bacon. Mix everything together and put cheese on top. Bake 350° for 1½ hrs. Put in oven until cheese is melted, then stir occasionally. Serves 10 to 15.

YUMA-ZETTA

Mrs. Sol Yoder, Linda Weaver,
and Kathryn Yoder

1 pkg. wide noodles
1/2 lb. yellow brick or Velveeta
   cheese
1½ lbs. hamburger

1 onion, cut fine
1 can Carnation milk
1 can tomato juice
1 minced green pepper (optional)
Salt and pepper to taste

Cook noodles 10 min. in salt water. Drain. Fry meat and onion together, brown and season. Put noodles and meat in layers - also cheese in 3-qt. casserole and bake at 350° for 1 hr. Add milk and tomato juice. Serves 10 to 12.

YUM-E-SETTI
Delores Hostetler

1 or 1½ lbs. hamburger
1 pkg. wide noodles
1 can cream of chicken soup
1 can cream of tomato soup

1 c. celery (cut fine-cooked tender)
½ lb. Velveeta cheese
Salt to taste

Fry hamburger in skillet, stirring occasionally. Cook noodles in hot water until tender, but not soft. Mix tomato soup and celery with hamburger and chicken soup with noodles. Put in layers in casserole. Cover with cheese and bake in a slow oven 275° for 1 hr.

YUM-YUM (RICE & HAMBURGER CASSEROLE) Elsie N. Yoder

Brown 2 lbs. or less hamburger with 1 c. chopped onion.

ADD:
1 can cream of chicken soup
1 can cream of mushroom soup
2 t. salt and pepper to taste
1 c. uncooked rice

1½ c. chopped celery
3 c. water
3 t. soy sauce

Bake in greased dish. Add chow mein noodles last 10 min. or buttered bread crumbs right away. Bake 300° for 1½ or 2 hrs. Serves 10 or more.

Rice and celery may be partially cooked. Shortens baking time.

BAKED CHICKEN & RICE
Mrs. Chris L. Miller

1 c. uncooked rice
1 c. chopped celery
1 c. cooked navy beans

4 c. water
1 pkg. onion soup mix

2 c. diced chicken meat

2 c. broth

In roaster, put rice, celery, and navy beans together. Make a gravy of chicken meat and broth, and add to rice mixture. Add water; mix all together. Sprinkle onion soup mix over top. Bake 325° for 2 hrs.

CHICKEN & RICE   Mrs. Crist Yoder, Sr.

1 c. rice	1 can mushroom soup
2 c. water	1 can cream of chicken soup
1 sm. onion	Add a little salt and pepper
1 fryer	1½ sticks butter or oleo

Mix uncooked rice, water, onion and soups together, then dip raw chicken in melted butter or oleo and add to the above ingredients. Put in a covered baking dish. Bake 275° for 2½ to 3 hrs.

CHICKEN & RICE   Verda Overholt, Mrs. Ernest W. Yoder

1¼ c. rice (uncooked)	1 can cream of chicken soup
1 pkg. dry onion soup	2 c. water
1 can cream of mushroom soup	1 to 2 chickens, cut up

Put this all together in pan, place chicken on top after rolling in melted oleo. Bake in covered 9x12" pan or casserole dish at 325° for 2½ hrs.

CHICKEN & RICE CASSEROLE   Mrs. Crist Yoder, Jr.,
Mrs. Nelson Yoder, Mrs. Leslie Yoder,
and Mrs. Levi Kauffman

1 can cream of celery soup	1½ c. milk
1 can cream of chicken soup	1 c. uncooked rice
1 whole chicken (cut up)	

Mix soups, milk and rice together. Put into casserole. Lay chicken on top of soup mixture and sprinkle with salt, pepper and paprika. Bake 350° for 2 hrs.

CHICKEN & RICE CASSEROLE   Lena Swartzentruber

1½ c. uncooked Minute rice	1 qt. cooked chicken (cut up)
1 can cream of celery soup	2 T. butter
1 can cream of chicken soup	Salt
1 soup can of water	Pepper

Mix all ingredients, put in casserole dish and bake at 300° for 1 hr.

CHICKEN & RICE DINNER

Mrs. Levi Kauffman, Ruth Yoder

3 c. cooked rice
1 c. grated cheese
1/2 c. parsley
1/3 c. onions, chopped
1/3 c. pimento
1 t. salt
3 eggs, beaten
1 1/2 c. milk

GRAVY:
1/4 c. butter
1/3 c. chopped onion
1/4 c. flour
2 c. chicken + broth
1 c. milk
Salt and pepper to taste
Cook till bubbly and serve on
baked rice.

Mix first 8 ingredients and bake in 2-qt. pan at 325° for 40 min. Then make the gravy. For serving: Cut the rice and chicken loaf into serving pieces and spoon gravy over it. Yum! Yum!

CHICKEN POT PIE

Mrs. Allen M. Yoder

1 chicken, cooked and cubed
1 can cream of chicken soup
3 c. chicken broth

1 pt. peas
1 pt. carrots (cooked)
Salt and pepper to taste

Combine above ingredients and pour in 9x12" pan. Pour crust over chicken mixture.

CRUST:
1 1/2 c. flour
1 T. baking powder
3/4 t. salt

1 1/2 c. milk
6 T. melted butter

Mix all ingredients and pour over chicken mixture, do not stir. Bake at 400° for 30 min. or until crust is finished. Serves 8.

CHICKEN POT PIE

Mrs. Allen E. Yoder

2 lg. baking hens, pressure
  cooked
2 to 3 qts. water
1 qt. canned broth
6 T. chicken seasoning

3 cans Lindy peas
3 pts. fine diced carrots
12 heaping T. clear gel or
  cornstarch to thicken
Salt and pepper to taste

Simmer together until carrots are soft and then add thickening. Use 12-qt. kettle.

CHICKEN VEGETABLE POT PIE   Kathryn Yoder

1-2½ to 3 lb. chicken
4 to 5 medium-sized potatoes,
   pared
5 stalks celery
½ lb. carrots
1 pt. English peas

3 c. chicken broth
½ c. butter or margarine
⅔ c. all-purpose flour
1 c. milk
1 chicken bouillon cube
Salt and pepper to taste

Cook chicken and cut into bite-sized pieces. Cut potatoes, celery and carrots into 1" chunks. Cook all vegetables until tender. Make a gravy with chicken broth, butter, flour, milk and bouillon cube. Mix all ingredients together and pour into 13x9x2" pan. Top with a pie crust or biscuits. Bake at 400° until biscuits or pie crust is brown. Serves 6 to 8.

CHICKEN AND BROCCOLI CASSEROLE   Ruth Weaver

1 whole chicken
2-10 oz. pkgs. frozen broccoli
2 cans cream of mushroom
   soup
¾ c. mayonnaise

2 T. lemon juice
1 c. bread crumbs
1 c. grated cheese
1 T. melted butter or oleo

Cook chicken and cut up. Cook broccoli and drain. Grease the bottom of dish with butter. Alternate layers of chicken and broccoli. Mix cream of mushroom soup with mayonnaise and lemon juice and pour over chicken and broccoli. Mix butter with bread crumbs and sprinkle on top. Sprinkle cheese on top 5 min. before removing from oven. Bake at 350° for 35 min.

CHICKEN CASSEROLE   Mrs. Bertha Yoder, Mrs. Louis Yoder

8 whole slices bread
4 c. cooked chicken (chopped)
¼ c. butter
½ c. salad dressing

4 eggs (beaten)
2 c. milk + chicken broth
1 t. salt
9 slices Velveeta cheese
2 cans cream of celery soup

Place bread in bottom of pan. Spread chicken over bread. Mix butter, salad dressing, eggs, milk and broth, and salt together and pour over chicken and bread. Place cheese on top of this. Spread celery soup over cheese. This can be covered and stored in refrigerator overnight before baking. Bake at 350° for 1 hr. and 15 min.

CHICKEN CASSEROLE
Alma Yoder, Mrs. Milton Yoder

2 c. chicken
1 c. cut-up celery
2 T. chopped onion
1-8 oz. pkg. noodles, partially
   cooked

1 can cream of chicken soup
1/2 c. mayonnaise
3 T. thin cream
2 c. crushed potato chips
Season with salt and pepper

Cook chicken, remove from bones. Cut in small pieces. Saute celery and chopped onion in small amount of butter until tender. Mix chicken, celery, onion, noodles, soup, mayonnaise, and cream (season) together. Place in 2-qt. greased casserole; cover with crushed potato chips. Bake at 350° for 45 min. Serves 6.

CHICKEN CASSEROLE
Mrs. Eli Hostetler

MIX TOGETHER:
1/4 c. melted butter
1/2 c. salad dressing
4 eggs, beaten

1 c. milk
1 c. broth
1 t. salt

9 slices toasted bread

4 c. cooked chicken

Put 9 slices of toasted bread in bottom of casserole dish. Then 4 c. of cooked chicken. Pour the mixture on the chicken and bread and 2 cans of celery soup. Top it with cheese and buttered crumbs. Cover and refrigerate overnight. Bake at 350° for 1 1/4 hrs.

CHICKEN & STUFFING CASSEROLE
Ruth Yoder

1 hen, cooked
6 c. bread crumbs
1/4 c. diced celery, cooked
1 T. chopped onion, cooked
1 T. parsley
GRAVY:
1 c. chicken broth
4 T. flour
Salt and pepper to taste

2 eggs, beaten
1/4 c. butter, melted
Sage, salt & pepper to taste
3 c. potatoes, cooked
1 1/2 c. carrots, cooked

1 can cream of chicken soup
1 soup can of milk

Mix bread crumbs, parsley, eggs, butter, seasonings and enough broth to moisten well, add celery and onions. Put in greased casserole. Dice or slice cooked carrots and potatoes and put on bread mixture. Put cut-up chicken meat on top of this and top with gravy. Make sauce with flour and chicken broth, add remaining ingredients and cook until thickened. Pour over stuffing casserole. Bake at 350° 30-40 min.

CHICKEN CRUNCH CASSEROLE

Delores Hostetler

2¹/₂ c. cooked chicken
1 c. rich milk
3 c. crushed potato chips
Paprika

1-10¹/₂ oz. can cream of
   mushroom soup
¹/₂ t. salt
4 T. cheese

Combine chicken, soup, milk, and salt. Heat to boiling. Spread 1¹/₂ c. potato chips in bottom of casserole. Pour in chicken mixture. Cover with remaining chips. Sprinkle with cheese and paprika and bake at 350° 25-30 min.

CLUB CHICKEN CASSEROLE

Mrs. William N. Yoder

¹/₄ c. butter
¹/₃ c. celery, chopped
¹/₄ c. flour
¹/₂ c. onions, diced
³/₄ c. evaporated milk
¹/₂ c. water

1 c. chicken broth
1 can cream of mushroom soup
2¹/₂ c. chopped, cooked chicken
3 c. cooked rice
1 t. salt

Melt butter and add flour, celery and onions. Brown slowly for 2 min., then add milk, water, chicken broth, and soup. Stir until thick. Remove from heat and add remaining ingredients. Stir lightly until mixed well. Pour in pan and bake at 350° for 40 min.

CHICKEN CHOW MEIN

Barbara Jean Hershberger

4 T. vegetable oil
1 can bean sprouts
2 c. thin onion strips
3 T. cornstarch
2¹/₂ c. diced celery
3 T. soy sauce

1 t. salt
2 c. diced, cooked chicken
2 t. sugar
1 or 2 cans chow mein noodles
1¹/₂ c. clear chicken stock

Heat oil in a 12" skillet over low heat. Mix in onions and celery; sprinkle with salt and sugar. Add chicken stock, cover and simmer gently about 10 min. Drain bean sprouts. Mix cornstarch and soy sauce until smooth with ¹/₄ c. of the bean liquid. Add to skillet; cook and stir until thickened. Add drained bean sprouts and chicken, mix and reheat. Serve with chow mein noodles. Can also be made with any meat preferred. It is good without bean sprouts also, and is good on cooked rice if preferred. Serves 4 to 6.

CHICKEN DIVANE   Ruth Yoder

3 pkgs. frozen broccoli
2 cans cream of chicken soup
1 lg. chicken (cooked), cut in
   pieces
1 c. mayonnaise

1½ T. melted butter
½ t. curry powder
¾ c. Cheddar cheese, grated
1 t. lemon juice
¾ c. bread crumbs

Cook and drain broccoli. Put in bottom of baking dish. Then add chicken. Mix together soup, mayonnaise, curry powder, and lemon juice. Heat. Pour over chicken mixture. Top with crumbs. Mix cheese and butter together and put on top of crumbs. Bake 350° 25-30 min.

CHICKEN TETRAZZINI   Ruth Yoder

1 chicken, cooked
1 pkg. spaghetti, 4 c. cooked
1 egg
1 c. chicken broth

½ c. cheese
1 can cream of mushroom soup
Salt and pepper to taste
1 T. oregano

Cook spaghetti, enough to make 4 c. Do not cook completely done. Mix together chicken, spaghetti, chicken broth, egg and cheese, mushroom soup, salt and pepper, and oregano. You can add any spices or flavorings you like. Bake at 300° for 45 min. Serves 8.

HUNTINGTON CHICKEN   Mrs. Norman Yoder, Mrs. Sol Yoder,
                              Mrs. Lloyd Swartzentruber,
              Barbara Jean Hershberger, Vernie Weaver

1 hen, cooked and boned
4 c. chicken broth
2 c. macaroni, cooked and
   drained
1 c. cheese

THICKENING FOR THE BROTH:
8 T. flour
¾ to 1 c. milk
Season with 1 T. chicken
   seasoning and salt to taste

Melt the cheese into the gravy. Pour over macaroni and chicken meat. Do not overstir or meat will get stringy. Pour into a large casserole dish and top with buttered bread crumbs. Bake at 350° for ½ hr. Serves 10.

111

SALMON CASSEROLE
Verda Overholt

8 oz. pkg. macaroni or spaghetti Salt and pepper
2 beaten eggs 1 can salmon
2 c. milk

Cook and drain macaroni or spaghetti. Combine all ingredients. Mix well and bake at 350° for 30 min.

BAKED TUNA WITH CHEESE SWIRLS
Mrs. Paul E. Yoder

1-6½ or 7 oz. can tuna 4 T. oleo
3 T. chopped onions ⅓ c. chopped green pepper
5 T. flour ¼ t. salt
1½ c. milk 1-10½ oz. cream of chicken soup
1 T. lemon juice 1-10½ oz. cream of celery soup

SWIRLS:
1 c. flour 2 T. shortening
⅓ c. milk 1½ t. baking powder
½ c. shredded process cheese ¼ t. salt

Drain oil from tuna and add oil to butter in saucepan. Add onion and pepper and brown slightly. blend in flour and salt and add milk gradually. Cook and stir till thick, then add soup, lemon juice and tuna (broken in pieces). Pour into casserole. Top with Swirls. Bake at 400° for 20 min., or until Swirls are brown.
SWIRLS: Sift flour, measure, add baking powder and salt. Mix with shortening until resembles coarse meal. Add milk; mix with fork. Turn on floured board. Roll in rectangle. Sprinkle cheese on top. Roll up like a jellyroll and cut in 8 slices. Place on top of tuna mixture. Serves 4 to 6.

CHEESY TUNA VEGETABLE BAKE
Lena Yoder

9¼ oz. can tuna, drained 10¾ oz. can cream of
  and flaked   mushroom soup
1 c. (4 oz.) shredded Cheddar 10 oz. (1½ c.) frozen peas
  or American cheese 8 oz. can buttermilk or country-
½ c. celery   style biscuits
3 T. chopped onion 1 T. margarine or butter, melted
½ c. milk ½ c. crushed potato chips

In ungreased 2-qt. casserole dish, spread tuna, sprinkle with cheese. In medium saucepan, combine celery, onion, milk, soup and peas; simmer while preparing biscuits. Separate biscuit dough into 10 biscuits, cut each biscuit into fourths. Pour hot soup mixture over tuna and cheese, arrange biscuit pieces over soup mixture. Drizzle with melted margarine. Sprinkle with potato chips. Bake at 375° 30-40 min. until golden brown. Serves 4 to 5.

112

TUNA NOODLE CASSEROLE   Linda Yoder

3 qts. boiling water
1 T. salt
2 c. uncooked noodles
2 T. butter
2 T. flour

1½ c. milk
½ t. salt and pepper
1 c. cheese, grated
1-7 oz. can tuna (drained)
1 sm. can mushrooms (or soup)

Cook noodles until tender and drain. Make White Sauce. Break tuna into large chunks and add oil. Add ¾ c. cheese and stir until melted. Add noodles and mix lightly. Put into 1½ qt. casserole and add remaining ingredients and sprinkle with remaining cheese. (I use mushroom soup and only 1 T. flour.) Bake at 350° for 20 min.

WHITE SAUCE:
4 T. butter or oil
4 T. flour

1 t. salt
2 c. milk

Melt butter in saucepan. Add flour and salt and stir till well blended. Slowly add milk until a smooth paste is formed.

CHEESE HAM CASSEROLE   Mrs. Melvin (Katherine) Yoder
                                     and Mrs. Ivan Yoder

2 c. cut-up ham
2 c. milk
1 can cream of celery soup
¼ c. onions, chopped
½ t. salt

2 c. uncooked noodles (broken up
  slightly)
1 can cream of mushroom soup
2 c. Cracker Barrel cheese, grated
1 can mushrooms (optional)

Mix ingredients and place in pan, cover and refrigerate overnight. Bake in 9x13" pan until bubbly 350° for 45 min. You may want to try chicken in place of ham. Serves 6.

HAM CASSEROLE   Mrs. Lloyd Swartzentruber

1-8 oz. pkg. egg noodles
¼ box Velveeta cheese
1 pt. peas

1 can cream of chicken soup
2 c. ham chunks
4 T. melted butter
1 c. graham crackers

Cook noodles as directed on package. Add cheese. cook peas till tender. Mix noodles, cheese, peas, soup and ham. Put into casserole and top with graham cracker crumbs that have been mixed with butter. Bake at 350° for 20 min. till brown.

HAM AND BROCCOLI CASSEROLE   Mrs. Eli Kauffman

1 pkg. frozen or 1 bunch fresh   1/2 c. shredded cheese
  broccoli, cooked   2 t. prepared mustard
4 slices cooked ham or 6 slices 1 t. salt
  bacon   1 T. minced onion
2 c. White Sauce

Arrange broccoli in bottom of 1 1/2 qt. casserole. Place ham on top. Prepare a White Sauce, add cheese, mustard, salt and onions and stir over low heat until cheese is melted. Pour sauce over meat and broccoli and bake at 400° 25-30 min. Serves 4.

WHITE SAUCE:
4 T. fat (butter preferred)   1 t. salt
4 T. flour   2 c. milk

HAM AND SCALLOPED POTATOES   Mary Plank

6 to 8 slices ham   1 c. grated Cheddar or American
8 to 10 medium potatoes,   cheese
  peeled & thinly sliced   1-10 oz. can cream of celery or
2 onions, peeled & thinly sliced   mushroom soup
                                 Paprika

Put half of ham, potatoes and onions in crock pot. Sprinkle with salt and pepper, then grated cheese. Repeat with remaining half. Spoon undiluted soup over top. Sprinkle with paprika. Cover and cook on low 8 to 10 hrs. (high: 4 hrs.).

SCALLOPED POTATOES WITH HAM   Mrs. Chris L. Miller

20 lbs. potatoes   1 1/2 c. flour
10 lbs. ham   1/2 lb. butter
1 gal. milk   1 lb. Velveeta cheese

Boil potatoes in skins. Peel and put through salad maker. Slice or chop ham. Mix milk, flour, butter together and heat. Add cheese to milk mixture. Mix all together and put in a large electric roaster. Bake at 200° for 3 hrs. Will serve 80 people when used as main dish or 100 people when served with a full course meal.

Add dill weed to scalloped potatoes for an extra flavor.

SCALLOPED POTATOES & HAM
Mrs. Norman Yoder

12 to 14 medium potatoes
1/4 lb. ham
8 slices Velveeta cheese

2 cans cream of chicken soup
1 3/4 to 2 c. milk
2 T. butter

Cook potatoes in skin and cool and remove peeling. Slice potatoes. Place in pan alternately with layers of ham. Melt butter in a kettle, add cream of chicken soup and milk till it's soupy like gravy. Heat and add Velveeta cheese. Sprinkle lightly with celery salt. Pour just enough gravy on to cover potatoes. Put in a slow oven. Just enough to make it real hot - so it doesn't cook.

FULL O' BOLONEY
Laura Whitt

1 1/2 c. cubed raw potatoes
1 can cream of celery soup,
    undiluted

1 1/2 c. cubed bologna (1/2 lb.)
2 lg. slices cheese, quartered

Mix all ingredients, except cheese. Bake in covered 1-1/2 qt. dish at 350° for 1 hr. and 15 min. Remove cover, top with cheese. Put under broiler until bubbly and browned.

HOT DOG CASSEROLE
(CHILDREN'S SPECIAL)
Mrs. Daniel Swartzentruber,
Ruth Yoder

5 slices bacon
1 can mushroom soup
1/2 c. water
1/2 t. salt

Dash of pepper
3 c. cooked, diced potatoes
1 c. canned green beans, drained
1/2 lb. franks, split & cut in half

In skillet, fry bacon, remove and crumble; set aside. Mix soup, water, salt, pepper, potatoes and green beens. Put into 1 1/2 qt. casserole dish. Stand franks around edge of casserole. Garnish with bacon. Bake at 350° for 30 min.

Blessed is he that expects nothing
for he shall never be disappointed.

115

HOT FRANK POTATO SALAD

Mrs. Alva Yoder

6 c. cooked, sliced potatoes
8 franks, sliced
2 hard-cooked eggs
1/2 lb. bacon
3/4 c. onions

1 1/2 t. salt
1 t. celery seed
3/4 c. vinegar
1 1/2 c. water
3 T. sugar
3 T. flour

Fry bacon until crisp, drain and crumble. Saute onions in 1/3 c. bacon drippings until tender. Add sugar, salt, celery seed, and flour. Stir in vinegar and water. Cook until thick. Combine with potatoes, bacon, franks, and eggs. Bake in covered 3 qt. casserole at 350° for 20 min. Serves 8.

PORK CHOP CASSEROLE

Mary Plank

6 to 8 pork chops
Salt and pepper
2 medium sweet potatoes
   (peeled and sliced)
1 lg. onion, sliced

1 lg. green pepper, sliced
1/2 t. leaf oregano
1/4 t. whole thyme
1-1 lb. can tomatoes

Trim fat from pork chops, season with salt and pepper and brown in skillet to remove excess fat. Drain and place in crock pot. Add remaining ingredients in order listed. Cover and cook on low 8 to 10 hrs. (High: 3 to 4 hrs.) Adjust seasonings to taste before serving.

White potatoes may be substituted for sweet potatoes if desired.

PORK CHOP SKILLET MEAL

Alma Yoder

4 T. lard or oil
4 pork chops
4 slices onion
4 rings of green pepper

1/2 c. uncooked rice
3 c. canned tomatoes
1 c. diced celery
Salt and pepper to taste

Brown chops on both sides in lard or oil (drain). Place slice of onion and ring of pepper on each chop. Add a T. of rice on each ring and pour tomatoes around meat. Add diced celery. Cover and simmer. 1 hr. Serves 4.

116

PORK CHOPS AND VEGETABLES   Verda Overholt

8 pork chops
1 onion
1 pt. peas
1 can cream of mushroom soup

6 potatoes
Dash of salt and pepper
$1/4$ c. oleo

Brown chops in grease. Take chops out of pan and pour off grease. Slice or dice potatoes and onions; put in bottom of pan. Add salt and pepper and peas. Dab oleo around on top, then lay chops on top and pour cream of mushroom soup which a little milk has been added to, over meat. Let simmer until everything is soft.

QUICHE LORRAINE   Mrs. L.D. Kauffman

5 slices crisply-fried bacon
$1/2$ c. milk
$1 1/2$ t. beef bouillon
3 eggs
$1/4$ c. grated Cheddar cheese
$1/4$ t. salt

$1/4$ t. paprika
$1/2$ t. dry mustard
2 t. flour
A dash of cayenne pepper
1 pie shell

Add bouillon to eggs and beat thoroughly. Slowly add milk, flour and seasoning. Crumble bacon; stir into egg mixture with cheese; pour into partially-baked 9" pie shell. Bake at 350° for 30 min. Serves 8 to 10.

SAUSAGE SQUASH CASSEROLE   Miriam Brenneman

1 lb. bulk pork sausage
1 clove garlic, crushed
4 c. sliced summer squash
$1/2$ c. dry bread crumbs
$1/2$ c. grated Parmesan cheese

$1/2$ c. milk
1 T. snipped parsley
$1/2$ t. salt
$1/2$ t. dried oregano, crushed
2 beaten eggs

Cook sausage and garlic till meat is brown; drain off excess fat. Cook squash, covered, in small amount of water till tender; drain. Stir squash and next 6 ingredients into meat; fold in eggs. Transfer to 10x6x1$1/2$" baking dish and bake 325° 25-30 min. Serves 4 to 6.

Notes

COOKIES & CANDY

ANGEL COOKIES

Irene Yoder

1/2 c. margarine
1 c. shortening
2 eggs
1 c. brown sugar
1 c. white sugar

2 t. vanilla
3 c. flour
2 t. cream of tartar
2 t. baking soda

Cream together margarine and shortening. Add eggs; mix well. Add brown and white sugars, and vanilla; combine thoroughly. Mix together flour, cream of tartar, and baking soda. Slowly add flour mixture to creamed mixture, mixing well. Drop by teaspoonfuls on ungreased cookie sheet. Bake at 350° for 8 min. Makes about 5 dozen cookies.

BUTTERMILK COOKIES

Mrs. Sol Yoder

2 c. brown sugar
1 c. melted lard (scant)
1 t. vanilla
2 eggs

2 t. baking powder
4 c. flour
1 c. buttermilk
2 t. soda
1 t. salt

Cream sugar and lard. (Crisco or other vegetable shortening may be used.) Add vanilla and eggs. Sift 1 c. flour with the baking powder and the salt and mix with the other flour. Add the soda to the buttermilk and stir well. Now blend flour mixture and buttermilk alternately into shortening mixture. Chill dough overnight. Place about 1/3 of dough on a floured cloth and roll out to about 1/8" thick. Cut with a cookie cutter and place on baking sheet with a potato turner (spatula). Use a well-greased cookie sheet. Dough may also be dropped by teaspoonfuls on cookie sheet if desired. Yield: approximately 4 dozen 4" cookies. Bake at 350° until brown.

Using an extra egg for soft cookies helps keep them soft.

A house should have a cookie jar for when it's half past three and children hurry home from school as hungry as can be. There's nothing quite so splendid as spicy, fluffy ginger cakes and sweet milk in a cup. A house should have a mother waiting with a hug. No matter what a boy brings home - a puppy or a bug. For children only loiter, when the bell rings to dismiss, if no one is home to greet them with a cookie and a kiss!

CARROT COOKIES
Bertha Swartzentruber

2½ c. sugar
3 c. shortening
3 c. cooked, mashed & cooled carrots

6 c. flour
6 t. baking powder
3 t. lemon flavoring

Mix all together at once and drop by the teaspoonful on cookie sheet. Bake at 375° for 8 min.
ICING FOR CARROT COOKIES: 3 T. soft butter, juice and grated rinds of 2 large oranges, enough powdered sugar to make thick frosting. Put on while cookies are still warm. Makes 6 dozen.

CEREAL COOKIES
Mari Yoder

1 c. white sugar
1 c. brown sugar
1 c. shortening
2 beaten eggs
1 t. vanilla
1 t. soda

½ t. salt
2 c. flour
1 c. crushed cornflakes or Rice Krispies
2 c. oatmeal
½ c. nuts (chopped)

Mix all ingredients and place in refrigerator until chilled. Drop on cookie sheets and bake at 350° till brown. Yield: approximately 6 dozen.

CHOCOLATE CHIP COOKIES
Mrs. Daniel Swartzentruber

1 c. softened shortening
¾ c. firmly-packed brown sugar
1 t. vanilla
2 eggs
1 t. salt
1-12 oz. pkg. chocolate chips

¾ c. white sugar
½ t. water
2 c. flour
1 t. baking soda
1 c. chopped nuts

Beat shortening, sugars, vanilla, water and eggs until light and fluffy. Mix flour with soda and salt; blend into shortening mixture. Stir in nuts and chips. Drop by teaspoonfuls on cookie sheet and bake at 375° for 10 min. Makes about 5 dozen.

CHOCOLATE CHIP-PEANUT BUTTER CRISPS   Elsie N. Yoder

1/2 c. granulated sugar	1 egg
1/2 c. brown sugar, packed	1/2 t. baking soda
1/2 c. peanut butter	1/2 t. baking powder
1/4 c. butter or margarine,	4 c. Rice Krispies
softened	1-6 oz. pkg. chocolate chips
1/4 c. shortening	

Mix sugar, peanut butter, shortening, egg, baking soda and baking powder in 4 qt. bowl thoroughly. Stir in cereal and chocolate chips. Shape dough, slightly rounded by teaspoon. Place about 2" apart on ungreased cookie sheet. Bake at 325°, 10-12 min. until golden brown. Cool 5 min. before removing from cookie sheet. Makes 3 ½ dozen.

Can substitute butterscotch chips for chocolate chips.

CHOCOLATE KISSES   Lorene Plank

2 c. sugar	2 c. unsifted flour
1/2 c. margarine (melted)	2 t. baking powder
4-1 oz. sqs. unsweetened	3/4 t. salt
chocolate (melted)	2 t. vanilla
2 eggs	3/4 c. powdered sugar

In a large mixing bowl, combine sugar, margarine and chocolate. Add eggs, one at a time and mix until well blended. Mix in vanilla. Combine flour, baking powder and salt and add gradually to chocolate mixture, mixing well after each addition. Cover and chill 2 hrs. or overnight. Drop mixture by rounded teaspoonfuls into powdered sugar coating, then shape into a kiss. Place on greased baking sheet 2" apart. Bake at 350° for 14 min. or until done. Makes 5 or 6 dozen.

To keep bugs off fresh paint,
mix in oil of citronella or vanilla with the paint.

121

COCONUT OATMEAL COOKIES   Barbara Jean Hershberger

1 c. brown sugar
1 c. white sugar
1 c. shortening
2 c. flour
1 c. coconut
3 c. quick-rolled oats

1/2 c. chopped nuts
2 eggs (beaten)
1 t. salt
1 t. soda
1 t. baking powder
1 t. vanilla

Blend sugar and shortening, add beaten eggs. Sift dry ingredients together and add to first mixture. Stir in vanilla, coconut, oatmeal and nuts. Mix well and drop by teaspoonfuls on greased cookie sheet. Flatten with bottom of glass and bake at 375° until light brown. Yield: 5 dozen.

COFFEE BREAK COOKIES   Mrs. Daniel Yoder

2 c. flour
1/2 t. baking powder
1 t. soda
1 c. shortening
1 c. chocolate chips, coconut,
   nuts or raisins

1/2 t. salt
1 c. white sugar
1 c. brown sugar
2 eggs
2 c. oatmeal
1 t. vanilla

Sift together dry ingredients. Blend sugars and shortening. Add eggs and vanilla; beat well. Add flour mixture, oatmeal and nuts (or chips). If stiff enough, press into small patties or add a little milk and drop from teaspoon onto greased cookie sheets. Bake at 375° until light brown (for 10 min.). Makes about 4 dozen.

CREAM CHEESE CRESCENTS   Lila Yder

1 c. butter, softened
1-8 oz. pkg. cream cheese
2 c. flour
2 t. sugar

1/2 t. salt
1 c. finely-chopped pecans
3/4 c. brown sugar
1 1/2 t. cinnamon

Combine butter and cream cheese, creaming until well blended. Add flour, salt and sugar to creamed mixture, mixing well. Shape dough into 4 equal balls. Roll each ball into circle on lightly-floured surface to about 1/4" thickness. Cut into 6 to 8 wedges. combine pecans, brown sugar, and cinnamon; sprinkle 1/2 of mixture onto each circle. Beginning at wide edge of dough, roll up each wedge and shape into a crescent. Place on ungreased cookie sheet, point-side down. Bake at 350° for 15 min. or until lightly brown. Makes 24.

DATE BALLS

Bertha C. Yoder

1 c. margarine or butter
2 c. light brown sugar (packed)
1 c. fine coconut

3 c. Rice Krispies
2 c. chopped pecans
1 lb. chopped dates

Cook butter, sugar, dates, and coconut over low heat for 5 min. Remove from heat. Add nuts and Rice Krispies. Dip out 1 T. at a time and form into balls. Roll balls in powdered sugar. Yield: 5 dozen.

A delicious Christmas treat.

FILLED COOKIES

Mary M. Yoder

2 c. brown sugar
1 c. shortening
2 eggs
1/2 t. soda in 1/2 c. milk
2 t. baking powder
4 c. flour

FILLING:
1 c. chopped raisins
1 c. sugar
1 c. water
1 heaping t. flour
1 heaping t. cornstarch

Boil raisins, sugar and water together 5 min. and thicken with flour and cornstarch mixed in a little water. Set aside to cool. Mix dough and roll out thin. Place 1 T. of cooled raisin mixture on a cut cookie and cover with another one. Bake at 350° till lightly browned. Makes 4 to 5 dozen.

MOTHER'S LIFETIME RECIPE

2 heaping cups of patience
1 heartful of love
2 handsful of generosity

Dash of laughter
1 headful of understanding

Sprinkle generously with kindness.
Add plenty of faith and mix well.
Spread over a period of a lifetime.
And serve everybody you meet.

FILLED JUMBO COOKIES

Mrs. Sol Yoder

1 c. shortening
2 c. brown sugar (packed)
3 eggs
1/2 c. water
1 t. vanilla

3 1/2 c. Gold Medal flour
1/2 t. salt
1 t. soda
1/8 t. cinnamon

Mix thoroughly shortening, sugar and eggs. Stir in water and vanilla. Sift together 1 c. flour and the other dry ingredients, mix with the rest of the flour and stir in. Drop by spoonfuls on ungreased cookie sheet. Place 1/2 t. of Filling on dough; cover with 1/2 t. dough. Bake at 350° 10-12 min. Makes approximately 5 dozen.

FILLING:
2 c. dates (cut small)
3/4 c. sugar

3/4 c. water
1/2 c. chopped nuts

Place all ingredients in saucepan and cook until thick, stirring constantly. Cool before using.

HALF BUSHEL COOKIES

Linda Kauffman

7 c. sugar
2 1/2 c. shortening
6 eggs
1/2 lb. nuts
1/2 lb. raisins
1 c. Karo syrup

2 c. milk
12 c. flour
4 3/4 c. oatmeal
2 T. soda
2 T. baking powder

Cream together sugar and shortening; add eggs and beat well. add remaining ingredients alternately, milk and syrup, with dry ingredients. Drop by teaspoonfuls on greased cookie sheets and bake at 350°. This makes about 1/2 bushel cookies!

Choose an author as you choose a friend.

IRISH DROP COOKIES   Irene Yoder

1¹/₂ c. raisins   2 c. sugar
¹/₂ c. boiling water   2 eggs
1 t. soda   ¹/₂ t. salt
²/₃ c. shortening   1 c. chopped nuts
1 t. cinnamon   1 t. nutmeg
3¹/₂ c. flour

Cream sugar and shortening. Cook raisins, add soda to 1/2 c. boiling water from the raisins. Add that to sugar and shortening. Add eggs, beat well. Then add spices, salt and flour. Add raisins and chopped nuts. Flatten dough. Bake at 350° for 10 min. Makes 7 dozen.

KRISPY KRUNCH COOKIES   Mrs. Stanley Yoder

1 c. shortening   1 c. white syrup
1 c. brown sugar   2 eggs
1 t. vanilla   2 c. flour
1 t. soda   1 t. baking powder
¹/₂ t. salt   2 c. Rice Krispies
2 c. rolled oats   1 c. coconut

Cream shortening and sugar. Add eggs, Karo and vanilla. Mix until smooth. Add sifted dry ingredients and mix well. Add rolled oats, Rice Krispies, and coconut. Roll into 1" balls. Place on greased cookie sheet and flatten with spatula dipped in milk. Chocolate chips may be used instead of coconut. Bake at 350° for 11 min. Makes approximately 5 dozen.

LEPP COOKIES   Mrs. Henry Overholt, Sr.

3 lbs. brown sugar, 2¹/₄ c.   1 T. soda
   packed = 1 lb.   1 t. cream of tartar
1 lb. lard = 2 c.   1 T. salt
1 qt. thick sour cream or   1 T. nutmeg
   buttermilk   1 T. maple extract
4 lbs. flour, 4 c. = 1 lb.

Mix sugar and lard until fluffy. Combine dry ingredients and add alternately with sour cream or buttermilk. Drop by teaspoonfuls on cookie sheet. Press down dough lightly with a fork that has been dipped in powdered sugar. bake at 350° 10-13 min. Makes approximately 5 dozen.

MEXICAN COOKIES

Ruby Swartzentruber

1 c. oleo or butter
3 heaping T. powdered sugar
2 c. flour

1 T. vanilla
1 c. chopped nuts

Mix and put in refrigerator until cold. Shape into balls about the size of a small walnut and bake at 325° for 20 min. until edges are slightly brown. While hot, dip in powdered sugar. Make 6 or 7 dozen.

MOLASSES COOKIES

Jo Ann Inhulsen

1 c. lard or vegetable shortening
1½ c. brown sugar
2 eggs
1 c. molasses
1 c. dark syrup

1½ c. sweet milk
3 t. soda
1 t. ginger
2 t. cinnamon
6 c. flour, approximately

Cream lard and sugar together. add eggs and mix well. Add molasses and syrup. Add dry ingredients with milk and mix well. May add more flour if cookies are flat when baked. Bake at 350° for 10 min. Yield: 6 to 7 dozen.

To keep cookies soft, put a piece of bread in the cookie jar with the cookies.

Let none escape, but try them all,
To boil or fry or bake.
We'll warrant they are just as good
As Mother used to make!

MOM'S COFFEE COOKIES   Mrs. Norman Yoder

2 c. brown sugar
1 c. shortening (½ butter & ½
  Crisco)
1 c. boiling water
1 t. instant coffee
1 t. soda

2 eggs, beaten
4 c. flour
3 t. baking powder
2 t. vanilla
½ c. chopped nuts

Cream together sugar and shortening. Dissolve coffee and soda in water and cool. Add the rest of the ingredients. Drop on cookie sheet and bake at 350° for 15 min. When cookies are cool, put Frosting on each cookie. Yield: 4 to 5 dozen.

FROSTING:
1 c. brown sugar
½ c. butter (1 stick)

¼ c. milk
1¾ to 2 c. powdered sugar

Melt butter, add brown sugar and milk. Boil over low heat 2 min., stirring constantly. Cool to lukewarm. Gradually add powdered sugar. Beat until thick. If icing becomes too thick, add hot water.

MOM'S FILLED COOKIES   Mrs. Eli Kauffman

1 c. sugar
½ c. shortening
½ c. milk
1 t. soda

3½ c. flour
¼ t. salt
1 t. vanilla
1 t. cream of tartar

FILLING:
1 c. raisins
3 medium apples
¾ c. nuts

½ c. sugar
2 T. cornstarch

Mix in order given and chill several hours or overnight. Roll out dough thin, cut with cookie cutter, and place 1 t. of Filling on cookie. Place another cookie on top. Press edges well. Bake at 350° for 15 min. Makes about 4 dozen.

FILLING: Grind apples and raisins, add sugar and cornstarch and cook 15 min., stirring constantly. Add nuts and cool.

MOTHER'S DATE NUT PINWHEELS   Chris Inhulsen

1/2 c. soft butter   1 egg
1/2 c. packed brown sugar   2 c. flour (sifted, plain)
1/2 c. white sugar   1/8 t. salt
1/2 t. vanilla extract   1/4 t. soda

FILLING:
1/2 pkg. dates   1/8 c. water
1/4 c. sugar   1 c. chopped pecans
Dash of salt

Cream butter and sugars. Add vanilla and egg and beat until light. Add sifted dry ingredients. Mix well. **Chill** (very important) until firm enough to roll (overnight). Halve dough, roll each half to 12x9" rectangle, spread with Filling, roll up tightly, wrap in waxed paper and freeze overnight. Slice 1/8" thick and bake on greased cookie sheet at 375° for 10 min.

MUNCHIE CRUNCHIE COOKIES   Delores Hostetler

1/2 c. brown sugar   1/2 c. pecans
1/2 c. white sugar   1 c. potato chips
1/2 c. butter   3 oz. butterscotch chips
1 egg   1 1/4 c. flour
1 t. vanilla   1/2 t. soda

Blend brown and white sugar, add butter and beat. Add egg and vanilla. Beat till fluffy. Sift flour and soda. Stir 1 c. flour mixture into sugar mixture. Mix chips and nuts and rest of flour together. Add to sugar mixture. Drop by teaspoonfuls on greased cookie sheet. Bake at 375° 10-12 min. Makes 2 dozen.

Life's fun when you go through each day
in a happy-go-lucky way.

OATMEAL COOKIES   Kathryn Yoder

1 c. oatmeal
3/4 c. flour
1/2 c. shortening
1/2 t. baking soda
1/2 c. packed brown sugar

1/2 c. nuts
1/4 c. sugar
1 egg
1/2 t. salt
1/2 t. vanilla

Measure all ingredients into large bowl. Mix well, then beat 4 min. Drop by teaspoonfuls on cookie sheet. Bake at 375° 10-12 min. Makes 2 dozen.

BEST EVER OATMEAL COOKIES   Sara Marie Yoder,
Mrs. Nelson Yoder,
Mrs. Raymond Weaver

1-6 oz. pkg. chocolate chips
1 c. brown sugar
1 c. white sugar
1 c. shortening
2 eggs
2 c. flour
1 c. nuts, chopped

2 c. oatmeal
1 t. almond extract
1 t. vanilla
1 t. salt
1 t. soda
1 t. baking powder

Mix sugar and shortening. Beat and add eggs and flavorings. Add dry ingredients and mix well. Drop by teaspoonfuls on greased cookie sheet. Bake at 350° 12-15 min. Yield: 4 dozen.

FAMOUS OATMEAL COOKIES   Marie King,
Mrs. Daniel Swartzentruber

3/4 c. shortening
1 c. firmly-packed brown sugar
1/2 c. white sugar
1 egg
1/4 c. water

1 t. vanilla
3 c. oatmeal
1 c. flour
1 t. salt
1/2 t. soda

Beat together shortening, sugars, egg, water and vanilla until creamy. Add combined remaining ingredients. Mix well. Drop by teaspoonfuls on greased cookie sheet. Bake at 350° 12-15 min. Makes 5 dozen cookies.

For variety, add chopped nuts, raisins, chocolate chips or coconut.

PEANUT BUTTER PINWHEELS

Mrs. Norman Yoder

$\frac{1}{2}$ c. shortening
1 c. sugar
$\frac{1}{2}$ c. peanut butter
1 egg
2 T. milk

$1\frac{1}{4}$ c. flour
$\frac{1}{2}$ t. soda
$\frac{1}{2}$ t. salt
1-6 oz. pkg. or 1 c. chocolate
chips

Cream shortening and sugar till light and fluffy. Beat in peanut butter, egg, and milk. Sift together flour, soda, and salt. Stir into mixture. Place dough on lightly-floured wax paper. Roll in a rectangle. Melt chocolate over hot water. cool slightly and spread over dough. Roll up dough like a jellyroll, lift wax paper slightly at each turn. Chill 20 to 30 min. Not too long or chocolate will break when slicing. Slice and place on ungreased cookie sheet. Bake at 375° 8-10 min. Makes 3 or 4 dozen.

PECAN CRISPIES

Mrs. Sol Yoder

$\frac{1}{2}$ c. shortening
$\frac{1}{2}$ c. butter
$2\frac{1}{2}$ c. brown sugar
2 beaten eggs

$2\frac{1}{2}$ c. flour
$\frac{1}{4}$ t. salt
$\frac{1}{2}$ t. soda
1 c. chopped nuts

Cream sugar and shortening. Add eggs, Mix well. Add flour, salt and soda. Add nuts last. Drop by teaspoonfuls on ungreased cookie sheet or make into a 3" roll, wrap in wax paper and chill overnight. Slice about $\frac{1}{8}$" thick, then bake at 375° 10-15 min. It gets too rich if you use all butter or oleo. Yield: approximately 60 cookies.

I don't sift my flour for cookies. I have better success that way.

PECAN FINGERS

Laura K. Yoder

1 c. butter (soft)
$\frac{1}{2}$ c. sugar (10X)
$\frac{1}{2}$ t. vanilla

$1\frac{3}{4}$ c. flour
1 c. chopped pecans
Powdered sugar

Beat butter till creamy; add sugar and blend well. Add vanilla; stir in flour, then nuts. Roll T. of dough between greased hands to form fingers. Place on baking sheet and bake at 350° 10-15 min. Roll while hot in powdered sugar. Yield: 5 to 6 dozen fingers.

Happiness is not having what you want,
but in wanting what you have.

PECAN PIE COOKIES
Irene Yoder

1 c. margarine
1/2 c. sugar
1/2 c. dark corn syrup

2 1/2 c. flour
2 eggs (separated)

PECAN FILLING:
1/2 c. powdered sugar
1/4 c. margarine

3 T. dark Karo
1/2 c. chopped pecans

Stir margarine and sugar on low speed, add corn syrup and egg yolks; beat until blended. Stir in flour gradually. Chill several hours. Roll into balls. Place on greased cookie sheets. Bake at 375° for 5 min. Remove from oven. Roll 1/2 t. of chilled Pecan Filling into ball, and firmly press into center of cookie. Return to oven; bake 5 min. longer, or until lightly browned. Makes about 3 dozen.

RAISIN DROP COOKIES
Alta Kauffman, Mrs. Nelson Yoder, and Lorene Plank

1 c. raisins
3/4 c. water
1 c. shortening
2 c. sugar
3 eggs
1 t. vanilla
3 1/2 c. flour

1 t. baking powder
1 t. soda
1 t. salt
1 t. cinnamon
1/4 t. cloves
1/4 t. nutmeg
1 c. nuts, chopped

Add water to raisins and boil 5 min. Cool. Cream shortening and sugar. Add vanilla, eggs, raisins and their liquid. Add sifted dry ingredients and mix thoroughly. Add nuts and drop from teaspoon onto greased cookie sheet. Bake at 350° 12-15 min. Yield: 6 dozen.

Planning your work is good, but doing it is even better.

RAISIN NUT COOKIES

Dorothy Yoder

1 c. raisins
3/4 c. boiling water
1 c. shortening
2 c. sugar
3 eggs
4 t. vanilla
4 c. flour

1 t. baking powder
1 t. soda
1 t. salt
1 t. cinnamon
1/2 t. cloves
1/2 t. nutmeg
2 c. chopped nuts

Add boiling water to raisins and cook for 5 min.; cool. Cream shortening and sugar together. Add eggs and vanilla and beat until fluffy. Add cooled raisins to creamed mixture and mix thoroughly. Sift flour; measure. Add salt, soda, baking powder, and spices. Sift again. Add sifted dry ingredients and chopped nuts and blend well into mixture. Drop by teaspoonfuls on greased baking sheet. Bake at 325° for 15 min. Makes 6 dozen cookies.

RANGER COOKIES

Mrs. Samuel Nisly, Mrs. Christ Yoder, Jr.

1 c. shortening
1 c. whtie sugar
1 c. brown sugar
2 eggs
1 t. vanilla
2 c. flour

1 t. salt
1 t. baking soda
1/2 t. baking powder
1 c. oatmeal
1 c. coconut
2 c. Rice Krispies or flaky cereal, crunched

Cream shortening with brown and white sugar; add eggs and vanilla and cream well. Sift flour with soda, salt, baking powder. Combine oatmeal, Rice Krispies and coconut. Fold dry ingredients into creamed mixture. Mix well. Drop by teaspoonfuls on cookie sheet. Bake at 350° 10-12 min. Do not overbake. Makes 4 to 5 dozen.

*(A child may not inherit his parents talents,
but he will absorb their values.)*

132

SOUR CREAM BALLS

Lila Yoder

1/2 c. butter
1 1/4 c. brown sugar
1 egg
2 c. flour

1/2 t. soda
1/2 t. salt
1 t. vanilla

TOPPING:
1 c. chopped nuts
1/2 c. brown sugar

1/4 c. sour cream

Cream butter, sugar, egg and vanilla. Add dry ingredients and shape into 1" balls. Punch centers down and fill with Topping. Bake at 350° for 10-12 min. Makes 3 to 4 dozen 1" balls.

SOUR CREAM COOKIES

Lila Yoder, Ruby Swartzentruber

1/2 c. shortening
2 c. brown sugar or white sugar
2 eggs
4 c. flour
1/2 t. salt

1 t. soda
1 c. sour cream
1 t. vanilla
1 T. lemon flavoring (optional)

Cream shortening, sugar, and eggs. Add dry ingredients alternately with sour cream, then add vanilla and lemon. Drop onto cookie sheet and sprinkle with sugar and cinnamon. Bake at 350° for 12 min. Makes about 4 dozen.

*The Christians' walk should contrast with the world,
not blend with it.*

SPICE COOKIES

Irene Yoder

2 c. brown sugar
1 c. shortening
1¼ c. milk
3 eggs
4 c. flour

2 t. soda
2 t. baking powder
1 t. cinnamon
1 t. cloves
1 t. vanilla
1 t. salt

Cream shortening and sugar. add milk, eggs, and vanilla; beat well. Sift all dry ingredients and mix with shortening mixture. Beat well and drop by the teaspoonfuls onto greased cookie sheet. Bake at 350° for 10 min. Let cookies cool, just a little, then put icing on. Yield: 5 or 6 dozen.

ICING:
6 T. butter
3 T. hot water

1 t. vanilla
Confectioners' sugar

Melt butter, stir in water and vanilla. Add confectioners' sugar till thick enough to spread.

WHOOPIE PIES

Mrs. Daniel Swartzentruber, Marie King and Kathy Yoder

1½ c. lard or shortening
3 c. sugar
3 eggs
3 t. vanilla
6 c. flour
1½ c. cocoa
3 t. salt
1½ c. buttermilk or sour milk

3 t. soda
1½ c. hot water
FILLING:
6 egg whites
6 t. vanilla
3 C. Crisco
10 T. milk
6 c. powdered sugar

Cream lard and sugar. Add well-beaten eggs and vanilla. Sift together flour, cocoa, and salt. Add alternately with buttermilk. Dissolve soda in hot water and add to mixture. Beat well. Drop by teaspoonfuls on cookie sheet. Bake at 400° 6-7 min.

FILLING: Beat egg whites till stiff. Mix in another bowl remaining ingredients. Add egg whites and beat vigorously until stiff. Put Filling between 2 cookies. Makes about 6 dozen whoopies.

WHOOPIE PIES

Lila Yoder

1½ c. sugar
1 c. shortening (half oleo)
2 eggs
4½ c. flour
2 t. soda
1 t. salt
2 t. vanilla
¾ c. cocoa

1 c. water
1 c. buttermilk
FILLING:
1 egg white, beaten stiff
3 c. powdered sugar
¾ c. oleo
1 t. vanilla

Mix together and drop by spoonfuls on baking sheet. Bake at 350°
for 12 min. When cool, put filling between 2 cookies. Makes 3 to 4
dozen whoopies.

ZUCCHINI COOKIES

Mary Lois Yoder

2 c. flour
1 t. baking powder
½ t. salt
¾ c. butter
¾ c. sugar
1 egg

Grated rind of 1 lemon
1 c. zucchini, grated
1 c. pecans
GLAZE:
1 c. powdered sugar
1½ T. lemon juice

Mix dry ingredients and set aside. Cream butter and sugar, then add
egg and rind. Stir in dry ingredients, then squash and pecans. Drop
by teaspoonfuls on greased cookie sheet. Bake at 375° 15-20 min.
GLAZE: Mix together and drizzle on cookies while still warm. Makes
4 dozen.

BROWNIES

Lorene Plank

4 rounded T. cocoa
⅔ c. + 2 t. shortening
2 c. sugar
4 eggs
1 t. vanilla

1¼ c. flour
1 t. baking powder
1 t. salt
1 c. (or less) pecans

Heat oven to 350°. Grease baking pan. Melt cocoa and shortening
together in large saucepan over low heat. Remove from heat. Mix in
sugar, eggs, and vanilla. Stir in remaining ingredients. Spread in
13x9" pan. Bake at 350° for 30 min. When done baking cut in
squares while still hot. Makes 15 large brownies.

BUTTERSCOTCH BROWNIES

Mrs. Loretta Brenneman

1/4 c. butter
1 c. brown sugar
1 egg, beaten
3/4 c. sifted all-purpose flour

1 t. baking powder
1/2 t. salt
1/2 t. vanilla
1/2 c. coarsely-chopped nuts

Melt butter over low heat. Remove from heat and add brown sugar. Stir until blended. Cool. Stir in egg. Sift flour, baking powder and salt together and stir in mixture. Add vanilla and nuts. Spread in well-greased 8" square pan. Bake at 325° for 20 min., until when lightly touched with finger, only a slight imprint remains. Don't overbake. Cut bars while still warm.

BUTTERSCOTCH SQUARES

Marie King

1/4 c. butter
1 c. brown sugar
1 egg
1 c. flour

1 t. baking powder
1/4 t. salt
1/2 c. chopped nuts
1 t. vanilla

Melt butter and blend with sugar, add egg, beat vigorously. Add dry ingredients, then nuts and vanilla. Spread in greased 8" pan. Bake at 350° for 30 min. Cut in squares or bars while warm.

CARAMEL PECAN DREAM BARS

Linda Kauffman

BASE:
1 pkg. yellow cake mix
1/3 c. butter (softened)
1 egg

FILLING:
14 oz. condensed milk
1 egg
1 t. vanilla
1 c. chopped pecans
1/2 c. Heath Bits O' Brickle baking chips

Heat oven to 325°. Grease 13x9x2" pan. In large bowl, combine cake mix, butter and egg. Mix at high speed till crumbly. Stir in nuts and chips. Pour over base in pan and spread to cover. Bake at 325° 20-25 min., or till brown. Don't overbake. (Center may appear slightly gooey.)

CHEESECAKE SQUARES

Elsie N. Yoder

1 c. all-purpose flour
1/3 c. packed bown sugar
6 T. softened butter or
  margarine
1-8 oz. pkg. cream cheese
  (softened)
1/4 c. granulated sugar
1 egg

1/4 t. finely-shredded lemon rind
2 T. lemon juice
1/2 t. vanilla
2 T. chopped walnuts
2 T. milk

Stir together flour and brown sugar. Cut in butter or margarine till mixture forms fine crumbs. Reserve 1 c. of mixture for topping. Press remaining over bottom of ungreased 8x8x2" baking pan. Bake at 350° for 12-15 min. In mixer bowl, cream the cream cheese and granulated sugar. Add milk, lemon rind, lemon juice, and vanilla; beat well. Spread over partially baked crust. Combine nuts with reserved crumbs; sprinkle over all - bake 20-25 min. Cool; cut into squares. Makes 16 squares.

CHINESE DATE YUMMIES

Lena Swartzentruber

1 c. sugar
3/4 c. flour
1 t. baking powder
1/4 t. salt

1 c. dates (chopped)
1 c. nuts (chopped)
2 eggs, well beaten

Sift flour, sugar, baking powder, and salt into bowl. Stir in dates and nuts. Then add eggs and mix well. Spread in pan and bake at 375° for 20 min. While still warm, cut into squares and roll in powdered sugar. Makes 2 dozen bars.

CHOCOLATE CHIP BARS

Ruth Yoder

1/2 c. butter
1 1/2 c. graham cracker crumbs
1 can Eagle Brand milk

1-6 oz. pkg. chocolate chips
3 1/2 oz. coconut
1 c. nuts

Melt butter and mix with graham crackers. Press into pan. Put Eagle Brand milk on cracker crumbs, then semi-sweet chocolate chips, coconut and nuts. Put in 13x9' pan and bake at 350° 25-30 min.

CHOCOLATE TOFFEE SQUARES   Mrs. Elmer M. Yoder (Esther)

1 c. butter, softened	1/4 t. salt
1 c. brown sugar, firmly packed	2 c. flour
1 egg yolk	1-6 oz. pkg. semi-sweet
1 t. vanilla	chocolate chips
	3/4 c. coarsely-chopped nuts

Beat butter and sugar until light and fluffy. Add egg yolk, vanilla and salt. Beat in flour just until combined. Turn into greased 13x9x2" pan and spread evenly. Bake at 350° for 25 min. or until golden brown. Remove from oven and immediately sprinkle with chocolate chips. Let stand until chocolate is soft; spread evenly over top. Sprinkle with nuts. Cut in squares while warm.

CONGO SQUARES   Mari Yoder

2 3/4 c. flour	1 c. shortening
1/2 t. salt	1 lb. brown sugar
2 1/2 t. baking powder	3 eggs
	1 pkg. chocolate bits
	1 c. pecans, chopped

Melt shortening. Add sugar. Mix well. add eggs, one at a time. Beat well. Add dry ingredients. Add chocolate bits and pecans. Pour into greased sheet cake pan and bake at 350° 25-30 min.

COWBOY COOKIES OR BARS   Mrs. Lloyd Swartzentruber

1 c. brown sugar	1 c. white sugar
1 c. oleo	2 eggs
1/2 t. salt	1 1/2 t. baking powder
1 1/2 t. vanilla	1/4 c. sour milk
2 c. flour	2 c. quick oatmeal
1 c. coconut	1 1/2 c. chocolate chips
	Confectioners' sugar

Mix well and spread on cookie sheet. Put nuts over top. Bake at 350° 25-30 min. Cut in squares while still warm. Sprinkle confectioners' sugar over top of cookies.

CREAM CHEESE BARS

Elsie N. Yoder

1 box butter cake mix
1/2 c. butter
2 eggs
1 t. vanilla

2 eggs
1 box powdered sugar
8 oz. cream cheese
1/2 c. butter
1 t. vanilla

Mix cake mix, butter, eggs, and vanilla by hand. Spread in 9x13" pan. Combine rest of ingredients and beat well. Spread over first layer and bake at 350° for 45 min.

CREAM CHEESE BROWNIES

Mrs. Leslie Yoder

1-4 oz. block German sweet
  chocolate
5 T. butter or margarine
1-3 oz. pkg. cream cheese
1 c. sugar
3 eggs

1/2 c. + 1 T. all-purpose flour
1 1/2 t. vanilla
1/2 t. baking powder
1/4 t. salt
1/2 c. chopped nuts

Melt chocolate and 3 T. butter over low heat, stirring occasionally; cool. blend remaining butter with cream cheese. Gradually add 1/4 c. sugar. Beat until fluffy. Blend in 1 egg and 1 T. flour, add 1/2 t. vanilla. Set aside. Beat 2 eggs until lightly-colored. Slowly add remaining sugar, beat until thickened. Add baking powder, salt and remaining flour, blend in chocolate mixture, remaining vanilla and nuts. Spread half of chocolate batter in a greased 8" pan, top with cream cheese mixture. Spoon remaining chocolate batter over top. Zigzag knife through batter to marbleize. Bake at 350° 35-40 min. Cut into bars or squares. Makes 16 to 20.

Of all home remedies, a good wife and mother is the best!

139

CREAM CHEESE SQUARES   Mari Yoder

BOTTOM LAYER   TOP LAYER:
1 box yellow cake mix   1 box confectioners' sugar
1/2 c. butter (melted)   8 oz. pkg. cream cheese
1 egg   2 eggs
1 c. pecans

Mix cake mix, butter, eggs, and pecans together. Pour in bottom of
pan. Combine rest of ingredients and pour over first layer. Bake in
9x13" pan at 350° until golden brown.

EASY SAUCEPAN BROWNIES   Lena Yoder

1/2 c. butter or margarine   2/3 c. sifted Martha White
2-1 oz. sqs. unsweetened   self-rising flour
   chocolate   1 t. vanilla
1 c. sugar   3/4 c. chopped nuts
2 eggs

Heat oven to 350°. Grease bottom of an 8" square pan. Melt butter
and chocolate in a saucepan over low heat. Remove from heat and
stir in remaining ingredients in order listed. Beat well. Bake at 350°
for 30 min. Cool and cut into squares. Makes 16 squares.

If using Martha White plain flour, add 1/4 t. salt and 1 1/2 t. baking
powder. You may also use Hershey's cocoa instead of squares. One
square (1 oz) = 3 T. unsweetened cocoa plus 1 T. shortening or oil.

LEMON BARS   Mrs. Loretta Brenneman

2 1/4 c. flour   2 c. sugar
1/2 c. powdered sugar   1/3 c. lemon juice
1 c. butter   1/2 t. baking powder
4 eggs

Mix 2 c. flour, powdered sugar and butter and pat into 13x9" pan.
Bake at 350° until light brown. Beat eggs and add 2 c. sugar, 1/4 c.
flour, lemon juice, and baking powder. Pour onto crust. Bake at 350°
20-25 min. Sprinkle with powdered sugar.

LEMON BARS DELUXE
Mrs. Levi Kauffman

2 c. flour
1/2 c. sugar
2 sticks butter

4 eggs
2 c. sugar
2/3 c. lemon juice
1/4 c. flour
1/2 t. baking powder

Combine flour and sugar. Cut in butter and press into 13x9" pan. Bake at 350° for 20 min. Mix next 5 ingredients and put on crust and bake an additional 25 min. Sprinkle powdered sugar on top.

LEMON SQUARES
Ellen R. Brenneman

1 c. flour
1/4 c. powdered sugar
1/2 c. butter
2 T. flour
1/2 t. baking powder

2 eggs, beaten
1 c. sugar
Rind of 1 lemon, grated
3 T. lemon juice
Powdered sugar

Combine 1 c. flour, 1/4 c. powdered sugar; add butter. Mix well. Press into 9" square pan. Bake at 350° for 20 min. Combine 2 T. flour and baking powder; set aside. Combine eggs, sugar, rind, lemon juice; beat well. Stir dry ingredients into egg mixture, pour over baked crust. Bake at 350° for 25 min. or until browned. Sprinkle powdered sugar on top.

MOUND BARS
Lorene Plank

2 c. graham cracker crumbs
1/2 c. oleo (melted)
1/2 c. sugar
1 pkg. coconut

1 can sweetened condensed milk
(Eagle Brand)
12 oz. pkg. melted chocolate
chips
2 T. peanut butter

LAYER 1: Mix graham cracker crumbs, melted oleo, and sugar and spread in 9x13" pan. Bake at 350° for 10 min.
LAYER 2: Mix coconut and condensed milk and spread over First Layer. Bake at 350° for 15 min.
LAYER 3: Spread melted chocolate chips and peanut butter on top while both are still hot. Cut into very small bars.

PEANUT BUTTER BARS

Bertha Swartzentruber

1 c. peanut butter
²/₃ c. butter (softened)
1 t. vanilla
2 c. brown sugar (firmly packed)
3 eggs
1 c. sifted flour

½ t. salt
¾ c. powdered sugar
2 t. water
¼ c. semi-sweet chocolate chips
1 t. shortening

Combine peanut butter, butter, and vanilla in a large bowl, beat until well-blended. Beat in sugar until light and fluffy. Beat in eggs, one at a time. Stir in flour and salt. When well blended, spread batter into well-greased cake pan. Bake in 13x9x2" pan. at 300° to 325° for 35 min. till center springs up when lightly touched. **Cool slightly.** Combine powdered sugar with water, stir until smooth, drizzle over warm cookies or bars in pan. Melt chocolate chips with shortening over low heat. Drizzle over top of white frosting. When cool, cut into bars. Makes 36 bars.

BONBONS (BUCKEYES)

Linda Yoder

9 T. melted margarine
1 lb. powdered sugar

1 c. peanut butter

Mix well and form into balls (size of hulled wanut). Refrigerate 1 hr. Dip in chocolate, leaving an area on top uncovered to resemble a buckeye. Makes 4 to 6 dozen.

CORNFLAKE CANDY

Vernie Weaver

1 c. white sugar
12 oz. crunchy peanut butter

1 c. white Karo
6 c. cornflakes

Bring sugar and Karo to a boil. Remove from stove, add peanut butter and cornflakes. When thoroughly mixed, shape intp patties with hands. Yield: 2 or 3 dozen patties.

Yesterday is gone, forget it.
Tomorrow may never come, don't worry about it.
Do a master job today.

DELICIOUS MARSHMALLOW TREATS — Donna Kauffman

1/4 c. margarine or butter
5 c. Rice Krispies

1-10 oz. pkg. regular
   marshmallows or
4 c. small marshmallows

Melt margarine in large saucepan over low heat. Add marshmallows and stir until completely melted. Cook over low heat 3 min. longer, stirring constantly. Remove from heat. Add Rice Krispies, stir until well-coated. Using buttered spatula or waxed paper, press mixture evenly into buttered 13x9" pan. Cut into squares.

$300 FUDGE — Verda Overholt

1 1/2 pkgs. semi-sweet
   chocolate bits
12 oz. marshmallows (small)
1/2 lb. oleo (melted)

1 lg. can evaporated milk
1 c. sugar

Put in large bowl, chocolate bits, marshmallows, and oleo. Mix well and set aside. Mix milk and sugar; boil exactly 9 min. Pour hot sauce over chocolate mixture; stir well until chocolate is melted. Pour in ungreased pan. Cool 2 hrs. Makes 5 lbs.

BEST EVER FUDGE — Mrs. Levi Kauffman

2 lg. Hershey bars
2 sm. pkgs. chocolate chips
1-7 oz. jar marshmallow creme
4 c. white sugar

1/2 c. butter
2 c. nuts
2 t. vanilla
1 can evaporated milk

First put milk and sugar in saucepan and boil hard for 6 min. (stir constantly to keep from scorching). Have rest of ingredients in large mixer bowl and pour boiling mixture over it and stir or mix well. Pour on greased cookie sheet or wax paper.

It's a little too much to save.
And a little too much to dump.
And there's nothing to do but eat it;
that makes the housewife plump!

143

PEANUT BUTTER REESE'S

Ramona Yoder

3 lbs. XXX sugar
1 lb. butter
1 qt. peanut butter

2 lg. pkgs. chocolate chips
2" sq. paraffin

Mix butter, sugar and peanut butter till smooth and creamy. Shape into balls and chill overnight. Melt chocolate chips and paraffin in double boiler. Dip balls into chocolate mixture, using toothpicks.

PECAN KISSES

Mrs. William N. Yoder

1 egg white
3/4 c. brown sugar

1/2 t. vanilla
2 c. pecan halves

Beat egg white until soft peaks form. Gradually mix in brown sugar and vanilla, fold in pecans. Place well-coated pecan halves on greased cookie sheet 1" apart. Turn oven off and let set for 30 min. Store in airtight container.

Freezes well.

SPICED PECANS

Vernie Brenneman,
Mrs. Crist Yoder, Sr.

1 egg white
1 t. cold water
1 lb. pecan halves

1/2 c. sugar
1 t. salt
1/2 t. cinnamon

Beat egg whites slightly, add water, beat until frothy, but not stiff. Fold in pecans. Combine sugar, salt, cinnamon and mix well. Spread on 9x12" buttered pan. Bake at 250° for 1 hr.

*Nothing annoys a woman more
than to have friends drop in unexpectedly,
and find the house looking as it usually does.*

SUPER DELICIOUS CARAMELS

Jo Ann Inhulsen

2 c. cream
2 c. sugar
1 t. butter

1½ c. light Karo
2 t. vanilla
Paraffin, size of walnut

Combine all ingredients except paraffin, vanilla and 1 c. cream; bring to a boil. Boil until firm ball stage or 244°, then add second c. of cream and boil until firm ball stage or 244° again. Add paraffin and vanilla. Put in buttered cake pan and cool. Add nuts, if desired. Cut in squares and wrap in wax paper.

You can make turtles by wrapping caramel around pecan halves and dipping in chocolate.

TURTLE CANDY

Viola Swartzentruber,
Irene Yoder

1 lb. brown sugar
½ lb. butter or oleo
1 c. light Karo

1 t. cream of tartar
1 can Eagle Brand milk

TOPPING:
1 box melted sweet chocolate or carob

Mix first 5 ingredients well and boil exactly 12 min., stirring constantly. Cool and pour over pecans on greased cookie sheet. Top with melted chocolate. Cut in squares and serve.

*"A little bit of this and a little bit of that,
makes you big and fat."*

145

Notes

DESSERTS

- TODAYS SPECIAL -
Cone .... 5¢
Double Dip .... 7¢

HAND CRANKED DAILY
- FRESH CREAM USED.

SMILE

APPLE DELICIOUS

Laura K. Yoder

6 apples, peeled and diced
1 c. water
2 c. sugar
1 t. cinnamon

1/2 t. nutmeg
2 T. clear gel
1 box cake mix
1/2 c. or 1 stick butter

Place sliced apples in loaf pan (set aside). Place water in saucepan. Mix spices, sugar and clear gel, make paste by using a little of the water in saucepan, then add to water and bring to boil. Pour over apples. Pour 1 box cake mix over apple mixture, and shred 1 stick butter over top. Bake in 13x9x2" pan at 350° for 35 min.

APPLE DELIGHT

Mrs. Eli Hostetler

1 1/4 c. flour
1 t. salt
1/2 c. shortening
1/4 c. water
1/2 c. brown sugar
1/2 c. white sugar

1/3 c. flour
1/4 t. salt
1 t. cinnamon
6 c. apples (diced)
1/4 c. butter

Make crust of first 4 ingredients. Form into dough and roll out, shaping dough into corners and up sides of pan. Combine sugars, flour, salt, and spices. Sprinkle half of this mixture over unbaked crust. Cut butter into remaining mixture until crumbly. Set aside for topping. Arrange apple slices in rows across pan, covering entire crust. Cover with crumbs. Bake in 15x10x1" pan at 350° for 30 min. Serve warm, plain or with ice cream.

APPLE GOODIE

Irene Yoder

3/4 c. sugar
1 T. flour
1/8 t. salt
1/2 t. cinnamon
2 c. sliced apples

TOPPING:
1/2 c. oatmeal
1/2 c. brown sugar
1/2 c. flour
1/4 c. butter
1/8 t. soda
1/8 t. baking powder

Mix sugar, flour, salt, and cinnamon together, and combine with sliced apples. Place in the bottom of a greased casserole. To make Topping, combine dry ingredients and rub in butter to make crumbs. Put crumbs on top of apple mixture. Bake at 375° for 35-40 min. Serve hot or cold with rich milk. Serves 6.

147

APPLE ROLL UPS

Ruth Yoder

6 baking apples
2 c. flour
2¹/₂ t. baking powder
¹/₂ t. salt
²/₃ c. shortening
²/₃ c. milk

SAUCE:
2 c. brown sugar
2 c. water
¹/₄ c. butter
¹/₄ t. cinnamon
¹/₄ t. nutmeg
Cook over low heat 10 min.

To make pastry, sift flour, baking powder, and salt together. Cut in shortening until particles are about the size of small peas. Sprinkle milk over mixture and press together lightly, working dough only enough to hold together. Roll pastry in 1 lg. piece ¹/₄" thick. Spread with ¹/₂ stick melted butter, ¹/₂ c. brown sugar, and 1 t. cinnamon. Add chopped apples and roll as a jellyroll; cut in slices 1¹/₄" thick. Place in a greased baking pan. Cover with sauce. Bake in oblong cake pan at 375° for 35-40 min. Serve with milk.

I get more hugs and kisses when I make this dish, than any other dish! Serve with milk and eat cheese along with it.

GERMAN APPLE CAKE

4 c. all-purpose flour
2 T. cornstarch
4 t. baking powder
2 eggs

2 sticks butter
1 c. sugar
Lemon rind
Apples
Cinnamon and sugar

Sift together flour, cornstarch, baking powder and sugar into a large bowl. Make a hole in dry ingredients. Into hole place 2 beaten eggs and butter; knead well. Work until good dough is made. Cut dough in half (recipe makes 2 cakes). Off of each half reserve small amount of dough to crumble on top. Roll out each half big enough to fill a 10" spring pan. Press dough into pan, raise edges up side. In center of cake place very thin sliced apples, 1 lemon rind per cake. Sprinkle brown sugar and cinnamon on top to taste. Bake in 2 cake pans at 350° for 40 min. Remove and sprinkle powdered sugar on top. Serves 14.

DELICIOUS APPLE SLICES

Mrs. Eli Hostetler

2 egg yolks (beaten)
1 T. lemon juice
8 T. cold water
2 c. flour
½ t. salt
1 c. shortening

8 apples
1 c. sugar
¼ t. salt
1 T. flour
½ t. cinnamon
½ t. nutmeg

Make dough for tops and bottoms of 14" oblong pan. Prepare ingredients in second column, core and slice apples. Lay apples on bottom crust and cover with remaining ingredients and crust. Bake at 350° till apples are soft. While still warm, brush with icing.

ICING: 1 c. powdered sugar, small piece of butter, 1 t. vanilla, just a bit of warm milk. Mix and make to spreading consistency, and brush over the apple slices while still warm.

SKILLET BAKED APPLES

Ruth Yoder

6 apples
2 c. water
1 c. brown sugar
3 T. cornstarch or clear gel
½ c. water

½ t. cinnamon
½ t. nutmeg
2 T. butter
A pinch of salt
½ c. pecans

Pare and core apples; cut apples in half. Put apples in skillet with 2 c. water; simmer until tender, about 15 min. When apples are done, remove from pan and put apples on serving dish. To your apple water, add brown sugar, cinnamon, nutmeg, butter, and salt. Mix together cornstarch and ½ c. water; stir into water mixture. Cook till clear. Put pecan on top of apples, then pour sauce over apples. Serve cool with whipped cream.

To prevent apples from cracking open when baking, prick them in several places with a silver fork before putting them in the oven.

BLUEBERRY BUCKLE

Alma Yoder

$^{1}/_{2}$ c. shortening
$^{3}/_{4}$ c. sugar
1 egg
2 c. sifted flour
2$^{1}/_{2}$ t. baking powder
$^{1}/_{4}$ t. salt

$^{1}/_{2}$ c. milk
2 c. fresh or frozen blueberries
$^{1}/_{2}$ c. sugar
$^{1}/_{2}$ c. sifted flour
$^{1}/_{2}$ t. cinnamon
$^{1}/_{4}$ c. butter

Thoroughly cream shortening and $^{3}/_{4}$ c. sugar; add egg and beat till light and fluffy. Stir together 2 c. flour, baking powder, and salt; add to creamed mixture alternately with milk. Spread in greased pan. Top with berries. Mix $^{1}/_{2}$ c. sugar, $^{1}/_{2}$ c. flour, and cinnamon; cut in butter till crumbly; sprinkle over berries. Bake in 11x7x1$^{1}/_{2}$" pan at 350° for 45 min. serve warm with milk.

BLUEBERRY SWIRL DELIGHT

Linda Kauffman,
Mrs. Allen M. Yoder

LAYER 1:
1$^{1}/_{2}$ c. flour
1 c. chopped pecans

$^{1}/_{2}$ c. butter

LAYER 2:
1 c. whipped cream or
Cool Whip
1 c. powdered sugar

1-8 oz. pkg. cream cheese

LAYER 3:
2 sm. pkgs. instant vanilla
pudding
3 c. milk

1$^{1}/_{2}$ c. blueberries

Mix ingredients for Layer 1 and press into 9x13x2" pan. Bake at 325° for 15 min. Beat together Layer 2 and spread over cooled crust. Beat together Layer 3, then stir in blueberries and spread on cream cheese layer. Set in refrigerator for 30 min. Top with whipped cream and garnish with blueberries. Serves 10 to 12.

Thy sandals, Lord, I find.
I think of how they trod the earth,
What time I scrub the floor.

CHEESECAKE   Marie King

1 c. sugar   1-13 oz. can evaporated milk
1-3 oz. box lemon jello   1-8 oz. pkg. cream cheese

Blend sugar and cream cheese together until well-blended. Add jello
which has been dissolved in 1 c. boiling water. Have the evaporated
milk cold enough to whip. Whip real well, then add sugar, cream
cheese and jello. Mix well. Chill in a graham cracker crust. Top with
favorite pie filling.
CRUST: 20 graham crackers (crushed), 1 T. powdered sugar, 1/2 c.
melted butter. Serves 10.

CHERRY TOPPED CHEESECAKE   Sara Marie Yoder

2 c. graham cracker crumbs   1 1/2 c. sugar
1/2 c. butter or margarine,   5 eggs
  melted   3 T. lemon juice
1/4 c. chopped pecans   1-24 oz. can cheery pie filling
3-8 oz. pkgs. cream cheese,
  softened

Combine graham cracker crumbs, butter and pecans; stir well. Press
mixture firmly into baking pan; set aside. Beat cream cheese until
soft and creamy; gradually add sugar, beating until fluffy. Add eggs,
one at a time, beating well after each addition. Stir in lemon juice.
Pour filling into crust; bake at 350° for 45 min., or until set. Cool.
Spread pie filling on top, chill thoroughly. Serves 15 to 18.

WHAT IS A GRANDMOTHER?

*A Grandmother is a lady who has no children of her own; she likes
other people's little girls. A grandfather is a man Grandmother
married. He goes for walks with the boys, and they talk about fishing
and tractors, and like that. Grandmas don't have to do anything but
be there. They usually are old, so they shouldn't play hard or run too
much. It is enough if they drive us to town and buy us a sucker or
a little toy. Or if they take us for walks, they should slow down when
we see things like pretty leaves or butterflies. They should never say
"Hurry up"! Usually they are fat, but not too fat to tie your shoes.
They wear glasses and bonnets. They can take their teeth and gums
off. It is better if they don't try to typewrite or play ball, except with
us. they don't talk baby talk like visitors do because it's so hard to
understand. Everyone should have a Grandma - especially if you
don't have television, because Grandmas are the only grownups who
have plenty of time!*

PEACHES 'N' CREAM CHEESECAKE

Elsie N. Yoder,
Ruth Yoder

¾ c. Pillsbury all-purpose flour
1 t. baking powder
½ t. salt
3¼ oz. pkg. dry vanilla
  pudding mix (not instant)
3 T. margarine or butter,
  softened
1 egg
½ c. milk

1-15 to 20 oz. can sliced peaches
  or pineapple chunks (drained
  well, reserve juice)
1-8 oz. pkg. cream cheese
  (softened)
½ c. sugar
3 T. reserved juice from fruit
1 T. sugar
½ t. cinnamon

Combine first 7 ingredients in large mixer bowl. Beat 2 min. at medium speed. Pour into greased 9" deep dish or 10" pie pan. Place fruit over batter. Combine cheese, sugar, and juice in mixing bowl. Beat 2 min. at medium speed. Spoon to within 1" of edge of batter. Combine sugar and cinnamon and sprinkle over cream cheese filling. Bake at 350° 30-35 min., until crust is golden brown. Serves 6 to 8.

Is very good served with ice cream.

CHERRY PIE DESSERT

Ruth Weaver

1 can cherry pie filling
1 lg. can sweetened crushed
  pineapple
1 white cake mix

½ c. coconut
½ c. pecans
½ lb. butter, melted

Pour cherry pie filling on bottom of 9x13" pan. Add pineapple on pie filling. Sprinkle cake mix on top of pineapple. Sprinkle coconut and pecans on top. Pour melted margarine over all of cake mix in pan, or as much as possible. Bake at 350° for 45 min.

You can live without music,
you can live without books,
but show me the one
that can live without cooks.

BAKED CHOCOLATE FLOAT
Kathy Yoder

1/2 c. sugar
1 c. water
8 lg. marshmallows
1 T. butter
1/2 t. vanilla

1/2 c. flour
1/4 t. salt
1/2 t. baking powder
3 T. cocoa
1/4 c. milk
1/4 c. chopped nuts

Cook 1/4 c. sugar and water 5 min. Pour into 1 qt. casserole. Top with marshmallows. Cream butter, 1/4 c. sugar and vanilla. Add flour, salt, baking powder, and cocoa alternately with milk. Add nuts. Drop from spoon over marshmallows. Cover. Bake in moderate oven 350° for 45 min.

CHOCOLATE ICE CREAM DESSERT
Alta Kauffman,
Mrs. Sol Yoder

2 c. vanilla wafer crumbs
1/2 c. butter
2 sqs. chocolate
2 c. powdered sugar

3 egg yolks, beaten
3 egg whites, beaten
1/2 gal. vanilla or peppermint
    ice cream
Chopped nuts, if desired

Butter a 12x14" (cake pan). Place 1 1/2 c. crumbs over the bottom. Melt butter and chocolate together. Add egg yolks and powdered sugar. Cook slowly for a few min., stirring frequently. Remove from heat and blend in egg whites very lightly. Spread over crumbs and cool. Slice ice cream and lay evenly over chocolate mixture. Top with remaining crumbs. Cover tightly with aluminum foil. Freeze until time to serve.

This can be made ahead of time and keeps well.

CHOCOLATE PUDDING CAKE
Marie King

3/4 c. sugar
1 c. flour
2 T. cocoa
2 t. baking powder

1/4 t. salt
1/2 c. milk
3 T. melted butter
1 t. vanilla

Mix well and pour in 9" pan. Then combine 1/2 c. sugar, 1/2 c. brown sugar and 1/4 c. cocoa. Mix well and sprinkle over batter, then pour 1 1/2 c. water on top. Bake at 350° for 40 min. Serve with ice cream or whipped cream.

153

CHOCOLATE SUNDAE DESSERT
Laura Whitt

20 chocolate Oreo cookies
¼ c. butter, melted
1-5⅓ oz. can evaporated milk
1 qt. vanilla ice cream

1 c. sugar
2 oz. unsweetened baking
  chocolate
½ c. chopped nuts

Crush cookies, add butter; blend well. Reserve about ½ c. for topping and press remaining crumbs into 9x13" pan. Freeze. Combine the sugar, milk and chocolate and bring to a boil. Cool. Layer softened ice cream over the frozen crumb crust. Pour cooked chocolate mixture over ice cream. Refreeze. Spread sweetened whipped cream over dessert. Sprinkle reserved crumbs and nuts over top. Cover pan tightly with foil and keep frozen until 15 min. before serving.

COTTAGE CAKE WITH TOPPING
Malinda Wingard

CAKE PART:
1 egg
2 T. butter
1 c. sugar
1 c. milk
2 c. sifted flour
4 t. baking powder

TOPPING SAUCE:
¾ c. sugar
4 T. butter
2 T. cream
2 c. milk
½ t. vanilla
1½ T. cornstarch

Beat egg. Gradually add sugar. Continue beating until stiff and fluffy. Add butter and milk. Add flour mixed with baking powder. Bake in well-greased 10x14" pan at 350° 25-30 min.

SAUCE: Caramelize sugar, butter and cream together; when brown, add milk and slowly bring to a boil. Add 1½ t. cornstarch in a little milk and bring to a boil. Add vanilla. Top pieces of cake with warm sauce, and a dip of ice cream. Serves 10 to 12.

*Even a woodpecker has found the way to progress
is to "use your head."*

FAST FRUIT COBBLER   Vernie Brenneman, Malinda Wingard

1 c. flour
1 c. sugar
2 t. baking powder
1 c. milk

1 t. vanilla
2 c. drained peaches
1/2 c. butter (melted)

Combine flour, sugar, and baking powder in 2 qt. baking dish Stir in milk and vanilla to make a thin batter. Place fruit over batter. Put butter over top. DO NOT STIR. Bake at 350° for 30 min. until nicely browned. Try any fruit in season. Serves 4 to 5.

PEACH COBBLER   Alma Yoder

BISCUIT TOPPER:
1 c. flour
2 T. sugar
1 1/2 t. baking powder
1/4 c. butter
1 egg, slightly beaten in
   1/4 c. milk

FILLING:
1 qt. peaches - canned or frozen
1 T. lemon
1 t.butter
3 T. tapioca (heaping)

FOR FILLING: Bring peaches to a boil - sprinkle tapioca over top, stir until thickened. Add lemon and butter; pour into pan.

BISCUIT TOPPING: Mix dry ingredients - cut in butter - then add egg and milk mixture. Mix and spoon 6 mounds on peach filling. Bake in 9" square cake pan at 375° for 25 min. Serve hot with milk. Serves 6.

PEACH COBBLER   Sara Marie Yoder, Mrs. Leslie Yoder

1/4 c. shortening
1 c. sugar
1 egg
1 1/2 c. flour
1/2 t. salt
2 t. baking powder

1 T. tapioca
1 T. lemon juice
2 T. butter
1/3 c. milk
2 c. peaches

Sift flour, baking powder, salt and sugar together. Cut shortening into dry ingredients. Beat egg and add milk. Combine with flour mixture. Pour peaches into a greased 9" shallow baking dish. Sprinkle with tapioca, add lemon juice and butter. Drop batter by mounds on peaches. Bake at 400° for 30 min. Serves 6.

155

PEACH COBBLER

Mrs. Allen M. Yoder

1½ c. flour
2 t. baking powder
½ t. salt
⅔ c. sugar
¼ c. shortening
1 egg

⅓ c. milk
1 qt. peaches (or any other fruit)
Tapioca
1 t. lemon juice
2 t. butter

Sift flour, baking powder, salt and sugar together. cut shortening into dry ingredients. Beat egg and add milk. Combine with flour mixture. Pour fruit into baking pan. Sprinkle with tapioca, add lemon juice and butter. Top with dough. Bake in 3 qt. baking pan at 375° for 45 min or until dough is done. Serve with milk. Serves 6.

MY FAVORITE PEACH COBBLER

Ruth Yoder

2 c. flour
1½ c. sugar
4 t. baking powder
½ t. salt
1 t. vanilla
1½ c. milk
Stick margarine

FILLING:
2 qts. peaches
½ stick butter
2 t. lemon juice
½ c. sugar
3 T. cornstarch or clear gel
¾ c. water

Combine flour, sugar, salt, and baking powder. Stir in mlik and vanilla; set aside. In saucepan put first 4 Filling ingredients; bring to a boil. Mix together cornstarch and water to make a paste, gradually add to Filling mixture, pour into pan and put cake mixture on peach filling. Melt stick butter and pour over batter. Mix together ¼ c. sugar and 1 t. cinnamon; sprinkle over top. Bake in 3 qt. baking dish at 350° for 40 min. Serve warm with milk. Serves 10.

RHUBARB COBBLER

Vernie Brenneman

4 c. chopped rhubarb
1 sm. box red jello
1 c. sugar
1½ c. flour
2 t. baking powder
1 egg

1 c. sugar
½ t. salt
½ c. butter
1 t. vanilla
1 t. cinnamon and 1 T. sugar
   mixed for topping

Combine rhubarb, 1 c. sugar and jello. Put in bottom of 9x12" pan. Sift flour, baking powder, and salt. In mixing bowl, cream butter, 1 c. sugar and egg. Add flour mixture alternately with milk. Put on top of rhubarb. Top with cinnamon and sugar. Bake at 350° for 35 min. Serves 8.

CREAM CHEESE AND JELLO

Mrs. Eli Hostetler

35 graham crackers
1/4 c. butter or margarine
2 T. sugar
1-3 oz. pkg. lemon jello
1 c. boiling water

1-8 oz. pkg. cream cheese
1 c. sugar
1 t. vanilla
2 pkgs. whipped topping

Mix graham cracker crumbs, sugar and margarine; put 3/4 c. of mixture in 9x13x2" pan and bake at 350° for 10 min. Dissolve jello in boiling water, cool. Soften cream cheese, add sugar. Mix till smooth. Add vanilla and jello mixture to cheese mixture, beat till smooth. Blend in the whipped topping. Pour mixture over crumbs and top with remaining crumbs.

CREAM PUFFS AND ECLAIRS

Laura K. Yoder

1 c. flour
1/4 t. salt
1 c. boiling water

1/2 c. butter
4 eggs

Place butter and boiling water in saucepan. Keep on low heat until butter is melted. Sift flour and salt together, and add all at one time to the boiling water and fat. Stir vigorously until mixture leaves sides of pan and forms a ball. Remove from heat and add unbeaten eggs, one at a time. Beat thoroughly after the addition of each egg. Drop by tablespoonfuls onto a greased baking sheet, placing about 2" apart. Bake at 425° for 30 min., or until beads of moisture no longer appear on surface. Makes 12 to 15 cream puffs. When cool, cut a slit in the top of each and fill with whipped cream or the following filling:

FILLING:
2 c. milk
2/3 c. sugar
3 eggs, separated

5 T. flour
1/4 t. salt
1 t. vanilla

Scald 1 1/2 c. milk in top of double boiler. Combine sugar, flour, and salt. Add remaining milk to dry ingredients to make smooth paste. Add paste to scalded milk and cook until thickened, stirring constantly. Slowly add beaten egg yolks and cook 2 more min.

*For Eclairs, put paste into pastry bag and force through a round hole 1" in diameter, and 3 1/2" to 4" long. Glaze with a chocolate icing.

CROWN JEWEL DESSERT

Irene Yoder

3 oz. box lime jello
3 oz. box cherry jello
3 oz. box orange jello
3 c. boiling water
2 c. cold water

1 c. pineapple juice
1/4 c. sugar
3 oz. box strawberry jello
2 c. whipping cream

Fix lime, cherry, orange jello with 1 c. boiling water and 1/2 c. cold water to each. Pour into cake pans to jell. After jelled, cut into 1/2" cubes. Heat pineapple juice and 1/4 c. sugar to a boil. Add strawberry jello. Stir until dissolved, then add 1/2 c. cold water. Put in icebox until thick. Whip cream. Fold in strawberry jello. Mix. Then fold in jello cubes. Put half of this into bowl. Then add half cracker crumbs (crumbs bellow). Put the rest of the jello in, then the rest of the crumbs on top.

CRACKER CRUMBS:
1 1/2 c. graham crackers
1/3 c. butter, melted

1/4 c. brown sugar

Crush graham crackers. Add melted butter and sugar. Mix well.

CAKE DESSERT

Mrs. Milton Yoder

1 sm. can fruit cocktail
1 c. sugar
1 t. soda
1/4 t. salt

1 1/2 c. flour
1 egg
TOPPING:
3/4 c. nuts
3/4 c. brown sugar

Drain fruit, saving 1/2 c. juice. Sift flour with sugar, soda and salt. Beat eggs well. Add 1/2 c. juice from fruit and mix slightly. Combine brown sugar and nuts and sprinkle over batter. Bake in 8" square pan at 350°. Serve with whipped cream.

DELIGHT

Mrs. Bertha Yoder,
Mrs. Ernest W. Yoder

2 pkgs. graham crackers
8 oz. pkg. cream cheese
1 pkg. Dream Whip or
Cool Whip
1 pt. fresh fruit

1/2 c. chopped nuts
1 c. butter
2 c. powdered sugar
1 sm. box Jell-O

Crush crackers and mix with nuts and butter. Press in bottom of 13x9" pan. Bake at 350° for 15 min. Let cool. Mix cream cheese and sugar together. Add Cool Whip and whip. Spread over crust. Top with fruit and Jell-O. (Prepare Jell-O as directed on box.) Cherry, peach, strawberry or blueberry.

DUMP SALAD OR DESSERT

Dorothy Yoder

1 lg. can cherry pie filling
1 lg. can crushed pineapple
(do not drain)

1 can sweetened condensed milk
1-12 oz. bowl Cool Whip

Mix all together in large bowl. Put in refrigerator 1 hr. before serving.

FROZEN FRUIT SALAD

Mrs. Sol Yoder

4 egg yolks
4 T. sugar
4 T. tarragon vinegar

1 can crushed pineapple
1/2 lb. marshmallows
1 c. pecans (chopped)
1 pt. whipping cream (whipped)

Cook first 3 ingredients until thick. Add the rest of the ingredients and pour in 12x14" oblong cake pan. Cover and freeze. Serves 16.

Other vinegar can be used.

FRUIT SLUSH

Kathy Yoder, Mrs. Chris L. Miller, and Kathy Hostetler

2 c. sugar
3 c. water
6 oz. frozen orange juice
   concentrate

20 oz. can crushed pineapple,
   undrained
6 or 7 bananas

Stir together sugar and water; boil 5 min. Add frozen orange juice concentrate made according to directions. Then add 20 oz. can pineapple, and bananas. Stir all together and place in freezer, stirring occasionally. Eat slushy. Serves 15.

FUDGE CAKE

Mrs. Bertha Yoder

2 T. butter
3/4 c. sugar
3 T. cocoa
1 c. flour
1/4 t. salt
1/2 c. milk
1 t. vanilla
2 t. baking powder

SAUCE:
1/2 c. white sugar
1/2 c. brown sugar
3 T. cocoa
1 c. milk
1 T. butter
1 t. vanilla

Melt butter and add sugar and cocoa. Mix well. Add dry ingredients alternately with milk and vanilla. Spread in pan and prepare sauce. Heat ingredients for Sauce, stirring until smooth. Pour over batter. Bake in 8x8" pan at 350° for 3/4 to 1 hr. Serve with ice cream.

You can't change the past,
but you can ruin a perfectly good present
by worrying about the future!

GINGERBREAD

Mrs. Harley Yoder

2 c. sifted cake flour
2 t. baking powder
1/2 t. baking soda
1/2 t. salt
2 t. ground ginger
1/4 t. ground cloves
1 1/4 t. cinnamon
1/4 t. nutmeg

3 T. cocoa
1/2 c. butter
1/2 c. dark brown sugar
1 lg. egg
1/2 c. Blackstrap molasses
1/2 c. honey
3/4 c. buttermilk
1/4 c. milk

Mix all dry ingredients in a large bowl and set aside. Beat egg into butter and sugar until light. Warm molasses and honey in saucepan. Remove from heat and stir in buttermilk and milk. Add molasses and egg mixture alternately to flour mixture. Pour into greased 12x8x2" pan. Bake at 350° for 30-35 min. Serves 8-10.

Serve topped with sweet whipped cream.

MY BEST GINGERBREAD

Sadie A. Yoder

1/2 c. sugar
1/2 c. butter
1 egg (beaten)
1 c. Brer Rabbit molasses
2 1/2 c. sifted flour
1 t. soda

1 t. cinnamon
1 t. ginger
1/2 t. cloves
1/2 t. salt
1 c. hot water

LEMON SAUCE FOR GINGERBREAD:

Ruth Yoder

1/2 c. sugar
1 1/2 t. cornstarch
1 1/2 c. boiling water

1/8 t. salt
2 t. butter
Grated rind & juice of 1 lemon

Cream butter and sugar, add beaten egg and molasses. Add dry ingredients. Add hot water last and beat until smooth. Bake in oblong pan at 350° for 35 min. Serve with whipped cream while still warm. Delicious.

LEMON SAUCE FOR GINGERBREAD: Combine sugar, salt and cornstarch, add boiling water and stir until a smooth paste. Cook slowly until thickened and clear, stir constantly. Remove from heat and add lemon rind, juice and butter. Makes about 1 1/2 c. Serve on warm gingerbread.

GRAHAM CRACKER FLUFF

Mrs. Crist Yoder, Jr.
Barbara Jean Hershberger

1 pkg. unflavored gelatin
1/3 c. cold water
1/2 c. sugar
3/4 c. rich milk
2 egg yolks
2 egg whites
1 c. cream, whipped

1 t. vanilla
Pinch of salt
CRUMBS:
12 to 16 graham crackers,
   crushed
3 T. melted butter
3 T. brown sugar

Soak gelatin in cold water. Mix together in double boiler 1/2 c. sugar, 3/4 c. milk, 2 egg yolks. Boil 1 min. Add gelatin mixture and mix. Set in cool place. When pudding has set, add 2 stiffly-beaten egg whites, 1 c. cream, whipped, 1 t. vanilla, and pinch of salt. Line bottom of dish with 2/3 of crumbs, then pour in pudding and put remaining crumbs on top. Set in refrigerator until ready to serve.

GRAHAM CRACKER FLUFF

Malinda Wingard,
Bertha Swartzentruber

2 eggs
1/2 c. white sugar
3/4 c. milk
1 c. whipping cream or
   1 1/2 c. Cool Whip
Pinch of salt

1 env. Knox gelatin
1 doz. graham crackers
1 1/2 T. brown sugar
1 T. butter
1 t. vanilla

FIRST STEP: Beat egg yolks gradually, add sugar and milk, bring to a boil. Remove from fire. add at once Knox gelatin (softened in cold water). Add flavoring and cool.

SECOND STEP: Melt together brown sugar and butter, mix with 1 doz. crushed crackers. Cool.

THIRD STEP: Beat egg whites stiff and whip cream. When first mixture is cool, add third mixture. Arrange your dish as you wish with second mixture. Chill thoroughly before serving. Serves 8 to 10.

Good exercise for the heart;
bending down and helping another up.

ICE CREAM DESSERT

Mrs. Ernest W. Yoder

FIRST PART:
60 Ritz crackers, crushed
1/2 c. oleo, melted

SECOND PART:
1 lg. box instant vanilla pudding
1 1/2 c. milk
1/2 gal. ice cream (vanilla)
3 Heath bars, crushed

FIRST PART: Melt oleo, pour over crackers. Press into 13x9" cake pan. Bake at 350° for 10 min. Cool.

SECOND PART: Mix pudding and milk. Add softened ice cream. Mix well. Pour over cooled cracker crust. Put in freezer. One hour before serving, take from freezer and top with Cool Whip. Garnish with Heath bars.

Chocolate chip ice cream can also be used in place of vanilla.

ICE CREAM SANDWICHES

Joyce Yoder

1/2 c. corn syrup
1/2 c. peanut butter
4 c. Rice Krispies

1 pt. ice cream (cut into 6 slices, 3x3x2")

Stir corn syrup and peanut butter together till smooth. Add cereal. Stir well. Press in buttered 9x9" cake pan. Place in freezer till firm. Cut cereal mix into 12x3" squares. Sandwich each slice of ice cream between 2 squares. Freeze till firm. Cut each in half. Serves 12.

BASIC ICE CREAM

Bertha Swartzentruber

2 T. Knox gelatin
3 c. milk
2 c. sugar
6 c. cream

5 t. vanilla
1/4 t. salt
6 eggs
1-3 1/4 oz. vanilla instant pudding

Soften gelatin in 1/2 c. milk. Scald 1 1/2 c. milk and put into gelatin mixture. Add sugar and salt until dissolved. Add remaining 1 c. milk, beat eggs 5 min. Add cream, pudding mix and vanilla.Then add gelatin mixture; pour into 1 gallon freezer.

BUTTER PECAN ICE CREAM

Verna Mae Wingard

2 sm. boxes instant pudding
2 or 3 eggs
1 t. salt
1 c. sugar

4 c. whole milk
3 c. cream
A little vanilla

BUTTER PECANS:
1 c. nuts
3 T. butter

¼ c. brown sugar

Beat eggs and add sugar; mix well. Add milk, cream, pudding, salt and vanilla. Put in freezer and add pecans when it starts to freeze. Makes 1 gal.
BUTTER PECANS: Melt butter and add pecans and brown sugar. Stir constantly until nuts are glazed.

BUTTER PECAN ICE CREAM

Sadie A. Yoder

3 sm. pkgs. instant vanilla
   pudding
1 sm. pkg. instant butterscotch
   pudding
½ t. maple flavoring

¾ c. sugar
1 can Eagle Brand milk
BUTTER PECANS:
2 T. butter
1 c. brown sugar
¾ c. pecans

Mix pudding as directed on box. Add remaining ingredients.
BUTTER PECANS: Put 2 T. butter in a skillet and melt. Add 1 c. brown sugar, ¾ c. pecans, stirring constantly, till slightly glazed. Remove from heat. Add nut mixture to pudding mixture and put in freezer can; add enough milk to make freezer can about ¾ full. Yields: 6 qts.

BUTTER PECAN ICE CREAM

Mrs. Stanley Yoder

1½ c. sugar
6 eggs (beaten)
2 T. vanilla

2 boxes instant vanilla pudding
Pinch of salt
2 pts. cream or rich milk

2 c. pecans
1 stick butter

About ½ c. brown sugar

Mix pudding as directed on box. Add all ingredients together and pour into freezer. Add toasted pecans and fill with milk. Freeze. Makes 5 qts.
To make toasted pecans: Melt margarine and add sugar and pecans. Toast for 20 min.

BUTTER PECAN ICE CREAM
Mrs. Eli Hostetler

2 qts. milk
9 T. flour
Pinch of salt
5 egg yolks

2 c. sugar
2¼ t. vanilla
2 cans evaporated milk
2¼ c. pecans
³/₈ c. butter
1½ c. brown sugar

Heat butter, brown sugar, and nuts in a saucepan. Keep it stirred to prevent from burning. Do not heat it too long or it will get hard. Bring milk to a boil. Add sugar. Make thickening with flour and evaporated milk. Bring to boil. Add salt, beten egg yolks and vanilla. Add toasted pecans and pour into freezer can and freeze. Makes 5 qts.

FIRST PRIZE ICE CREAM
Mary Lois Yoder

2 cans Eagle Brand milk
5 c. milk
2 c. heavy cream

2 T. vanilla
½ t. salt
3 c. of your favorite fruit
(optional)

Mix together in freezer can and freeze with ice cream freezer. Makes 4 qts.

HOMEMADE DAIRY QUEEN ICE CREAM
Beula Yoder,
Mrs. Milton Yoder

2 envs. Knox gelatin
½ c. cold water
4 c. whole milk
2 c. sugar

2 t. vanilla
½ t. salt
3 c. cream

Soak Knox gelatin in cold water. Heat milk - do not boil. Remove from heat, and add gelatin, sugar, vanilla and salt. Cool and add cream. Chill 5 to 6 hrs. Pour into 4- to 6-qt. ice cream freezer can.

Add marshmallow creme to your favorite homemade ice cream recipe.

ORANGE ICE CREAM

Mrs. Chris L. Miller

2 c. sugar
5 eggs
2 c. heavy cream

2-3 oz. pkgs. orange Jell-O
1 c. boiling water

Beat together sugar, eggs, and cream. Dissolve the Jell-O in the boiling water - cool. Mix all together and put in freezer can. Add whole milk to fill a 1-gallon freezer to within 2" of top. Any other flavor Jell-O may be used or unflavored gelatin, with vanilla added.

Add a can of crushed pineapple to orange ice cream for orange-pineapple flavor ice cream.

VANILLA ICE CREAM

Kathryn Yoder

2½ qts. milk
5 c. sugar
½ t. salt
3 pkgs. Knox gelatin
3 heaping T. flour

1 c. cold water
1 pt. milk
1 qt. heavy cream
2 cans evaporated milk
3 to 4 T. vanilla

Mix 2½ qts. milk, sugar, and salt and bring to a boil. Soak gelatin in cold water. Mix flour with enough milk to make a smooth sauce. Stir flour into hot milk, stirring constantly until mixture comes to a boil. Add gelatin and remove from heat. Chill and stir occasionally until it begins to thicken, then add 1 pt. milk, cream, evaporated milk and vanilla. Cool 5 to 6 hrs. before freezing. 8 qt. freezer

VANILLA ICE CREAM

Mrs. Isaac Plank

2 eggs
⅛ t. salt
2 c. milk
1½ t. vanilla extract

1 c. sugar
½ box instant vanilla pudding
2 c. half and half

Beat eggs in mixing bowl until fluffy. Add remaining ingredients and continue beating until sugar and vanilla pudding are dissolved. Pour mixture into 2 qt. ice cream can and freeze.

166

VELVET ICE CREAM
Lela Brenneman, Elsie N. Yoder

1 qt. milk
2 c. sugar
2 T. cornstarch
4 egg yolks, beaten

1/4 t. salt
1 t. vanilla
3 c. heavy cream whipped
4 egg whites, stiffly beaten

Heat milk to scalding. Mix the sugar with the cornstarch and egg yolk. Gradually add the scalded milk and cook until mixture begins to thicken, stirring constantly. Remove from heat, add salt and flavoring, set aside to cool. Fold in egg whites and whipped cream into cooled custard and freeze. Makes 4 quarts.

For maple ice cream, use brown sugar instead of white, and 1/2 t. maple flavoring instead of vanilla.

BUTTER CRISP ICE CREAM TOPPING
Mrs. Lloyd Swartzentruber

1/2 c. finely-crushed cornflakes
1/4 c. brown sugar

1/2 c. chopped pecans

Blend in 2 T. melted butter

Mix well and spread on cookie sheet and bake. Stir frequently. Serve on ice cream.

HOT FUDGE FOR SUNDAES
Mrs. Allen M. Yoder

2 c. sugar
2/3 c. cocoa
1/4 t. salt
1 1/2 c. water

2 T. butter
1/2 c. water
4 T. cornstarch
1 t. vanilla

Mix sugar, cocoa, and salt together. Add 1 1/2 c. water. Bring to boil. Mix cornstarch and water together and add to above mixture. Cook till thick. Add butter and vanilla.

167

SONNY'S SYRUP

Ellen R. Brenneman

2 c. white sugar
1/4 c. flour
2 c. water
1 t. vanilla

2/3 c. cocoa
1/4 t. salt
2 T. butter

Mix dry ingredients, add water. Cook until smooth. Cool. Add butter and vanilla. Delicious on vanilla ice cream!

LEMON CREAM CHEESE DESSERT

Ruby Swartzentruber

3 c. Cherrios cereal, finely crushed
1/3 c. melted butter
1 T. sugar
1 t. ground cinnamon

1-8 oz. pkg. cream cheese (softened)
1-4 oz. can sweetened condensed milk
1/4 c. lemon juice
1 t. vanilla

Heat oven to 375°. Mix cereal, margarine, sugar and cinnamon in small bowl. Reserve 2 T. Press remaining cereal mixture in ungreased square pan. Bake in 8x8x2" pan for about 9 min. Cool. Beat cream cheese in large mixer bowl until light and fluffy. Mix in milk gradually. Stir in lemon juice and vanilla. Pour over baked cereal mixture in pan. Sprinkle reserved cereal mixture over top. Refrigerate until firm - 3 to 4 hrs. Top with fresh fruit if desired. Makes 9 to 12 servings.

LEMON CREAM CHEESE DESSERT

Linda Yoder

1-8 oz. pkg. cream cheese
2 c. milk

1 pkg. instant lemon pudding
1-9" graham cracker crust (baked)

CRUST:
1 pkg. graham crackers
1/4 c. sugar

1/4 c. butter

Mix Crust and press into 9x13" pan and bake at 325° for 10-15 min. Mix cream cheese until soft. Gradually add 1/2 c. milk until smooth and creamy. Add 1 1/2 c. milk and pudding mix. Beat slowly with beater for 1 min. Pour at once into cooled Crust. Chill 1 hr. or till firm.

LEMON DELIGHT

Kathy Yoder, Mrs. Crist Yoder, Jr.

1 c. flour
1/2 c. melted butter
1/2 c. chopped nuts
2 sm. boxes instant lemon
  pudding

1/2 c. Cool Whip
1-8 oz. bar cream cheese
1 c. powdered sugar
3 c. milk

Mix butter, flour and nuts together. work like pie dough, put in an 8x8" cake pan and bake at 375° for 15 min. Beat Cool Whip, cream cheese and powdered sugar together and put on baked crust after cooled. Mix lemon pudding with milk and let set a few minutes and pour over cream cheese mixture. Top with Cool Whip or whipping cream.

LEMON FLUFF SQUARES

Mrs. Chris L. Miller

CRUMB CRUST:
1 c. quick-rolled oats
1/3 c. flour
1/2 t. salt
1/2 c. brown sugar
1/3 c. melted butter

FILLING:
1 env. unflavored gelatin
1/2 c. cold water
4 egg yolks (beaten)
1/2 c. sugar
1 t. grated lemon rind
1/2 c. lemon juice
4 egg whites
1/2 c. sugar

FOR CRUST: Combine oats, flour, brown sugar and salt in shallow 8" square baking pan, add melted butter and mix thoroughly. Toast in 350° oven about 10 min. Cool, tossing occasionally with fork.

FOR FILLING: Soften gelatin in cold water, combine egg yolks, sugar, lemon juice, and rind in saucepan; cook over low heat, stirring constantly until mixture boils. Remove from heat, add softened gelatin and stir until dissolved. Cool thoroughly. Beat egg whites until foamy. Gradually add sugar and continue beating until mixture stands in soft peaks. Carefully fold cooled gelatin mixture into beaten egg whites. Pack half of crumbs into bottom of an 8" square pan. Gently pour filling on top of crust, sprinkle remaining crumb crust on top of filling. Chill until set.

FROZEN LEMON DESSERT

Sadie A. Yoder

1¾ c. graham crackers
½ c. melted butter
2 T. sugar
1 c. sugar
½ c. lemon juice

5 egg yolks
Dash of salt
Grated lemon rinds

5 egg whites
¾ c. evaporated milk

Mix together the first 3 ingredients, forming crumbs and press 3/4 of the crumbs in an 8" square pan. Combine the rest of ingredients in top of a double boiler. Cook until thick, stirring occasionally. Cool. Beat egg whites and 3/4 c. evaporated milk, fold into mixture. Pour into dish and top with remaining crumbs. Freeze. Serves 10.

LEMON SPONGE CUSTARD

Mrs. Leslie Yoder

1½ c. sugar
6 T. butter
6 T. flour
4 eggs, separated

Juice of 1 lemon
1 t. grated lemon rind
2 c. milk

Cream sugar and butter in a bowl. Add the flour and mix well. Add beaten egg yolks, lemon juice, grated rind and milk, and mix well. Fold in beaten egg whites and pour into a greased and floured 8" square pan. Place in a pan of warm water to bake and bake at 325° for 50 min. to 1 hr. Then invert onto serving plate. Serves 6 to 8.

PAP (BRY)

Alma Yoder

Bring 2 c. milk to a boil.

MAKE PASTE OF:
3 rounded T. cornstarch
3 level T. sugar

¼ t. salt
¼ c. milk

Add to boiling milk and cook 1 min., stirring constantly. Serve, sprinkled with brown sugar.

"Very good for baby's first food."

PEACHES AND CREAM DELIGHT
Laura Whitt

2 pkgs. lemon Jell-O
1 c. boiling water
1 c. orange juice

1 env. Dream Whip
1-8 oz. pkg. cream cheese
1 can peach pie filling

Dissolve 1 package. lemon Jell-O with 1 c. water. Add orange juice. Chill until syrupy. Mix Dream Whip according to directions and add cream cheese. Chill. After syrupy, mix the two together. Pour into pan and let set until completely set. Dissolve remaining package of Jell-O in 1 c. boiling water, add pie filling, and pour on top. Chill until completely set.

PEANUT BUTTER CRUMB DELIGHT
Vernie Brenneman

1 lg. box instant pudding
  (vanilla)
2½ c. milk
1½ c. drained pineapple
  chunks

½ c. peanut butter
2 c. graham cracker crumbs
½ c. light brown sugar

Prepare pudding using 2½ c. milk. When thick, fold in pineapple. In a separate bowl, blend peanut butter, graham cracker crumbs and sugar. Put half of topping mixture in buttered pan. Top with half the pudding mixture and repeat. Chill. Top with whipped cream if desired. Serves 8.

PINEAPPLE-PEACH DESSERT
Mrs. Stanley Yoder

1-20 oz. can crushed pineapple
1-8¾ oz. can sliced peaches
  (drained)
1 pkg. white cake mix

1¼ c. chopped pecans
½ c. butter (1 stick)

Spread pineapple and drained peaches in bottom of 13x9" loaf baking pan. Combine cake mix, pecans, and margarine. (Mixture will be crumbly.) Sprinkle over fruit. Bake at 350° 45-50 min. till golden brown. Serve warm with whipped cream or ice cream. Serves 12.

QUICK PINEAPPLE ROLLS

Ruth Yoder

1 c. crushed pineapple
1/4 c. butter (melted)
1/2 c. brown sugar, firmly packed

1 t. cinnamon
1 can refrigerated biscuits

Drain pineapple, mix with butter, brown sugar and cinnamon. Spoon into large muffin cups, greased. Open 1 can biscuits, place a biscuit in each cup, over pineapple mixture. Bake at 425° for 10-12 min. Let cool 5 min., then invert to remove from pan.

SCALLOPED PINEAPPLE

Mrs. Marlene Swartzentruber

3 eggs, well beaten
2 c. sugar
1-20 oz. can crushed pineapple,
    undrained

4 c. 1" cubes fresh bread
1 c. butter, cut up

Combine all ingredients in a medium mixing bowl and mix well. Pour into a greased 13x9x2" pan. Bake at 350° for 1 hr. Serves 10 to 12.

BREAD PUDDING

Mrs. Daniel Swartzentruber,
Mrs. Henry Overholt, Sr.

4 eggs
1 c. brown sugar

3 c. milk
6 slices bread
1 c. raisins

Put raisins in bottom of 9x13" pan. Put bread on top of raisins. Beat eggs, brown sugar, and milk and pour over bread. Sprinkle nutmeg on top. Bake at 350° for 20 min. Serves 8 to 10.

CHOCOLATE FUDGE PUDDING
Ruth Yoder

5 T. butter
1 c. sugar
1 sq. chocolate
1 t. vanilla
1½ c. flour

2 t. baking powder
½ t. salt
¾ c. milk
½ c. nutmeats

TOPPING:
¾ c. brown sugar
5 T. white sugar

2 T. cocoa
1½ c. boiling water

Blend butter, sugar, melted chocolate, and vanilla. Sift flour, salt, and baking powder. Gradually add milk and dry ingredients to chocolate mixture. Stir in nuts and spread in greased pan. Mix cocoa, brown and white sugar and sprinkle over batter. Pour boiling water over but do not stir. Bake in 8x8" pan at 350° for ¾ to 1 hr. Serve bottom side up with whipped cream.

CHOCOLATE PUDDING
Mrs. Allen M. Yoder

1 c. sugar
⅓ c. cocoa
⅔ c. flour
½ t. salt

4 egg yolks (beaten)
4 c. milk
½ c. marshmallows
2 t. butter
1 t. vanilla

Mix sugar, cocoa, flour and salt together. Mix egg yolks and milk together and gradually add to dry ingredients. Cook till thick. Add marshmallows, butter and vanilla. This can also be used as pie filling.

Good advice --- "No" thyself!

CINNAMON PUDDING

Laura K. Yoder, Kathy Hostetler

PART 1:
3 c. brown sugar
2¼ c. water
6 T. butter
⅛ t. salt
Mix and bring to boil
  (set aside)

PART 2:
1 c. sugar
2 T. butter
1 c. milk
1⅔ c. flour
2 t. baking powder
2 t. cinnamon
½ t. salt

Cream together sugar and butter. Sift together flour, baking powder, salt, and cinnamon and add alternately with milk to creamed mixture, and pour into loaf pan, then pour Part 1 over Part 2 and bake in 13x9x2" pan at 325° for 45 min. Serve with whipped cream, or ice cream.

CINNAMON PUDDING

Lorene Plank

3 c. brown sugar
2¼ c. cold water
3 T. butter (oleo)
1½ c. white sugar
3 T. butter (oleo)

1 T. baking powder
1½ c. milk
3 c. flour (scant)
1½ t. cinnamon

Mix brown sugar, cold water and 3 T. butter together and bring to a boil. This is your syrup mixture. Next, mix sugar, flour, baking powder and cinnamon together. Add 3 T. butter and milk. Pour this dough mixture in pan and put syrup on top. Sprinkle with nuts, if desired. Bake in 13x9x2" pan at 350° for 45 min. Serves approximately 18.

This is delicious with ice cream.

People are lonely because they build walls instead of bridges.

CINNAMON PUDDING

Verda Overholt

LIQUID:
1½ c. brown sugar
1½ c. cold water
2 T. butter
Mix and bring to boiling point.

BATTER:
1 c. sugar
1⅔ c. flour
2 T. oleo
2 t. cinnamon
1 c. milk
2 t. baking powder

Put batter into loaf cake pan first, then pour liquid over top. Bake in loaf pan at 350° for 30 min. Serve warm. Delicious with ice cream.

CREAMY TAPIOCA PUDDING

Mary M. Yoder

2 c. milk
1 T. Minute or baby pearl
  tapioca
½ t. salt

2 egg yolks
⅓ c. sugar
1 t. vanilla
½ t. maple flavoring

Bring milk to a boil, reserving 2 T. to mix with egg yolks. Sprinkle a little sugar in pan to prevent the milk from scorching. When milk is at the boiling point, stir tapioca in. For Minute tapioca, cook only 5 min. - for baby pearl, cook 20 min. or until clear. Beat egg yolks, salt and sugar and 2 T. milk real well. Add egg mixture to milk and stir till ready to boil. Do not boil or it will curdle. Remove from heat, add vanilla and maple. Cool 20 min. and stir. Can be served hot or cold.

GRAHAM PUDDING

Lena Yoder

2½ c. whole wheat flour
1 t. soda
1 c. milk
1 c. syrup

Dash of salt
½ c. sugar
2 eggs
1 t. vanilla

Mix all ingredients at once. Pour into greased 9x13" loaf pan. Bake at 350° for 30 min. Eat with milk and brown sugar.

GRAPE-NUT PUDDING
Dorothy Yoder

6 T. flour
12 T. Grape-Nuts
12 T. melted butter
3 c. sugar
6 egg yolks

3 c. milk
9 t. grated lemon rind
9 T. lemon juice
6 stiffly-beaten egg whites

Mix flour, Grape-Nuts, and melted butter. Add sugar, egg yolks and milk, lemon rind and lemon juice; then last of all add stiffly-beaten egg whites. Pour into 2 qt. casserole and set in pan of water. Bake at 325° for 1 hr. Serve cold. If knife comes out rather clean, it is done. Grease casserole with butter.

GRAPE-NUT PUDDING
Mrs. William N. Yoder

1/2 c. butter
2 c. sugar
2 c.milk
4 eggs

6 T. Grape-Nut cereal
4 T. flour
Grated rind and juice of 2 lemons

Melt the butter and mix flour with it. Add sugar. slowly add milk and beaten eggs. Then add Grape-Nuts, juice and lemon rind. Put in bowl and set in pan of water and bake at 350° for 40 min.

GRAPE-NUT PUFF PUDDING
Vernie Brenneman

1 t. grated lemon rind
4 T. butter
2 egg yolks, well beaten
4 T. Grape-Nuts

2 T. flour
1 c. sugar
3 T. lemon juice
1 c. milk
2 egg whites, stiffly beaten

Add lemon rind to butter and cream well. Add sugar, slowly beating after each addition. Add egg yolks and beat. Then add lemon juice. Add flour, Grape-Nuts, and milk, mixing well. Fold in egg whites. Turn into greased 9x6" baking dish and place in pan of hot water. Bake in slow oven 325° for 1 hr. and 15 min. Serves 8.

HOT FUDGE PUDDING

Lena Swartzentruber

1 c. flour
¾ c. sugar
2 t. cocoa
2 t. baking powder

¼ t. salt
2 T. melted shortening
½ c. milk
¾ c. nuts

1 c. brown sugar
2 t. cocoa

1¾ c. hot water

Sift dry ingredients, add milk and beat, then add shortening and nuts. Put in 9" square baking dish. Then put brown sugar and cocoa mixture across the top. Pour hot water over all and bake at 350° for 40-45 min.

ICE CREAM PUDDING

Esther Ruth Yoder

½ gal. vanilla ice cream
2 sm. boxes instant vanilla
   pudding
1½ c. milk

2 pkgs. Dream whip
5 Ritz crackers
½ c. butter

Beat first 3 ingredients together. Make Dream Whip and fold in. Put this in a serving dish. Then break up crackers and mix in melted butter and sprinkle over top. Put in freezer several hours before using.

May use other flavors. Butterscotch, chocolate or coconut are real good.

JELLO TAPIOCA

Esther Ruth Yoder

4 c. boiling water
½ c. pearl tapioca
   (medium-size)
A little salt

1 sm. box raspberry jello
1 c. sugar

Boil tapioca, salt and water for 20 min. Then add jello and sugar. Let jell, then add fruit (if desired) and 1-8 oz. Cool Whip or whipped cream. We like it better without the fruit. Serves 6.

LEMON CRUNCH PUDDING   Mrs. Rufus L. Yoder

1/2 c. Grape-Nuts   1/4 c. firmly-packed brown sugar
2 T. melted butter   1 sm. box lemon pudding

Combine cereal, sugar and butter. Set aside. Prepare pudding
mixture as directed on lemon pudding box. Spoon warm pudding and
cereal mixture into a serving dish. Chill. Serve with whipped cream
or Dream Whip.

LEMON FLUFF PUDDING   Mrs. Rufus L. Yoder

1 sm. box Jell-O raspberry   1-8 oz. pkg. cream cheese
  or lemon   1 c. sugar
1 c. boiling water   1/2 can evaporated milk

GRAHAM CRACKER MIXTURE:
1 3/4 c. graham cracker crumbs   1/2 c. melted butter or margarine
1 T. sugar

Melt Jell-O in boiling water. Cool. Cream 8 oz. cream cheese with
sugar. Whip chilled evaporated milk. Add whipped cream to Jell-O
mixture. Add cream cheese and sugar mixture. Mix together graham
cracker mixture and press most of mixture into bottom of the pan.
Set aside a small amount. Pour pudding mixture into graham
cracker-lined pan and sprinkle remaining crumbs on top.

MARSHMALLOW PUDDING   Bertha Swartzentruber

1 c. milk   1 c. whipped cream
28 marshmallows   1 c. pineapple

GRAHAM CRACKER CRUST:
1 3/4 c. crushed graham   1 T. sugar
  crackers   1/2 t. cinnamon
1/2 c. melted butter

Heat milk and add marshmallows and stir till marshmallows are
dissolved. Remove from heat and cool. Add whipped cream and
pineapple after it is cooled and pour into graham cracker crust in 9"
square pan. Serves approximately 6.

This is better to eat when partly frozen. Will also keep in freezer for
a long time.

OZARK PUDDING
Mary M. Yoder

⅔ c. sugar
1 egg
¼ c. flour
1¼ t. baking powder
½ c. cream

¼ t. salt
1 t. vanilla
½ c. chopped nuts
1 c. chopped apples

Mix sugar and egg well. Then mix flour, baking powder, salt and vanilla and add to first mixture. Fold in the nuts and apples. Spread real thin in 8" or 9" pan. Bake at 350° for 35 min. When served, break up in pieces and fold in whipped cream.

Can be doubled or more for a larger quantity. I use 4 recipes for company.

PEACH PUDDING
Verda Overholt

1 c. flour
¾ c. sugar
2 t. baking powder
¼ t. salt
½ c. milk

16 oz. sliced peaches (drained)
1 c. brown sugar
1 t. cinnamon
1 c. boiling water
3 T. cooking oil

Mix flour, sugar, baking powder and salt. Beat in milk and oil until smooth. Pour into greased 8x8x2" baking pan. Arrange peaches on top. Mix brown sugar and cinnamon. Sprinkle over peaches, then pour boiling water over peaches. Bake at 350° for 1 hr. and 10 min. until wooden pick inserted in middle comes out clean. Serve warm with ice cream or whipped cream.

SAUCY FUDGE PUDDING
Mrs. Daniel Yoder,
Verda Mae Wingard

1 c. sugar
4 T. shortening
2 c. flour
1 t. salt
1 c. milk
1 t. soda (put in milk)

2 t. vanilla
2 T. cocoa
½ c. chopped nuts
1⅔ c. hot water
1½ c. brown sugar
1½ T. cocoa

Cream together sugar, shortening. Then add next 7 ingredients. Stir together hot water, brown sugar, cocoa, and pour on top of batter in well-greased 9x13" cake pan. Bake at 350° for 45 min. Serve warm with ice cream.

VANILLA PUDDING

Mrs. Allen M. Yoder

4 c. milk
2 eggs
4½ T. cornstarch

½ c. white sugar
¼ c. brown sugar
2 t. vanilla

Bring milk to a boiling point. Mix eggs, cornstarch, and sugars together and beat. Add to milk at boiling point. Don't let it come to a full boil. Remove from heat, add vanilla. Use in any of your pudding recipes.

ROLL CAKE

Elsie N. Yoder

4 eggs
1 scant c. sugar
1 heaping c. flour

2 t. baking powder
1 T. hot water
1 t. vanilla

FILLING:
1 box chocolate pie filling made as directed on box.

ICING:
3 oz. bitter chocolate
1 egg
6 oz. cream cheese

1 t. vanilla
Pinch of salt
5 c. confectioners' sugar

Beat eggs and sugar to a creamy batter. Add water and vanilla and dry ingredients. Bake in a large 10x15" cookie sheet. Bake at 375° for 10-15 min. Turn out on a towel that has been sprinkled with powdered sugar and roll into towel. When cool, fill with chocolate filling and roll. Spread icing over top. Makes 2.

ICING: Melt chocolate; add egg and cream cheese. Whip. Add vanilla and salt. Then gradually add confectioners' sugar, beating until light and fluffy. If too thin, add more sugar; if too thick, add cream.

CHERRY JUBILEE ROLL

Lela Brenneman

CAKE ROLL:
3 eggs
1/2 t. salt
3/4 c. sugar
3/4 t. vanilla extract
3/4 c. pancake mix

CHERRY JUBILEE SAUCE:
1-1 lb. can sweet Bing cherries, drained, reserving liquid
1 T. cornstarch mixed with 1 T. cold water

Heat oven to 400°. Grease bottom of pan. Line with wax paper, grease again and flour. Beat eggs and salt until thick and lemon-colored. Add sugar gradually, beating constantly. Stir in extract and pancake mix. Spread evenly in 15 1/2 x 10 1/2 x 1" jellyroll pan. Bake at 400° for 8-10 min. Immediately loosen edges and turn out on kitchen towel sprinkled with powdered sugar. Carefully peel paper from cake. Roll cake in towel, starting at narrow end. Cool about 30 min., unroll, spread with filling and reroll. Chill or freeze, depending on filling used.

CHERRY JUBILEE SAUCE: Stir cornstarch mix into reserved liquid in medium saucepan. Heat till bubbling and cook till clear and slightly thickened, stir in cherries. Serve warm over ice cream roll.

FOR CHERRY JUBILEE ROLL: Spread slightly softened, very rich packaged ice cream, either vanilla or cherry vanilla, about 1/2" thick over cake, carefully roll up and freeze. When ready to serve, slice 1" to 2" slices from roll and serve with warm cherry sauce.

FOR CHERRY PIE ROLL: Spread cake roll with 1 can prepared cherry pie filling. Roll. When ready to serve slice cherry roll and serve with sweetened whipped cream or vanilla ice cream on top of slice.

COCOA CREAM ROLL

Elsie N. Yoder

3 eggs
2 T. cocoa
1 c. sugar
4 t. cold water
1 scant c. flour
1 1/4 t. baking powder
1/4 t. salt
1 t. vanilla

2 T. hot melted butter
COCONUT PECAN FROSTING:
1-8 oz. cream cheese, softened
1/2 c. butter or margarine, softened
1-16 oz. pkg. powdered sugar
1 t. vanilla
Dash of salt
1/2 c. flaked coconut
1/2 c. chopped pecans

Beat eggs and sugar to a creamy batter. Add water, cocoa, and dry ingredients. Gradually add vanilla and hot butter last. Bake on 10x15" cookie sheet in quick oven at 375° 10-15 min. Turn out on a towel that has been sprinkled with powdered sugar. Roll with the towel. When cool, fill and frost with Coconut Pecan Frosting or your favorite icing. Makes 1.

181

JELLYROLL
Ellen R. Brenneman

2 eggs
1 c. sugar
4 T. cold water
Approximately 1½ c. jelly

1 c. flour
1 t. baking powder
½ t. salt

Separate eggs, beat yolks. Slowly add sugar while beating. Add water, beat well. Add dry ingredients and egg whites. Put in 10x15" pan and bake at 350° for 10 min. Flip on a powdered sugar-floured towel. Roll up and cool. Unroll and fill with jelly, jam or pudding. Serves 8 to 10.

LEMON ROLL
Mrs. Eli Kauffman

3 eggs
1 c. sugar
¼ c. water
1 t. vanilla

1 c. flour
3 t. baking powder
½ t. salt
1 box lemon pie filling

Beat eggs and add sugar, mix with water and vanilla. Add flour, baking powder and salt and mix well and bake on 10x15" cookie sheet at 375° for 12 min. To cool, put on a tea towel sprinkled with powdered sugar and roll. When cool, unroll. Spread with lemon pie filling and roll again.

To clean chimneys and stovepipes,
put a piece of zinc on the live coals in the stove.

SNOW-CAPPED LEMON ROLL

Mrs. William N. Yoder
(Yoder's Bakery recipe), Marie King

4 egg yolks	4 egg whites
2/3 c. sugar	2/3 c. sifted flour
1/2 t. grated lemon rind	1/4 t. salt
1 T. lemon juice	Lemon filling and meringue

LEMON FILLING:

3/4 c. sugar	2 slightly-beaten egg yolks
2 T. cornstarch	1 t. grated lemon rind
Dash of salt	3 T. lemon juice
3/4 c. cold water	1 t. butter

Beat egg yolks, gradually add 1/3 c. sugar, beating constantly. Stir in lemon rind and juice. Beat egg whites till soft peaks form, gradually add remaining 1/3 c. sugar and beat till stiff peaks form. Gently fold yolks into whites. Sift together flour and salt, fold into egg mixture. Spread into 15 1/2x10 1/2x1" greased and floured pan. Bake at 350° for 15 min., loosen sides, immediately, put on towel sprinkled with powdered sugar, roll cake and towel together. Cool. Prepare Lemon Filling. Unroll cake, spread with filling. Roll again. Top with meringue (top and sides). Bake at 350° until brown, about 15 min.

LEMON FILLING: In saucepan, combine sugar, cornstarch, and salt; gradually add water. Stir in egg yolks, lemon rind and juice. Cook and stir over medium heat till thickened and bubbly. Boil 1 min. remove from heat. Stir in butter. Cool to room temperature without stirring.

MERINGUE: Beat 2 egg whites till soft peaks form. Gradually add 1/4 c. sugar, beating till stiff. Spread on roll.

THE OLD PANTRY

It stood next to the kitchen,
Only a door between;
It held the many goodies
About which children dream:

Sweet jellies, red and purple,
(Wild strawberry and grape);
Fresh pies and homemade cookies
And tasty chocolate cake.

It stood next to the kitchen,
With just a door between . . .
The old pantry at Grandma's
Where goodies reigned supreme.

183

PUMPKIN ROLL   Mrs. Allen M. Yoder, Mrs. Elmer M. Yoder

3 eggs
1 c. white sugar
2/3 c. pumpkin
1 t. lemon juice
3/4 c. flour
1 t. baking powder

2 t. cinnamon
1 t. ginger
1/2 t. nutmeg
1/2 t. salt
1 c. nuts, chopped

Beat eggs on high speed of mixer for 5 min. Gradually beat in sugar, add pumpkin and lemon juice. Mix together flour, baking powder, salt and spices. Fold into pumpkin mixture. Spread into greased and floured cookie sheet pan. Top with nuts. Bake at 375° for 15 min. When baked, turn out on towel sprinkled with powdered sugar. Starting at narrow end, roll towel and cake together, cool, unroll.

FILLING:
1 c. powdered sugar
4 T. butter
2-3 oz. pkgs. cream cheese

1 t. vanilla
1 t. lemon juice

Beat until smooth. Spread over cake, roll, chill.

PUMPKIN TORTE   Jo Ann Inhulsen

24 graham crackers, crushed
1/3 c. sugar
1/2 c. butter
2 eggs, beaten
3/4 c. sugar
8 oz. cream cheese
2 c. pumpkin
3 egg yolks
1/2 c. sugar

1/2 c. milk
1/2 t. salt
1 T. cinnamon
1 env. plain gelatin
1/4 c. cold water
3 egg whites
1/4 c. sugar
1/2 pt. whipping cream

Mix graham crackers, 1/3 c. sugar and butter and press into 9x13" pan. Mix eggs, 3/4 c. sugar and cream cheese and pour over crust. Bake at 350° for 20 min. Cook pumpkin, egg yolks, 1/2 c. sugar, milk, salt and cinnamon until mixture thickens. Remove from heat and add gelatin, dissolved in cold water. Cool. Beat egg whites, 1/4 c. sugar and fold in pumpkin mixture. Pour over cooled, baked crust. Top with whipped cream.

SHORTCAKE

Mrs. Henry Overholt, Sr.

2 c. flour
3 t. baking powder
1/2 t. salt

1/4 c. sugar
1/3 c. butter
3/4 to 1 c. milk

Cream sugar and butter - not with electric mixer. Add rest of ingredients and mix lightly by hand. Bake in 9x13" pan at 450° for 15-20 min. Good with strawberries or other fruit. Top with whipped cream.

STRAWBERRY CHIFFON SQUARES

Kathy Yoder

1/4 c. butter
1 1/2 c. crushed vanilla wafers
1-3 oz. pkg. strawberry gelatin
3/4 c. boiling water

1-14 oz. can sweetened
  condensed milk
10 oz. sliced frozen strawberries
  in syrup
4 c. miniature marshmallows
1 c. whipping cream (whipped)

Melt butter, stir in vanilla wafer crumbs. Pat firmly in bottom of 11x7" baking dish. Chill. In large bowl, dissolve gelatin in boiling water. Stir in sweetened condensed milk and undrained strawberries. Fold in marshmallows and whipped cream. Pour into dish. Chill 2 hrs. If desired, garnish with whipped topping and strawberries. Refrigerate. Serves 12.

STRAWBERRY DELIGHT

Sara Marie Yoder

2 pkgs. graham crackers
1 c. melted butter
8 oz. cream cheese
1 pkg. Dream Whip
2 c. powdered sugar

1 sm. box strawberry jello
3 c. boiling water
2 heaping t. tapioca
1/2 c. sugar
1 qt. fresh strawberries

Crush graham crackers and add butter. Press in 9x13" pan and bake at 350° for 15 min. Set aside and let cool. Mix cream cheese, Dream Whip, and sugar until smooth. Pour over crust. Mix jello, water, tapioca, and sugar. Cook until tapioca is clear. Cool and add strawberries. Pour over second layer and top with whipped cream.

STRAWBERRY DELIGHT

Tillie Yoder

1ST LAYER:
1 c. flour
1/2 c. melted butter

1/2 c. pecans

Mix butter, flour and nuts together. Press in 9x13" pan and bake at 350° for 10-15 min. Cool.

2ND LAYER:
1-8 oz. pkg. cream cheese
1 c. powdered sugar

1 c. Dream Whip or Cool Whip

Beat Cool Whip, cream cheese, and powdered sugar together. Put on baked crust after cooled.

3RD LAYER:
1 c. water
1 c. sugar
3 T. cornstarch
3 T. strawberry jello

1/4 t. lemon juice
Dash of salt
1 qt. strawberries (sliced)

Mix sugar and 3/4 c. water. Bring it to a boil, then add cornstarch and 1/4 c. water to thicken. After thickened, remove from heat and stir in dry jello, salt, and lemon juice. Cool and add fresh strawberries. You may substitute peaches and peach jello for strawberries and strawberry jello.

What you are is God's gift to you.
What you become is your gift to God.

STRAWBERRY DESSERT
Naomi Yoder

FIRST:
1 c. flour
1/2 c. butter
1/2 c. nuts (chopped)
1/3 c. sugar

SECOND:
2 cans sweetened condensed
milk
16 oz. cream cheese
1 c. Cool Whip
2/3 c. lemon juice

Mix all of first column together well and put in bottom of 9x13" pan. Bake at 350° for 15 min. Cool. Mix ingredients in column 2 and pour over first column. Last add third column. Serves 12.

THIRD:
1 pt. fresh strawberries, sliced   3 T. cornstarch
1 lg. box strawberry jello   3 c. water
1 1/3 c. sugar

Mix jello, sugar, water and cornstarch. Cook till clear. **Cool.** Slice strawberries over top of second layer. Pour cooled mixture over strawberries. Refrigerate.

STRAWBERRY DESSERT
Ellen R. Brenneman

1 c. flour
1/2 stick melted butter
1/4 c. brown sugar
1 c. nuts, chopped

2 egg whites
2/3 c. sugar
2 T. lemon juice
10 oz. crushed strawberries
1 lg. Cool Whip

Mix flour, butter, brown sugar, and nuts. Bake in 6x6" pan at 300° for 20 min. Let cool. Pack 2/3 of mixture in bottom of pan for crust. Beat egg whites, add sugar. Slowly add lemon juice, a drop at a time. Add berries. Beat 20 min. at high speed. Beating is the secret. Stir in large size (13 oz.) Cool Whip. Spread on crumb mixture. Sprinkle rest of crumbs on top, cover and freeze. Serves 8.

STRAWBERRY YUM-YUM

Delores Hostetler

1. c. flour
½ c. butter
½ c. brown sugar
½ c. pecans
2 egg whites

1 c. white sugar
2 t. lemon juice
1 pt. frozen strawberries
1-9 oz. container Cool Whip

Mix first 4 ingredients until crumbly. Press into pan and bake at 300° for 20 min. Cool and break into crumbs. Next, combine the egg whites, lemon juice, sugar and strawberries, and beat at medium speed for 15-20 min. Fold berry mix into whipped topping. Put ½ of the crumbs into bottom of pan. Spread berry mix over crumbs and top with remaining crumbs. Freeze.

VELVET MAPLE CREAM

Mary Lois Yoder

1⅓ c. brown sugar
1 c. sour cream

1 T. maple extract
1 c. whipping cream

Blend together sugar, sour cream, and maple until sugar is dissolved. Fold in whipped cream; chill. Just before serving, add 4 c. fresh blueberries, or your favorite fruit. Serve over slices of angel food cake.

YOGURT FRUIT SALAD

Linda Kauffman

1-8 oz. carton orange yogurt
2 T. mayonnaise
1-20 oz. can pineapple chunks,
  drained
1-16 oz. can fruit cocktail,
  drained

1-11 oz. can mandarin oranges,
1 c. sliced fresh strawberries
1 c. seedless grapes, halved
2 bananas, sliced

Combine yogurt and mayonnaise. Stir well and chill. Combine all fruit except bananas and chill. Stir in yogurt mixture and bananas just before serving.

BEEF INTERNATIONAL

Mrs. Leslie Yoder

2 lbs. round steak
2 medium onions
1 can cream of celery soup
2 peppers
2 T. butter

1 T. Worcestershire sauce
Salt and pepper
1/2 c. water
1/2 c. mayonnaise
3 oz. mushrooms

Cut steaks in bite-size pieces. Fry steak, onions and pepper until done. Combine remaining ingredients and add to meat mixture and simmer 1/2 hr.

POOR MAN'S BEEF STROGANOFF WITH MUSHROOM SOUP

Dorothy Yoder

1 lb. ground beef
1 T. margarine
1/2 c. sour cream
1/2 t. paprika

1 c. chopped onion
1 can condensed cream of
    mushroom soup

Brown beef and onion in oleo. Add soup, sour cream and paprika. You also can use Carnation milk and put lemon juice - enough to sour it - if you don't have sour cream. Simmer 20 min. Serve over hot noodles. Best to take off some grease.

To prevent splashing when frying meat, sprinkle a little salt into the pan before putting the margarine in.

SCRUMPTIOUS BEEF

Mrs. Leslie Yoder

1 to 2 lbs. beef as for stew
8 oz. mushrooms
1 can beef broth

2 onions, chopped
1 can cream of celery soup
2 envs. onion gravy mix

Do not brown meat. Place everything in a roaster or casserole. No need to mix. Place in oven, uncovered. Bake at 350° for 2 to 3 hrs. Serve with rice.

PEPPER STEAK

Alma Yoder

1½ lb. round steak, cut into
  ¼" strips after being
  trimmed of fat and bone
½ t. salt
2 medium onions, sliced
1 c. broth (beef bouillon)

3 T. soy sauce
1 clove garlic, sliced
1 green pepper, sliced
2 T. cornstarch
¼ c. cold water
2 tomatoes, cut in wedges

Brown meat thoroughly in lightly-greased skillet. Mix soy sauce and beef broth; add to meat, cover and simmer 35-45 min. Add onion, garlic, and green pepper to meat. Stir - cook until tender. Blend cornstarch and water, stir gradually into meat mixture. Cook till thick - add tomatoes - heat - serve over steamed rice. Serves 4.

POOR MAN'S STEAK

Ellen R. Brenneman, Alta Kauffmann,
Esther Ruth Yoder

1 lb. hamburger
1 c. milk
1 onion, chopped fine

1 c. soda crackers, crushed
1 t. salt
½ t. pepper

Mix well and shape in narrow loaf. Let set for at least 8 hrs. or overnight in refrigerator. Slice in pieces and fry until brown. Put slices in layers in a roaster and spread mushroom soup on each piece. Use 1 can soup. Bake at 350° for 1 hr. Serves 10.

The only way to help yourself is to help others.

BAR-B-QUE HAMBURGERS Mrs. Noah Yoder, Mrs. Ivan Yoder

1½ lbs. hamburger
¾ c. oatmeal
1 c. canned or plain milk
1 t. salt
Shape patties and brown in skillet.

BAR-B-QUE SAUCE:
2 T. sugar
2 T. vinegar
1 t. Worcestershire sauce
1 c. catsup
½ c. chopped celery
½ c. water
¾ c. onion, chopped

Pour Bar-B-Que Sauce over patties and bake in slow oven for 1 hr.

BARBECUED MEATBALLS Linda Weaver

3 lbs. hamburger
1 can evaporated milk
2 c. quick oatmeal
2 eggs
1 c. chopped onions
½ t. garlic powder
2 t. salt

½ t. pepper
2 t. chili powder
SAUCE:
2 c. catsup
1½ c. brown sugar
½ t. garlic powder
½ c. chopped onions

Mix and shape into balls. Place in flat pan - 1 layer to a pan. Heat sauce and pour over meatballs. Bake 350° for 1 hr.

MUSHROOM MEATBALLS Mrs. Elmer M. Yoder (Esther)

1 lb. ground beef
⅔ c. fine bread crumbs
2 T. minced onion
2 T. chopped parsley

1 egg. slightly beaten
1½ t. salt
2 cans cream of mushroom soup
¼ c. water

Combine ground beef, bread crumbs, onion, parsley, egg and salt. Stir soup until smooth. Blend in water. Put ¼ c. of soup mixture into the meat; mix well. Shape into balls about 1" in diameter. Brown meatballs in skillet. Pour in remaining mushroom sauce. Cover and bake at 350° or cook slowly on top of range about 30 min.

191

SWEET & SOUR MEATBALLS
Elsie Yoder

1 lb. hamburger
1 sm. onion
1 clove garlic
1/3 c. milk
1 egg
1/2 c. bread crumbs
3/4 t. salt

1/4 t. seasoning salt
1/4 t. pepper
1/4 t. Accent
2 carrots (cut in strips)
1 onion (cut in chunks)
1 bell pepper (cut in strips)
1-10 oz. jar sweet & sour sauce

Beat egg in mixer bowl. Add milk, bread crumbs and seasonings. Add hamburger and mix. Shape in small balls. Brown in small amount of oil over medium heat. Stir-fry carrots, onions, pepper over medium heat a few minutes. Put the hamburger balls and the sweet and sour sauce and vegetables in a saucepan and heat through.

TACO MEATBALLS
Ms. Ernest W. Yoder,
Mrs. William N. Yoder

1 lb. hamburger
1 c. onion (chopped)
1 c. peppers (chopped)
1 c. celery (chopped)

2 c. cooked rice
2 eggs (beaten)
2 t. garlic salt
1-8 oz. can taco sauce
1 can condensed Cheddar
    cheese soup

Mix first 7 ingredients and form into 12 meatballs. Place in 2-qt. casserole. Bake, uncovered, at 350° for 30 min. Blend and heat Cheddar cheese soup and taco sauce. Pour over meatballs. Bake another 30 min. (covered). Serves 6 to 8.

CHEESE 'N RICE MEAT LOAF
Mrs. Alva Yoder

1 can Campbell's Cheddar
    cheese soup
1 1/2 lbs. hamburger
1/2 c. chopped onions

1/2 c. Minute rice (uncooked)
1 t. salt
3 strips bacon, cut in half

Combine 1/2 can soup with remaining ingredients except bacon. Bake at 350° for 1 hr. Top with remaining soup and bacon and bake 5 min.

MEAT LOAF

Bertha Swartzentruber

1½ lbs. ground beef
1 c. tomato juice
¾ c. oats (uncooked)
1 egg, beaten

¼ c. chopped onions
1½ t. salt
¼ t. ground pepper
¼ c. chopped sweet peppers

Combine all ingredients and press in ungreased 9x13" loaf pan. Bake at 350° for 1 hr. Let stand about 5 min. before serving. Serves approximately 8.

MEAT LOAF

Vernie Weaver

3 lbs. ground beef
4 eggs, beaten
4 t. salt
3/4 c. tomato juice

1 1/2 c. quick oats
1/2 c. onion
1/2 t. pepper
3/4 c. milk

Mix all together and press into 9x13" pan. Bake at 350° for 1 hr. Serves 16.

MEAT LOAF

Mrs. Floyd E. Yoder

2 lbs. hamburger
2 eggs
2 T. onion
6 oz. tomato juice

20 crackers, crushed
1 T. Worcestershire sauce
1 1/2 t. salt
1/2 t. pepper

Mix all together, put in 9x9" pan and bake at 350° for 1 hr. Serves 10.

MEAT LOAF

Sara Marie Yoder

2 lbs. ground beef
2 eggs
1 c. cracker crumbs
1-8 oz. can tomato sauce

1 medium onion
1/2 t. salt
1/4 t. pepper
Bacon strips

In medium-size mixing bowl, combine all ingredients. Knead mixture well. Form into loaf and place in baking dish; then top with bacon strips. Bake at 375° for 1 hr.

ITALIAN MEAT LOAF

Ruth Yoder

1 c. cracker crumbs
1½ lbs. hamburger
1 can tomato paste

2 eggs
1 medium onion, chopped
¼ c. green pepper, chopped
¾ t. salt - dash of pepper

FILLING:
1-12 oz. carton cottage cheese
1-3 oz. can mushrooms, drained
1 T. parsley

¼ t. oregano
2 T. Parmesan cheese

Mix meat loaf ingredients together and put half of mixture in baking dish, place Filling in the center and top with the rest of the meat loaf. Bake at 350° for 1 hr.

MEATLESS MEAT LOAF OR COTTAGE CHEESE LOAF

Chris Inhulsen, Mary M. Yoder, Mrs. Levi Kauffman

5 eggs, beaten
½ c. onions, chopped
3 T. dry bouillon (beef)
1 stick melted margarine
1 c. chopped pecans

1 T. Accent
2 pts. cottage cheese
½ c. milk
1-7 oz. pkg. Special K
1 T. chopped green pepper

Mix all ingredients and bake at 350° for 1 hr.

Delicious meatless main dish.

POT ROAST MEAT LOAF

Lela Brenneman

1 lb. ground beef
⅔ c. Pet evaporated milk
⅓ c. fine, dry bread crumbs
¼ c. catsup or chili sauce

1 t. salt
2 t. Worcestershire sauce
¼ t. pepper

Mix in a 1½-qt. bowl. Wet hands and shape into loaf in center of pan. Peel and slice ¼" thick 3 medium potatoes and 3 medium onions. Peel and quarter lengthwise 3 medium carrots. Mix 2 t. dried parsley flakes, 1 t. salt, a few grains of pepper. Place vegetables in layer around meat. Sprinkle each layer with part of salt mixture. Cover tightly with foil. Bake in 13x9x2" pan at 375° for 1 hr. or until vegetables are tender. Uncover and bake 10 min. more to brown meat. Serves 4.

194

PRIZE WINNING MEAT LOAF — Marie King, Mrs. Nelson Yoder

1½ lbs. ground beef
1 c. tomato juice
¾ c. oatmeal
1 egg beaten

¼ c. chopped onion
1½ t. salt
¼ t. pepper

Combine all ingredients. Mix well. Press firmly into ungreased 8" pan. Bake at 350° for 1 hr. Let stand 5 min. before slicing. Serves 8.

PRIZE WINNING MEAT LOAF — Vernie Brenneman

1½ lbs. hamburger
1 c. oatmeal, uncooked
¼ c. chopped onion
1½ t. salt

¼ t. pepper
1 c. tomato juice
1 egg, beaten

TOPPING:
⅓ c. catsup
2 T. brown sugar

1 t. mustard
2 drops liquid smoke flavoring

Mix all together, then top with Topping before baking in 9x6" pan at 350° for 45 min. Serves 8.

SKILLET MEAT LOAF — Mrs. Noah Yoder

2 lbs. ground beef
2 eggs
1 c. cracker crumbs
1-8 oz. can tomato sauce

2 T. dehydrated onion flakes
½ t. salt
¼ t. pepper
¼ c. margarine or butter

In medium-sized mixing bowl, combine all ingredients except butter. Knead mixture well. Place mixture on a sheet of waxed paper and mold into loaf, 6" wide and 15" long and 2" high. Preheat electric skillet, uncovered, at 225° for about 3 to 4 min. Melt ¼ c. butter or margarine in skillet, spreading evenly to cover cooking surface. Place meat loaf in center of skillet. Cover and cook for 35-40 min.

MOCK TURKEY

Mrs. Alva Yoder
Mrs. Noah Yoder

2 lbs. hamburger
1 can cream of celery soup
1 can cream of chicken soup

4 c. milk
1 loaf bread, crumbled

Brown hamburger in butter, mix together and place in pan and bake at 350° for 45 min.

PIZZA

Mrs. Milton Yoder

1½ to 2 lbs. hamburger
¼ t. chili powder
Salt and pepper
½ c. Parmesan cheese
1 pepper, diced
¾ c. chopped ham
1 pack mozzarella cheese

¼ t. taco seasoning
1 t. Italian seasoning
1½ c. pizza sauce
1 sm. onion
1 sm. jar mushrooms or 1 can
   mushroom soup
Pepperoni

Fry hamburger. Add taco seasoning, chili, salt, pepper, and Italian seasoning. Bake a pizza crust till partly baked. Layer in this order - crust, pizza sauce, ¼ c. Parmesan cheese, hamburger mixture, onion, pepper, mushrooms or mushroom soup, ham, pepperoni, mozzarella cheese, ¼ c. Parmesan cheese. Bake at 350° for 20 min. Serves 4 to 6.

In cooking, and in life as well
The only way that one can tell
What recipe is best, no doubt
is read it through and try it out.

PIZZA
Mrs. William N. Yoder

1-8 oz. can tomato sauce
1 T. sugar
1 T. minced onion
2 T. mustard

¼ t. oregano
1 lb. hamburger
Grated cheese on top

Fry hamburger - set aside. Combine all ingredients, bring to boil and simmer 10 min. Pour sauce over partly-baked crust. Then add hamburger, and spread cheese on top. If desired, you can put green pepper, onions and pepperoni on top.

PIZZA DOUGH:
1 c. Bisquick
1 t. mustard

¼ c. milk

Stir milk and mustard together. Blend in Bisquick and knead 1 min. Press into pizza pan. Prick with fork and bake in hot oven, 425° for 5-7 min.

CRAZY CRUST PIZZA
Mrs. Chris L. Miller

1 c. flour
⅔ c. milk
2 eggs
1 t. oregano
⅛ t. pepper
⅛ t. salt

TOPPING:
1½ lbs. ground beef, fried
1 c. pizza sauce
1 c. shredded cheese

Mix thoroughly first 6 ingredients. Grease and flour skillet. Put first mixture in electric skillet, heat at 375° until set, then add pizza sauce, hamburger and cheese on top.

INDIVIDUAL PIZZA
Ruth Yoder

1 lb. hamburger
½ lb. sausage
1 can cream of mushroom
   soup

1½ t. pizza seasoning
1 c. catsup
10 slices Velveeta cheese
1 pkg. refrigerator biscuits

Fry hamburger and sausage; drain off fat. To hamburger and sausage add pizza seasoning and catsup. Flatten biscuits on cookie sheet. Put equal amounts of hamburger mixture on each biscuit. Put slices of cheese on each and cover with mushroom soup.

197

BAKED CHUCK ROAST

Mrs. Levi Kauffman,
Alta Kauffman, Ruth Yoder

3 to 5 lb. beef roast

12 oz. Coca-Cola
1 pkg. onion soup mix

Place roast in baking dish unseasoned. Sprinkle with onion soup mix. Pour Coca-Cola. Cover and seal tightly with aluminum foil. Bake at 300° for 3½ hrs. or until tender. This has an excellent flavor.

MARINATED CHUCK ROAST

Beulah Yoder

3 to 5 lb. chuck roast
1 c. strong coffee
½ c. soy sauce

1 T. Worcestershire sauce
1 T. vinegar
Meat tenderizer

Sprinkle meat with tenderizer. Mix together other ingredients and pour over meat in a covered pan, turning every few hours. Let stand overnight in refrigerator or several hours at room temperature. Charcoal broil 45 min. to 1 hr. Baste often with marinade. Slice thin and serve. Serves 4 to 6, depending on size of roast.

SAVORY SWEET POT ROAST

Linda Yoder

3 or 4 lb. blade roast
1 sliced onion (medium)
1 can cream of mushroom soup
½ c. water
¼ c. brown sugar

¼ c. vinegar
2 t. salt
1 t. mustard
1 t. Worcestershire sauce

Brown meat on both sides. Add onion. Blend together remaining ingredients and pour over meat. Cover and simmer for 2½ to 3 hrs., or until tender. Serves 6.

COUNTRY FRIED STEAK

Mrs. Crist Yoder, Jr.

6 medium cubed steaks
1 lg. onion, chopped

1 can cream of mushroom soup
Water
Salt and pepper

Flour each steak and fry in skillet until brown. Salt and pepper steaks and place in baking dish. Spread cream of mushroom soup over each steak and add onions. Almost cover with water and bake at 325° until tender, approximately 2 hrs.

BAKED HERB CHICKEN

Mrs. Loretta Brenneman

1-3 lb. fryer, cut up
1 can mushroom soup
1 t. grated lemon rind (optional)
2 T. lemon juice

½ t. salt
¼ t. sweet basil
¼ t. oregano

Arrange fryer in 9x13" baking dish. Combine rest of ingredients and pour over chicken. Bake uncovered at 325° for 1¼ hrs.

You can also bake it at 250° for 2½ to 3 hrs. Makes a good Sunday dinner.

CRISPY FRIED CHICKEN

Mrs. Ernest W. Yoder

1 whole chicken
½ c. butter
1 c. Crisco

1 c. milk
2 c. flour
Lawry's seasoned salt

Heat butter and Crisco in electric frypan at 375° to 400°. Cut up chicken. Dip 1 piece of chicken at a time into milk, then into flour. Fry till golden brown on both sides. When frying, season with Lawry's salt. Place chicken in roasting pan without a lid. Bake at 250° for 1 hr.

This makes the chicken crisp and it isn't greasy.

CORN CRISP CHICKEN

Mrs. Henry Overholt, Sr.

1 chicken, fryer size
1/2 c. Pet evaporated milk
  (thin milk just won't do)

1 c. cornflake crumbs
1 t. Accent
1 t. salt
1/2 t. pepper

Dip 1 cut-up chicken in evaporated milk. Roll in mixture of cornflakes and seasonings. Bake in shallow pan lined with Reynold's Wrap. Bake at 350° for 1 hr. Serves 6.

FRIED CHICKEN

Mrs. Raymond Weaver

3 1/2 lb. fryer
1 c. flour

2 t. salt
1/8 t. pepper

Cut chicken into serving pieces. Wash pieces of chicken, drain. Mix flour, salt and pepper together. shake chicken in flour mixture. Melt fat to a depth of 1/2" in a skillet. When fat is moderately hot, add pieces of chicken. For a crisp crust, fry chicken for 20 min. with skillet covered. Turn chicken every 5 min. You may eat right away or steam in the oven at 325° for 1 hr. Serves 6.

Don't crowd chicken in the skillet.

GOLDEN BAKED CHICKEN

Miriam Brenneman

1/4 c. butter
1/2 c. flour
1 t. salt
1 t. dry mustard

1 t. paprika
1 t. pepper
1-2 1/2 to 3 lb. broiler-fryer,
  cut up

Melt 2 T. butter in 13x9x2" baking pan. Combine next 5 ingredients; stir well. Dredge chicken in flour mixture, coating well. Place chicken in baking pan and dot with remaining butter. Bake at 350° for 1 hr. Serves 4.

OVEN BARBECUED CHICKEN

Linda Yoder

1 frying chicken

SAUCE:
1/2 c. catsup
1/4 c. vinegar

1/2 c. sugar
A little chili & paprika

Roll chicken in flour and brown. Place in casserole and pour barbecue sauce over all. Bake in slow oven 250° for 2 hrs. or till tender.

OVEN FRIED CHICKEN

Alma Yoder

2 1/2 to 3 lb. broiler or fryer
    chicken
1/2 c. melted butter

2 c. crushed cornflake crumbs
Seasoned salt and dash of pepper

Cut chicken in serving pieces - dip in melted butter - sprinkle with seasoned salt and pepper - roll in cornflake crumbs - place skin-side up in baking pan (not touching). Sprinkle with remaining butter and crumbs. Bake in large shallow baking pan at 350° for 1 hr. Serves 4 to 6.

OVEN FRIED CHICKEN

Mrs. Lloyd Swartzentruber

1 stick oleo
1 fryer

3/4 c. buttermilk

FLOUR MIXTURE:
1 c. flour
3/4 t. parsley flakes
2 t. paprika
1 t. seasoned salt

1/4 t. pepper
1/4 t. thyme
1 t. salt

Cook chicken 15 min. and drain well. Dip in buttermilk. Dredge in flour mixture. Place in single layer in baking dish with melted oleo. Bake at 400° for 30 min., turn chicken and bake 45 min.

PARTY PERFECT CHICKEN
Mrs. L.D. Kauffman, Ruth Yoder

2 frying chickens, cut up
6 T. flour
2½ t. salt
1 t. ginger
1⅓ t. pepper
CURRY GLAZE:
6 slices bacon, diced
1 medium onion, chopped

2 T. flour
1 T. sugar
1 T. curry powder
2 T. appleasuce
2 T. ketchup
2 T. lemon juice
1-10 oz. can beef broth
Salt to taste

Coat chicken with flour and spice mixture. Fry bacon until crisp and drain. Add onion to bacon fat, fry till glossy; drain. Pour bacon grease into pan big enough to hold chicken pieces, lying flat. Turn chicken once to grease both sides. Bake at 350° for 20 min. In the meantime, combine bacon, onion and remaining Curry Glaze ingredients in a saucepan. Bring to a boil; reduce heat and simmer for 15 min. When chicken has baked 20 min., spoon half of Curry Glaze over chicken. Bake for 20 more min. Spoon remaining glaze over chicken and bake another 20 min. or until chicken is tender.

SHAKE AND BAKE CHICKEN
Ruth Yoder

2 c. flour
2 t. baking powder
2 t. paprika
½ c. instant potato powder

½ c. seasoning salt
2 T. salt
2 T. pepper
½ c. water

Cover chicken with shake and bake mixture; place in a baking pan. Add ½ c. water into the baking dish. Cover loosely with tin foil. Bake at 300° for 1½ hrs. Uncover and bake 15 more min.

When a painting job is done, and you close the lid on the can,
add the plastic wrap between can and cover
and close up - no scummy layer on top of paint.

SHAKE AND BAKE CHICKEN   Lela Brenneman

1 pkg. soda crackers	1 t. oregano
¹/₄ t. thyme	¹/₄ t. salt
¹/₂ t. poultry seasoning	A little pepper

Put crackers in blender to make crumbs. Add the rest of seasoning. Dip chicken pieces in melted butter, then roll in cracker crumbs, or put chicken and crumbs in covered bowl and shake. Place in pan skin-side up and bake at 250° for 3 to 3¹/₂ hrs.

SILLA'S SOUR CREAM CHICKEN   Ruth Yoder

16 oz. sour cream	¹/₂ c. celery
1 can mushroom soup	¹/₂ c. onions
1 can mushrooms	¹/₂ c. green pepper

Fry celery, onion, and green pepper in butter till tender. Add sour cream, soup and mushrooms. Pour this sauce over chicken that has been baked till tender. Bake ¹/₂ hr. at 350°. Serve over rice.

CHICKEN & DRESSING   Malinda Wingard

1-3 lb. chicken	2 T. McKay's chicken seasoning
1-1 lb. loaf white bread (not homemade)	2 t. salt - add to water to cook chicken
5 eggs	¹/₄ t. sage
1 stick oleo	1 t. nutmeg
5 c. chicken broth	¹/₂ t. black pepper

Cut chicken lengthwise in half, place in crock pot (slow cooker) on high control, with 1 qt. water and 2 t. salt. When soft, debone and cut in pieces. (Set aside.) Brown oleo slightly, pour in baking pan (set aside). Mix with diced bread, sage, nutmeg, black pepper. Pour beaten eggs over bread. Mix McKay's seasoning with broth (if you don't have 5 c. broth, add water to make that amount). Pour over bread the warm broth (not boiling hot), add chicken. Now you may stir, but cautiously. Pour dressing into buttered 10x14" pan and bake at 325° for 45 min. Serves 10

Use spices and herbs sparingly. They are best when you have to guess which ones are really used. This dressing can be kept in freezer for weeks. When put in oven cold, the temperature and baking time need a change. When put in oven hard frozen, set temperature at 220° for the first few hrs., it can then be increased for browning.

CHICKEN & DRESSING   Mrs. Lloyd Swartzentruber

1/2 loaf bread	1 sm. onion
3 pieces celery	3 eggs
1/2 c. milk	1 t. sage
1 t. salt	4 c. chicken broth
Chicken or turkey meat, as desired	

Mix well, put in casserole. Bake at 375° for 20 min., then reduce heat to 200° and bake 50 more min.

HOMESTEAD CHICKEN & DRESSING   Ruth Yoder

12 chicken drumsticks	1/2 c. onion
1/2 t. salt	1/2 c. celery
1/4 t. black pepper	1/2 c. green pepper
3 t. butter	1 c. uncooked rice
1/4 lb. pork sausage	12 oz. corn
	2 c. chicken broth

Sprinkle chicken parts with salt and pepper. In a large skillet, melt butter over medium heat. Brown chicken parts on all sides. Remove from pan, saute sausage, onion, celery, green pepper in pan until sausage is done and vegetables are tender. Add rice, corn and broth to sausage mixture and bring to a boil, place rice mixture in a greased 9x13" pan. Arrange chicken on top, cover and bake at 350° for 45 min. till chicken is tender. Serves 6.

KATIE'S CHICKEN AND DRESSING   Ruth Yoder

2 loaves white bread	1 pt. onions, partly cooked
6 eggs	1 qt. celery, partly cooked
1 T. salt	1 T. sage
1 T. poultry seasoning	Milk and chicken broth to make
2 t. pepper	it moist
	1 cooked chicken, boned

Mix all together and put in loaf pan and bake at 350° for 1 hr. Serve with chicken gravy.

SCALLOPED CHICKEN

Mrs. Henry Overholt, Sr.,
Linda Weaver

16 slices white bread,
  cubed & sliced
4 c. cooked chicken
1 c. chopped onions
1 c. chopped celery, uncooked
1 c. mayonnaise

$\frac{1}{2}$ t. salt
$\frac{1}{8}$ t. pepper
$\frac{1}{4}$ t. curry powder
3 eggs
3 c. milk

Mix all together and put in 9x13" pan. Before baking, spread 1 can of mushroom soup over top. Bake at 325° for 2 hrs. Sprinkle 1 c. shredded cheese over the top for the last 10 min., also sliced cheese can be used. This may be fixed the day before and put in refrigerator overnight. Serves 15.

CHICKEN AND GRAVY

Verda Overholt

6 pieces chicken, raw
1 can cream of chicken soup

$\frac{1}{2}$ can water
Italian seasoning

Place chicken in casserole dish, sprinkle with Italian seasoning. Pour cream of chicken soup and water over top. Cover and bake at 350° for 1$\frac{1}{2}$ hrs.

PINEAPPLE GLAZED HAM

Ruth Yoder

1-10 lb. ham
1 c. brown sugar
3 T. honey

2 T. mustard
1-8 oz. Sprite
1 c. pineapple
$\frac{1}{4}$ t. cloves

After ham is baked, combine ingredients and put on top of ham. Bake 30 more min. May add 1 c. chopped pecans for a crunchy ham.

GOOD PORK CHOPS

Mary Plank

6 to 8 lean pork chops (1" thick)
$\frac{1}{2}$ c. flour
1 T. salt

1$\frac{1}{2}$ t. dry mustard
$\frac{1}{2}$ t. garlic powder
1 can chicken and rice soup

Dredge pork chops in mixture of flour, salt, dry mustard and garlic powder. Brown in oil in large skillet. Place browned pork chops in crock pot. Add can of soup. Cover and cook on low for 6 to 8 hrs. (High: 3$\frac{1}{2}$ hrs.)

SWEET AND SOUR PORK CHOPS
Anna Yoder

6 medium pork chops
4 medium onions, sliced
4 T. brown sugar

2 T. vinegar
1 c. water
Salt and pepper

In heavy skillet, brown pork chops in small amount of fat. Add remaining ingredients. Cover and simmer 1 hr., or until pork chops are tender.

MOCK HAM LOAF
Ruth Weaver, Lela Brenneman

1 lb. hamburger
1/2 lb. hot dogs (ground)
1 c. cracker crumbs or oatmeal
1 egg (beaten)
1 t. salt

Pepper to taste
GLAZE:
3/4 c. brown sugar
1/2 c. water
1/2 t. dry mustard
1 T. vinegar

Mix well, add 1/2 of Glaze to hamburger mixture. Put in 9x5x3" loaf pan and pour remaining Glaze on top. Bake at 350° for 1 hr.

FISH ALMONDINE
Alta Kauffman

Roll fish in seasoned flour (salt and pepper). Fry fish in butter on medium heat. Toast sliced almonds in butter. Sprinkle salt and lemon juice over almonds. Spread almonds over fried fish. Serve.

SALMON LOAF
Mrs. Paul E. Yoder

1-15 1/2 oz. can salmon
2 eggs
1 t. dry mustard
1/2 c. milk
1/2 c. finely-chopped celery
3/4 t. salt

1/8 t. pepper
2 c. bread crumbs
3 T. finely-cut parsley
2 T. finely-cut onion
2 T. finely-cut pimento

Put canned salmon with liquid into bowl. Remove skin and bones. Beat eggs with mustard, salt and pepper. With fork, mix all ingredients together. Put in greased 9x13" pan and bake at 375° for 45 min. Serves 6.

TUNA PATTIES IN SAUCE
Ruth Yoder, Mary Lois Yoder

2-7 oz. cans tuna
1/4 can cream of mushroom
  soup
1/2 c. quick oats

1/4 c. minced onion
1 egg
3 t. lemon juice

3/4 can cream of mushroom
  soup
1/3 c. milk

2 T. mayonnaise

Mix together and form into 8 patties, roll in cracker crumbs and fry in 2 T. butter. Mix 3/4 can of soup, milk and mayonnaise; heat and pour over patties and serve.

To prevent an odor in frying fish, put a teaspoon of peanut butter in the pan with oil. The fish will look and taste better.

THE KITCHEN PRAYER

Lord of all pots and pans and things
since I've not time to be
A saint by doing lovely things
or watching late with thee
Or dreaming in the dawn light
or storming Heaven's gates
Make me a saint by getting meals
and washing up the plates
Although I must have Martha's hands,
I have Mary's mind
And when I black the boots and shoes
Thy sandals, Lord, I find.
I think of how they trod the earth,
What time I scrub the floor
Accept this meditation, Lord,
I haven't time for more.
Warm all the kitchen with thy love,
and light it with thy peace
Forgive me all my worrying,
and make my grumbling cease.
Thou who didst love to give men food,
in room or by the sea
Accept this service that I do,
I do it unto Thee.

Notes

MICROWAVE

APPLES 'N DUMPLINGS

Linda Kauffman

1-8 oz. can refrigerated biscuits
4 medium cooking apples,
  peeled and sliced
1/2 c. chopped nuts

1/2 c. water
1/2 c. corn syrup
1/2 c. firmly-packed brown sugar
1/4 c. butter

Separate biscuits and cut each in half. Arrange in 2 qt. (12x7") baking dish. Top with apples and nuts. In 2 c. measure, combine water, syrup, brown sugar and butter. Cook, uncovered, 2 min., 30 sec., or until it boils. Pour over apples. Cook, covered with wax paper, 9-10 min., or until apples are tender. Serve warm with rich milk or ice cream. Serves 6 to 8.

This dish freezes well. Thaw and reheat to serve.

BLACK FOREST CHEESECAKE

Laura K. Yoder

CRUST:
24 sm. chocolate wafers (1 c.)
1/8 c. sugar

4 T. butter (softened)

FILLING:
4-3 oz. pkgs. cream cheese
2 eggs
1/2 c. sugar

1 t. vanilla
1/3 c. chocolate morsels
1 can cherry pie filling

Make fine crumbs of wafers in blender, add butter and sugar and stir until blended. Line bottom of 9" pie plate with crumb mixture and bake in microwave 2 min., turning every 20 sec. Cool. Place 1 egg and 2 pkgs. cream cheese in bowl and beat until creamed, add remaining egg and cream cheese, sugar, and vanilla; beat until thoroughly blended. Melt chocolate morsels in microwave 2 1/2 to 3 min. Using fork, swirl melted chocolate into filling, using minimum number of strokes. Pour into crust and bake 4-5 min. until outer edge of filling is set. Turn 1/4 turn every min. Cool to room temperature. Spread 1 can cherry pie filling over top and chill before serving.

CHICKEN DIVAN

Laura K. Yoder

2-10 oz. pkgs. frozen broccoli (cooked)
4 chicken breasts, cooked, boned & sliced

½ c. shredded cheese
½ c. soft bread crumbs
1½ T. melted butter

MIX:
1 c. mayonnaise
1 t. lemon juice

½ t. curry powder

Arrange items in order given in 2 qt. pan and bake on high 8 to 10 min. Halfway through baking time, rotate pan for even baking. Serves 6.

CREAMY CHICKEN STEW

Mrs. Allen E. Yoder

2 medium potatoes, cut into sm. pieces
2 c. thickly-sliced carrots
1 c. thickly-sliced celery
1 lg. onion, cut into ⅛'s

2 cans cream of chicken soup
2 t. salt
¼ t. pepper
1 chicken, cut into pieces

Combine all ingredients except chicken in 4 qt. casserole. Place chicken, skin-side down, on top of vegetables. Cover tightly. Microwave for 25 min. on HIGH. Stir, turning and rearranging chicken; Microwave for 35 min. on SIMMER. Let stand, covered, for 5 min. Serves 4 to 6.

A house is not a home unless it contains
food for the soul as well as the body.

FAVORITE MEAT LOAF

Linda Kauffman

1-8 oz. can tomato sauce,
   divided
$1/4$ c. brown sugar
1 t. mustard
2 eggs, lightly beaten

$1/3$ c. cracker crumbs
2 lbs. lean ground beef
$1 1/2$ t. salt
$1/4$ t. pepper
1 medium onion, minced

In small bowl, combine tomato sauce, brown sugar and mustard. Set aside. In large mixing bowl, combine eggs, onions, cracker crumbs, ground beef and seasonings. Add $1/2$ c. of tomato sauce in mixture and mix well. Place meat mixture in glass ring mold. Pour remaining tomato sauce over top of meat. Cook, uncovered, on High for 12-14 min. Let stand, covered, 5-10 min. before serving. Serves 6 to 7.

You can make your own ring mold by placing a small glass or custard cup in center of round casserole dish.

FREEZER TO OVEN CASSEROLE

Laura K. Yoder

1 lb. ground beef
1 sm. onion
$1/2$ green pepper
1 pkg. tater tots

1 sm. jar mushrooms
1 can cream of chicken soup
1 can cream of celery soup
1 c. peas or carrots

Cook ground beef with onion and pepper on high heat until meat is browned, and onion and peppers are soft (about 5 min.). Add salt and pepper; stir. Spread tater tots over meat mixture - mix together the soups, peas, and mushrooms, and pour over top of tater tots. Bake in 2 qt. casserole in microwave on High for 15 min.

HOT SCOTCH

Linda Kauffman

1 mug of milk
1 marshmallow

1 to 2 T. butterscotch chips

Heat a mug of milk $1 1/2$ min. on High. Add chips and stir. Garnish with a marshmallow and enjoy! Children love it. Serves 1.

211

LAST MINUTE SHORTCAKE
Laura K. Yoder

1 c. unsifted flour
3 T. sugar
1 t. baking powder
1/4 t. salt

1/4 c. butter
1/3 c. milk
1 egg

In mixing bowl, combine flour, sugar, baking powder and salt. Cut in butter. Add milk and egg; mix with fork and stir until just moistened. Spoon into 4 to 5 dessert or custard dishes (1 c. size). Cook, uncovered, 2 1/2 to 3 min., or until shortcakes are firm and no longer doughy. Best while warm or reheat about 30 sec. To serve, top with strawberries and whipped cream. (If desired, use 1 1/2 c.. biscuit mix, adding only the sugar, milk, and egg.) Serves 4 to 5.

MICROWAVE FUDGE
Laura K. Yoder

1 lb. 10X sugar
1/2 c. cocoa
1/4 c. milk

1 stick butter
1 t. vanilla
1/2 c. chopped nuts

Blend sugar and cocoa in 8x8x2" glass baking dish. Pour in milk and place butter on top. Cook in microwave on high for 2 min. Remove and stir just to mix ingredients. Add vanilla and nuts. Stir until well-blended. Refrigerate for 1 hr. Cut and serve.

MUNCHING PEANUT BRITTLE
Laura K. Yoder

1 c. raw peanuts
1 c. sugar
1/2 c. white corn syrup
1/8 t. salt

1 t. butter
1 t. vanilla
1 t. baking soda

Stir together peanuts, sugar, syrup, and salt in 1 1/2 qt. casserole. Place in microwave oven and cook 7 to 8 min., stirring well after 4 min. Add butter and vanilla to syrup mixture, blending well. Return to oven and cook 1 or 2 min. more. Peanuts will be lightly-browned, and syrup very hot. Add baking soda and gently stir until light and foamy. Pour mixture onto lightly-greased cookie sheet; let cool 1/2 to 1 hr. When cooled, break into small pieces and store in airtight container. Makes 1 lb.

212

NO-FUSS CARAMEL CORN
Mrs. Samuel Nisley

5 qts. popped corn
1 1/2 c. peanuts
1 c. packed brown sugar
1/2 c. butter

1/4 c. light corn syrup
1/2 t. salt
1/2 t. baking soda

Place popped corn and peanuts in large brown paper bag. Set aside. Combine brown sugar, butter, corn syrup and salt in 2 qt. glass bowl or casserole. Microwave (High setting) 3 to 4 min., stirring after each min. until mixture comes to a boil. Microwave 2 min. more. Stir in baking soda. Pour syrup mixture over popped corn and peanuts in bag. Close bag and shake well. Microwave (High setting) 1 1/2 min. Shake bag well. Microwave 1 1/2 min. more. Shake bag and pour caramelized popcorn into large roasting pan. Cool and stir to separate caramel corn kernels. Makes 5 qts.

NUTTY CHOCOLATE MARSHMALLOWS
Martina Kauffman

1 c. chocolate chips
1/4 c. milk

25-30 lg. marshmallows
1 c. chopped nuts

In small glass casserole or mixing bowl, combine chocolate chips and milk. Cook, uncovered on High, 1 min. and 30 sec., or until chocolate melts, stirring twice. Place a toothpick in each marshmallow. Dip marshmallows in chocolate and roll in nuts. Serve warm or cold. Marshmallows can also be rolled in coconut or graham cracker crumbs. (If chocolate mixture begins to cool while dipping marshmallows, return to oven for a few seconds.)

*Sharing's such a simple way
of sweetening someone else's day.*

STUFFED MEAT LOAF ROLL
Laura K. Yoder

1-2¹/₂ oz. jar sliced mushrooms
²/₃ c. milk and mushroom liquid
  (combined)
1¹/₂ lbs. ground beef (lean)
¹/₂ c. dry bread crumbs
1 egg
2 t. salt

1 c. Cheddar cheese (grated)
1¹/₂ t. Worcestershire sauce
1 T. minced onion
¹/₃ t. pepper
¹/₂ c. ketchup

In mixing bowl, combine all ingredients except cheese and ketchup. Mix until properly combined, but not overmixed. On a sheet of waxed paper, spread mixture into a 9x12" rectangle, or until meat is about ¹/₂" thick. Sprinkle cheese over meat. Using the waxed paper to start, roll the meat, starting at smaller end; place the seam-side down in 1¹/₂ qt. baking dish. Spread top with tomato sauce or ketchup. Cook, uncovered, about 16 min., rotating once during cooking time. Let dish stand 10 min. before serving. Serves 6.

SUSAN'S CARAMEL TOPPING
Ruth Yoder

1 T. cornstarch
1¹/₂ c. light brown sugar
¹/₂ c. evaporated milk
2 T. light Karo

¹/₈ t. salt
¹/₄ c. butter
1 t. vanilla

Mix all ingredients together, but vanilla. Put in microwave 2 min. Stir and cook till thickened. Add vanilla. Serve over ice cream. If you want to **really** make it good, fry pecans in butter and add to caramel!

SWEET POTATO CASSEROLE
Laura K. Yoder

4 c. grated raw sweet potatoes
1 c. corn syrup
1 c. sugar
1 c. milk
1 t. allspice
¹/₂ t. cloves

1 stick butter
¹/₂ c. choped pecans
1 c. raisins
3 eggs (beaten)
1 t. cinnamon

In a 3 qt. glass dish, melt butter for 30 sec. on High. Mix all other ingredients, then add butter and mix well. Pour back into glass dish, spread until evenly distributed. Cover with waxed paper and cook on High for 7 min., rotating every 2 min. After this 7 min., stir, bringing outer edges to center, and cook for 10 more min., uncovered, rotating every 3 min. This can be served with sweetened whipped cream and garnished with maraschino cherries.

SWEET POTATO CASSEROLE   Linda Kauffman

3 to 4 c. sweet potatoes
2 eggs
1/4 c. evaporated milk
1 t. vanilla
3/4 c. sugar
1/2 t. salt
3 T. butter

1/4 c. orange juice
1/2 t. nutmeg
TOPPING:
1/3 c. butter
3/4 c. brown sugar
1/2 c. flour
1 c. pecans

Cook 3 medium potatoes in microwave for 10 to12 min. Wrap in foil for 5 to 10 min. to soften. Place potatoes, eggs, milk, vanilla, sugar, salt, butter, orange juice and nutmeg in food processor or mixer and blend well. Pour into buttered 12x7$\frac{1}{2}$x2" dish and microwave on High 10 to12 min., stirring once. For Topping, cut butter into sugar and flour, adding nuts last. Place on top of sweet potatoes and microwave 5 to 7 additional min. on 80% power. Serves 8.

TURTLES   Laura K. Yoder

1-14 oz. pkg. caramels
2 T. evaporated milk
1 T. butter

5 oz. pecan halves
1-6 oz. pkg. chocolate morsels
1-1" sq. paraffin

Place caramels, milk, and butter in 1 qt. casserole. Heat in micro-wave on Medium-High for 4-5 min., or until caramels are melted. Arrange pecan halves in groups of 3 on buttered baking sheet; spoon about 1 T. warm caramel mixture over each group of pecans. Refrigerate for 30 min. Place chocolate chips and paraffin in 2 c. glass measure. Heat in microwave for 5 to 6 min. Stir mixture and spoon over caramel to cover. Cool before removing from baking sheet. Makes 2 to 2$\frac{1}{2}$ dozen.

May be stored in single layer in tightly covered container for as long as 3 weeks.

Notes

ORIENTAL FOODS

CHINESE EGG ROLLS

Elsie N. Yoder

1 lb. hamburger
1 sm. onion
2 cloves garlic (crushed)
1 t. salt
½ t. seasoned salt
¼ t. black pepper

½ t. Accent
¼ c. soy sauce
1 egg
1 lg. carrot
1 c. cabbage
Pastry wrappers

Cut carrot very fine or put in blender with water and then drain off water. Mix all ingredients and spread very thin over pastry wrappers and roll. Deep-fry until brown.

LAOTIAN EGG ROLLS

Alta Kauffman

FILLING FOR EGG ROLLS:
2 lbs. lean hamburger or
   ground pork (raw)
½ c. cabbage, shredded
1 medium potato, shredded
1 sm. onion, chopped
¾ c. soaked rice noodles or
   sticks
2 eggs, beaten

1½ t. salt
1½ t. Accent
¼ t. black pepper
¼ t. red pepper
1½ t. soy sauce
¼ t. fish sauce
1½ t. sugar

Rice paper for wrapping rolls

Soak rice noodles in hot water for several min. Drain. Thoroughly mix all the ingredients for the filling. To prepare rice paper, dip each sheet in very warm water. Place softened sheet on flat surface. The sheets are shaped like a pie wedge. Put approximately ¼ c. of filling on the rounded side of sheet. Fold the sides over the filling, then roll up from the bottom. Fry in oil ¼" deep in skillet till brown. Turn and brown on all sides. Yields approximately 25 rolls. Serve with sauce.

Rice paper, rice noodles and fish sauce may be bought at the Oriental food store.

SAUCE TO DIP EGG ROLLS IN:

1 c. brown sugar
1 c. water
½ t. Accent
½ t. lemon juice

¼ t. fish sauce
Dash of red pepper
½ c. chopped, salted peanuts

Boil brown sugar and water for several min. Remove from heat and add remaining ingredients. Cool.

LAOTIAN FRIED EGG ROLLS
Laura K. Yoder

1 lb. hamburger
1 lb. sausage
1 medium potato (chopped fine)
1 medium onion (chopped fine)
1/2 pkg. bean thread or rice
   noodles
2 eggs (beaten)
1 T. Worcestershire sauce
1/2 t. Accent

1 t. salt
1/2 t. red pepper
1/2 t. black pepper
1 pkg. rice paper
SAUCE:
2 c. boiling water
3/4 c. brown sugar
1/8 t. each: salt and Accent
1 c. peanuts

Soak bean thread in very hot water until soft; drain. Mix together all ingredients (like mixing meat loaf). Cut rice paper in half for big rolls and 1/4's for small ones; dip into a pan of very hot water; soak for 8 sec. Place "serving spoon" full of meat mixture on rice paper and roll securely. Fry in hot oil until golden brown and crisp on both sides.
SAUCE: Dissolve brown sugar in boiling water; add salt, pepper, Accent, and chopped peanuts. I like to serve the sauce in individual cups, since you dip the egg roll into the sauce before each bite.

SALAD TYPE EGG ROLLS
Laura K. Yoder

1/2 head lettuce (finely chopped)
1 finely-diced cucumber
1/2 medium onion (finely
   chopped)
6 eggs, beaten together with
   1 T. soy sauce and
   1/8 t. each: salt, pepper
   and 1/2 t. Accent

6 medium pork chops
2 T. soy sauce
1 T. accent
1/2 t. red pepper
1/2 t. salt
1 pkg. rice paper
2 bundles Oriental-style noodles-
   prepared according to pkg.
   directions

Cut pork chops into small cubes, and mix with soy sauce, Accent, salt, and red pepper; let stand 1/2 hr. while you shred onion, lettuce, and cucumber. Fry the egg mixture (forming a solid mass), let cool, then cut into strips, about 3" long and 1/2" wide, until done. Set aside. Cut rice paper in half, dip in very hot water for about 8 sec. spread on table and put small portion of lettuce, cucumber, onion, then 1 strip of egg, small portion of noodles, and about 5 or 6 pieces of meat and wrap securely.

Serve by dipping into sauce (same as Fried Egg Rolls).

SALAD (LAOTIAN STYLE)   Alta Kauffman

1 head lettuce (medium size)
1 cucumber
1/3 c. chopped peanuts
1/4 lb. ground pork or beef
6 hard-boiled eggs
1 T. chopped onions

DRESSING:
6 hard-boiled egg yolks
1/2 c. water
1/2 c. sugar
1 t. lemon juice
1 1/4 t. salt

Cut up lettuce, cucumber, and onion. Separate egg yolks and whites of boiled eggs. Slice the egg whites and add to lettuce. Fry the pork (or beef) in a small skillet and sprinkle a little salt, red and black pepper, Accent and garlic salt while frying. Set aside till cool. Add chopped peanuts and cooled meat to lettuce.
DRESSING: Put all ingredients in blender and mix well. Stir into lettuce mixture and serve.

EGG DROP SOUP   Mrs. Elmer M. Yoder (Esther)

1/2 c. water
1 T. cornstarch
4 c. water

4 t. chicken-flavored instant
   bouillon
2 eggs, well beaten
Sliced green onion

Stir cornstarch into 1/2 c. water, in a 1-cup measure. Combine water, cornstarch mixture, and bouillon in medium saucepan. Cook, stirring occasionally, until bouillon dissolves. **Slowly** pour in the egg and stir. Heat through. Garnish with onion, using the green tops also. Celery may also be added.

EGG FOO YUNG   Mrs. Lloyd Swartzentruber

1 pkg. fried Rice-A-Roni with
   almonds
6 eggs
1/2 t. salt
1 c. chopped meat

1/4 c. sliced or chopped green
   onion
1 T. soy sauce
Dash of pepper
1-16 oz. can bean sprouts

SAUCE: Combine 2 T. cornstarch, 2 T. soy sauce and 2 c. water. Cook till thick and serve over patties.
Prepare Rice-A-Roni according to directions on package, and mix with all other ingredients to fry. Cool. Beat eggs with soy sauce, salt, pepper. Add meat (chicken, beef, ham or pork), bean sprouts and onion. Drop by 1/2 cupfuls on greased or oiled skillet. Fry till brown on each side. Then serve this with **cooked** rice and top with sauce. Serves 4.

FORMOSAN FRIED CABBAGE
Mrs. Eli Hostetler,
Mrs. Eli Kauffman, and Lela Brenneman

4 strips bacon
1/2 medium onion, chopped
1/2 medium cabbage, coarsely
  chopped

Celery, carrots, and red peppers
  (as many as you wish)
1 T. soy sauce

One-half pound sausage may be substituted for bacon. Stir-fry all ingredients together. Serve over rice and pass additional soy sauce.

FRIED RICE
Vernie Weaver

1 qt. cubed fresh pork
1 lg. onion
Soy sauce

2 c. rice
Salt and pepper
6 eggs

Cook rice in 4 c. salt water with 1/2 onion for 20 min. Fry pork until done and throw in rest of onion and cooked rice. Fry and mix together until well blended. Add eggs and fry until well mixed and done. Either add soy sauce now or at the table. Serves 15-20.

LAOTIAN CHICKEN & BROCCOLI
Linda Kauffman,
Fannie Carol Yoder

3 medium fryers
1 lg. head cauliflower
2 lg. bunches broccoli
1 T. Accent
3 T. seasoning salt

1 1/2 t. salt
3/4 t. red pepper
1/2 t. garlic salt
3/4 t. ginger

Chop raw chicken into 2-3" pieces with cleaver on chop block. Add all seasonings listed above; mix well and set aside for 30 min. or longer. Cut broccoli and cauliflower into thin strips. Add all seasonings listed above. Mix well and set aside also for 30 min. **Note:** Use above amounts of seasonings for both chicken and vegetables, each. Fry chicken in small amount of very hot oil in large skillet or pot. Fry till tender; then add vegetable mixture and stir-fry on high heat approximately 10 min. or until crunchy-tender. Mix 1 1/2 T. cornstarch in with 1 1/2 to 2 c. water and stir this in and bring to boil. Serve with sticky rice. Serves 14.

You may use beef or pork instead of chicken.

LAOS CHICKEN & VEGETABLES STIR
Lena Yoder

8 c. chopped chicken on bone
6 c. broccoli
2 medium onions
2 T. fish sauce
1 T. fresh garlic (chopped)
1½ t. ginger

¼ t. pepper
1 t. Season-All
½ t. garlic salt
½ t. red pepper
2½ t. Accent
4 t. salt

Chop up chicken into 1½" pieces (or take off bone if desired) and slice 1 onion very thin lengthwise. Add all seasonings except fresh garlic and fish sauce. Mix chicken, onion and seasonings well and let set 1 to 2 hrs. One hour before serving, fry chicken and onion mixture in 4 T. oil and 1 T. fresh garlic, finely chopped. Simmer until well done. Slice 6 c. fresh broccoli and second onion very thin. Stir-fry broccoli and onion into boiling chicken mixture ½ hr. before serving. When vegetables are hot and crunchy, add fish sauce. Simmer 5 more min. Serve with sticky rice.

Cabbage, Frenched green beans and cauliflower can be used as well.

LAOS EGG SANDWICH
Marquita Yoder

2 eggs
2 t. diced onion

2 T. tomato, chopped fine
⅛ t. salt

Beat eggs; add remaining ingredients, and fry in hot skillet. Spread 1 piece of bread with mayonnaise and 1 piece with ketchup. Put hot egg mixture between, and enjoy.

LAOS HAMBURGERS
Lena Yoder

2 lbs. hamburger
2 c. shredded fresh cabbage or
  rice noodles, precooked
2 t. fish sauce
1 t. salt

½ t. black pepper
¼ t. red pepper
½ t. Accent
½ t. garlic salt

Mix hamburger with finely-shredded cabbage and all above ingredients. Make small patties and fry until crisp and dark brown in ½ c. oil. Eat with sticky rice.

You may wish to cut down on pepper if you don't like hot foods.

MEXICAN FLOUR TORTILLAS

Lena Yoder

4 c. all-purpose flour
1/2 t. baking powder
2 t. salt

2 t. shortening
2 c. hot water

Combine flour, baking powder, and salt; cut in shortening until mixture resembles coarse meat. Stir in water and mix well; knead dough until it is very elastic, about 10 min. Divide dough into balls (the size of small eggs), roll out each ball with a rolling pin 7" or 8" in diameter. Heat a lightly-greased skillet over medium heat. Cook until llightly-browned on both sides. Serve hot with refried beans or use for tostatas. Makes 16 to 20 tortillas.

PANCIT

Elsie N. Yoder

1/2 lb. chicken breast
1 1/2 c. carrots (cut fine)
1 c. celery (cut fine)
1 c. cabbage (cut fine)
1 sm. onion
1 garlic clove (crushed)

1/3 c. soy sauce
1 t. salt
1 t. seasoned salt
1 t. Accent
1/3 t. pepper
1-8 oz. rice noodles or egg
     noodles

Make in wok or skillet to stir-fry. Cut uncooked chicken in small pieces, add soy sauce and let stand 1 day if possible. Brown meat, onion, and garlic until meat is done. Add carrots and celery and stir-fry until heated through. Do not overcook. Add cabbage. Stir-fry a few minutes longer. Add noodles that had been soaked in hot water and drained. Keep adding enough water to make it slightly moist but not wet. Add salt, seasoned salt, black pepper, and Accent.

Use meat of your choice - pork chops or shrimp.

When painting woodwork, cover door knobs,
locks and other hardware with vaseline.
If paint splashes where it shouldn't, it can be wiped off easily.

PANCIT

Katie Hershberger

2 c. fryer meat, cut in bite-size
pieces
2 c. carrots, sliced very thin
2 c. celery, cut real thin
3 c. shredded cabbage

1 good-size garlic clove, minced
¼ to ⅓ c. soy sauce
2 to 3 T. Mazola corn oil
1 medium-size onion, chopped
1 pkg. fine noodles

Use a large kettle (about 6 qts.). Put oil in kettle and heat it. Now add garlic and onions and fry a few min., then add soy sauce and chicken and stir about 5 min. or till chicken is about tender. Next add carrots and stir a few min., then add celery. Stir a few min. or till crispie-soft. Last of all, add cabbage and stir about 1 min. Cut it off-it's finished.

TIP: The vegetables can be cut oriental-style to make it look like Chinese food.
TIP: Cook chicken boney pieces and cook noodles in broth and cook only a minute or so and turn heat off and cover tight till ready to use. To serve, put noodles on large platter and put Pancit on top.
TIP: I like to have everything ready before starting with Pancit-it's best if you can eat as soon as it's finished. (This serves 8 people.)

STICKY RICE

Fannie Carol Yoder, Linda Kauffman

6 c. sticky rice

Soak sticky rice in pan of warm water (enough to cover well) for 3-5 hrs. Drain and steam in basket or steamer with 4 c. water in bottom of pan for 10-15 min. Check for doneness - when rice is soft and sticks together. Dump out on large tray and stir well with wooden spoon for 3-4 min. Pack into serving basket or bowl. Serve with Laotian food. Sticky rice may be bought at oriental food stores. Serves 12-14.

*Housework is something you do
that nobody notices unless you don't do it!*

223

STIR-FRIED LAOS FOOD

Laura K. Yoder

STEP 1:
3 lbs. pork chops (chopped fine) 2 t. salt
3 T. soy sauce   ½ t. black and red pepper

STEP 2:
1 bundle broccoli (peel, stem   2 t. salt
  & shave pieces)   ½ t. red pepper
1 head cauliflower (finely   ½ t. black pepper
  chopped)   1½ t. Accent
4 medium squash (thinly sliced) ½ t. garlic salt
1 lg. sweet onion (finely shaved) 1 t. seasoned salt

STEP 1: Marinate meat in soy sauce, salt, and peppers for 1 hr., then fry in small amount of very hot grease; when meat is tender, mix about 1½ T. clear gel or cornstarch with 2 c. water, and add to meat, to make gravy.
STEP 2: Mix together all the seasoning, and sprinkle over prepared vegetbles and let set 1 hr., then stir-fry in very hot pan with about 2 T. vegetable oil, until tender-crisp.

Serve these 2 dishes separately or mixed together, and serve with Sticky Rice.

LAOS SWEET ROAST

Lena Yoder

2½ lbs. lean roast   1 t. salt
3 T. oil   1 t. garlic salt
1¼ c. water   1 t. Accent
½ c. white sugar   2 T. fish sauce
¼ c. brown sugar   Red and black pepper to taste
1 lg. onion

Cut roast in 1" strips and brown in oil. Add water and simmer for 1 hr., then add rest of ingredients, simmer 1 more hr. or until meat is tender. Meat will turn dark, with a thick syrup. Extra water may added if needed to cook roast until tender. Cut into smaller strips and serve with rice. Serves 6.

PASTRIES & PIES

SUCCESSFUL MERINGUE

Malinda Wingard

2 t. cornstarch
2 T. cold water
½ c. boiling water

3 egg whites
6 T. sugar
⅛ t. salt
½ t. vanilla

Mix cold water with cornstarch. Stir into boiling water. Cook until thick and clear. Beat egg whites, gradually beat in sugar, salt and vanilla. Beat into cooled, cooked mixture; continue beating until mixture stands in peaks. Spread on pie. Brown in preheated oven, 375°. This makes a tender meringue and will not weep. Spreads a 9" pie. Bake 375° for 10 min.

ELEGANT PASTRY SHELL

Mrs. Ivan Yoder

1½ c. flour
½ t. salt
½ c. shortening

1 egg yolk
4 to 5 T. ice water
2 t. lemon juice

Combine flour and salt, cut in shortening until pieces are the size of small peas. Blend together egg yolk, 4 T. ice water and lemon juice. Add liquid to flour mixture, mixing lightly with fork until dough just sticks together. Add more water if necessary. Press dough into ball on lightly-floured surface or pastry cloth and roll into circle 10" in diameter, ⅛" thick. Trim edge, fold under excess crust and flute edge. Prick bottom and sides with tines of fork. If using 9" metal pie pan, bake at 450° for 8-10 min. If using 9" glass pie pan, bake at 425° for 8-10 min., until golden brown. Cool on wire rack.

Yields 1 single crust. Also, if you aren't real fond of lemon, only put 1 t. of lemon into crust.

Dust your pie pans with flour before liing them with dough. This will prevent the pie from sticking after it has been baked.

*When adding egg yolks into hot mixtures - stir a small amount
of the hot mixture into the egg yolks first to warm them,
then stir warmed egg yolk mixture into the remaining hot mixture.*

PIE CRUST

Mrs. Norman Yoder

2¼ c. flour
⅔ c. shortening

½ t. salt
⅓ c. cold water

Mix flour and salt in mixing bowl. Cut shortening into flour with 2 knives. Do not overmix. These are sufficiently blended when particles are the size of peas. Add water gradually and toss lightly with a fork. Roll dough into a round ball, handling as little as possible. Divide dough in half and roll out on floured table. Makes 2 9" crusts. Bake at 450° for 12-15 min. or until golden brown.

Never fails.

PIE CRUST

Mrs. Bertha Yoder

3 c. flour
1 t. salt
1 egg yolk
1 t. vinegar

1 c. shortening
½ c. warm water
1 T. sugar
Pinch of baking powder

Mix flour and shortening together. Add rest of ingredients. This makes 3-9" pie shells. Bake at 450° for 12-15 min., or until golden brown.

NEVER FAILING PIE CRUST

Kathy Yoder

4 c. flour
1¾ c. shortening
1 T. sugar
2 t. salt

1 T. vinegar
1 egg
½ c. water

Combine flour, shortening, sugar, salt and vinegar together. Then add egg and water; mix well. Refrigerate 10 min. Makes 6 pie crusts. Bake at 350° for 10-15 min.

The secret of happy living is not to do what you like,
but to like what you do.

NEVER FAIL PIE CRUST

Mari Yoder

1½ c. flour
¾ c. shortening
½ T. vinegar
1 t. sugar

1 egg
3½ T. water
¼ t. salt

Mix flour, shortening till crumbly. Set aside. Mix egg, water, salt, sugar and vinegar together, then add to flour mixture. Makes 2-9" crusts. Bake at 350° for 10-15 min.

NEVER FAIL PIE CRUST

Mrs. Loretta Brenneman

1½ c. flour
1 t. salt
½ c. + 2 T. shortening

¾ t. vinegar
¼ c. water

Thoroughly mix flour, salt and shortening. Put vinegar into cup and add water. Mix with flour mixture. Makes 2-9' crusts. Bake at 350° for 10-15 min.

Delicious **flaky** crust!

NEVER FAIL PIE CRUST

Beulah Yoder

3 c. flour
½ t. salt
1 t. sugar
⅛ t. baking powder

1 c. shortening
1 egg
¼ t. vinegar
5 T. water or milk

In a large mixing bowl, combine the flour, salt, sugar, and baking powder. Add shortening and blend with a pastry blender or fork until mixture resembles fine crumbs. In a small bowl, beat the egg and add vinegar and water. Pour over flour and mix with fork until dough forms. Roll out for pie. Makes 3 crusts. Bake at 350° for 10-15 min.

A pie crust will be more easily made and better if all ingredients are cool.

"NO ROLL" PIE CRUST

Mrs. Norman Yoder

1½ c. flour
1½ T. sugar
2 T. milk

½ t. salt
½ c. Wesson oil

Mix together till crumbly, then press in pan. Makes 1-9" crust. Bake at 350° for 20 min.

Real flaky.

SOFT FLAKY PIE DOUGH

Delores Hostetler

1 c. shortening
1 t. salt

3 c. flour
½ c. milk

Mix shortening, salt and flour by hand, then add milk and mix lightly with fork till well-blended. Makes 3-9" pie shells. Bake at 450° for 12-15 min., or until golden brown.

ANNA'S VANILLA CRUMB PIE

Marie Swartzentruber

FILLING:
2 pts. water
2 well-beaten eggs
2 heaping T. flour

2 c. sugar
1 c. dark Karo
1 c. pancake syrup

CRUMBS:
½ c. sugar
2 c. flour
½ t. cream of tartar

½ c. lard
1 t. soda

FILLING: Boil and let cool; pour over pie crusts, put crumbs on top and bake at 350°.
CRUST: Mix till crumbly.
Makes 2 pies.

APPLE PIE

Mrs. L.D. Kauffman

1¼ c. sugar
1 c. water

2 cinamon sticks
1 t. whole nutmeg

Simmer together for 15 min. Strain and bring to a boil and add 1 heaping T. clear gel or cornstarch with ½ c. of water. Peel and slice 4 or 5 apples and add to the above mixture. Add ¼ stick margarine and stir real well. Fill pie crust and cover with a top crust and fasten edges securely. Moisten top with milk and sprinkle with sugar. Bake in 9" pie pan at 350° for 45 min.

CHEESE APPLE PIE

Mrs. Allen M. Yoder

⅔ c. sugar
¼ c. flour
1 t. cinnamon

⅛ t. nutmeg
3 c. sliced apples
Pinch of salt

Mix all ingredients and pour into unbaked 9" pie shell. Pour Topping on and bake at 375° for 35 min.

TOPPING:
¼ c. sugar
⅛ c. flour
½ c. grated cheese

3 T. butter
Pinch of salt

Combine sugar, flour, and salt. Cut in cheese and butter. Spread over filling.

IMPOSSIBLE FRENCH APPLE PIE

Mrs. Alva Yoder,
Laura K. Yoder

6 c. sliced, pared, tart apples
1¼ t. cinnamon
¼ t. nutmeg
1 c. sugar

¾ c. milk
½ c. Bisquick baking mix
2 eggs
1 T. margarine or butter, softened
Streusel

STREUSEL:
1 c. Bisquick baking mix
⅔ c. chopped nuts

⅓ c. packed brown sugar
3 T. margarine or butter

Heat oven to 325°. Grease pie plate, 10x1½". Mix apples and spices. Put into plate. Beat remaining ingredients except Streusel until smooth, 15 seconds in blender on high or 1 min. with hand beater. Pour into plate. Sprinkle with Streusel. Bake at 325° for 55-60 min., or until knife inserted in center comes out clean.
STREUSEL: Mix until crumbly.

SOUR CREAM APPLE CRUMB PIE

Ramona Yoder

6 apples, pared and sliced
1/2 c. raisins
6 T. sugar
2 T. flour
1 c. sour cream
1 egg, beaten
1 t. vanilla
A pinch of salt

CRUMB TOPPING:
1/2 c. flour
1/4 c. white sugar
1/4 c. brown sugar
1 t. cinnamon
Sprinkle of nutmeg
1/3 c. butter

Fill unbaked 9" pastry shell with apples and raisins together. Stir sugar and flour together and fold in cream, beaten egg, vanilla and salt. Spoon cream mixture over apples and raisins. Bake at 350° for 40 min., or until pie is golden brown. Combine flour, sugars, cinnamon and nutmeg. Blend in 1/2 stick plus 1 T. butter, until mixture is crumbly. Spoon crumbs over top of pie and bake 15 min. or until lightly browned.

BANANA CREAM PIE

Mrs. Norman Yoder

3/4 c. sugar
3 T. cornstarch
1/4 t. salt
2 eggs, separated

2 c. milk
1 T. butter
1 t. vanilla
2 bananas

Combine sugar, salt and cornstarch. Add 1 1/2 c. milk. Cook on medium heat, stirring constantly, until thickened. Beat egg yolks and add to remaining milk. Add egg mixture slowly to custard and cook 2 more min. Remove from heat and add butter and vanilla. Chill. Slice bananas and cover bottom of a baked pie crust. Spoon in 1/2 of custard and add more sliced bananas. Spoon in the rest of the custard and top with Cool whip or meringue. Place a few sliced bananas on top. Makes 1-9" pie.

People are usually down on anything they are not up on.

BANANA SPLIT PIE
Verna Mae Wingard

1 c. sugar
1-8 oz. pkg. cream cheese
5 T. milk
2 bananas
1 sm. can pineapple, drained

1-9" graham cracker crust

GARNISH WITH:
Cool Whip
Chopped nuts
Chopped cherries

Mix cream cheese, sugar, and milk together and pour into bottom of graham cracker crust. Slice bananas on top of mixture. Pour drained pineapple on top of that. Spread top with Cool Whip and garnish with nuts and cherries. Serves 6.

CAROLYN'S BLUEBERRY PIE
Ruth Yoder

3 c. water
2 c. sugar
7 heaping t. cornstarch or
   clear gel

1 sm. pkg. blackberry jello
2 t. lemon juice
4 c. frozen blueberries

Cook first 3 ingredients until thickened, remove from heat, add jello and lemon juice. Cool and add berries, pour into unbaked pie shells, cover with topping.

1 c. brown sugar
1 c. oatmeal

1 c. flour
1 stick butter

Mix well and put on pies. Bake at 350° till golden brown. Try using whole blackberries (drained) instead of blueberries. Delicious! Makes 2 pies.

If you are thick and tired, cut out the rich food and late hours.

BUTTERSCOTCH PIE

Mrs. Eli Hostetler

FIRST PART:
1/2 c. brown sugar
3 T. boiling water
1 T. butter
1/2 t. salt
1/2 t. vanilla
1/8 t. soda

SECOND PART:
1 egg yolk
1/2 c. flour
1/4 c. granulated sugar
1 1/2 c. boiling water

Combine brown sugar, 3 T. boiling water, butter, and salt. When mixture begins to boil, add soda. Boil until syrup forms a hard ball in cold water. Combine egg yolk, flour, and granulated sugar, slowly add boiling water. Add second mixture to first and bring to a boil. When filling is cold, beat with spoon until fluffy. Pour into baked pie shell. Top with whipped cream.

Three recipes make 2 nice full pies.

CHERRY CHEESE PIE

Kathy Hostetler

1-9" graham cracker crumb crust
1-8 oz. pkg. cream cheese
1-14 oz. can Eagle Brand
    sweetened condensed milk
1/3 c. lemon juice
1 t. vanilla
1-21 oz. cherry pie filling

In large mixing bowl, beat cream cheese until fluffy. Beat in condensed milk until smooth. Stir in lemon and vanilla. Pour into crust. Chill 3 hrs. or until set. Top with pie filling.

CHERRY TOPPED CHEESE PIE

Kathryn Yoder, Linda Weaver

1 pkg. graham crackers
1/4 c. sugar
1/3 c. softened butter
8 oz. pkg. softened cream cheese
1/2 c. sugar
2 c. thawed Cool Whip
1 can cherry pie filling

In plastic bag, finely roll graham crackers. Mix sugar and butter with graham cracker crumbs. Press in pan. Beat together cream cheese and sugar till creamy. Blend in Cool Whip and pour in unbaked 9" graham cracker crust. Top with cherry pie filling. Chill at least 3 hrs. before serving. Serves 6-8.

CHOCOLATE PIE

Mrs. Isaac Plank

2½ c. sugar
2⅔ T. cornstarch
4⅔ c. milk
1⅓ T. butter
2 t. cocoa

1⅓ t. salt
5 T. flour
4 egg yolks
2⅔ t. vanilla

Bring milk to a boil. Separate eggs. Beat egg yolks, add sugar, salt, cornstarch, flour, cocoa, using enough milk to make smooth paste. Add to boiling milk and cook till thick. Remove from heat, add butter and vanilla. Put in 2-8' baked pie shells. Top with a meringue.

Add a T. of cornstarch to the sugar when making meringue for pie. It won't weep!

COCONUT CREAM PIE

Ruth Yoder

2 c. milk
½ c. sugar
4 T. cornstarch
2 eggs, separated
1 T. butter

½ t. salt
1¼ c. shredded coconut
1 t. vanilla
1-9" pie crust

Scald 1½ c. milk in double boiler. Combine sugar, salt and cornstarch. Add remaining milk and cook until thickened; beat egg yolks. Pour small amount of hot mixture over yolks before adding them to milk. Cook 2 min. longer; remove from heat. Add butter, vanilla and ¾ c. shredded coconut. Cool and pour into baked crust. Cover with meringue made by adding 4 T. sugar to beaten egg whites. Sprinkle remaining coconut over top and bake at 350° until golden brown. Makes 1-9" pie.

COCONUT MACAROON PIE

Mrs. Levi Kauffman, Beulah Yoder

3 eggs
1 c. sugar
½ t. salt
1 T. flour

3 T. butter
¾ c. milk
½ t. vanilla
1½ c. coconut

Beat eggs, sugar, and salt. Add flour and butter. Blend and add milk, vanilla, and 1 c. coconut. Put in shell and sprinkle ½ c. coconut on top and bake at 325° for 1 hr. Makes 1-8" pie.

COFFEE ANGEL PIE

Mary Lois Yoder

1 can condensed milk
1 c. strong coffee
1 c. pecans
1½ c. cream

MERINGUE SHELL:
4 egg whites
¼ t. cream of tartar
¼ t. salt
1 c. sugar
1 T. instant coffee

Preheat oven. Combine egg whites, cream of tartar, and salt. Beat until soft peaks form. Gradually add sugar, 1 T. at a time, beating well after each addition. Add coffee with last of sugar till stiff glossy peaks form. Spread ½ of meringue on bottom of 10' pie plate. Swirl or pipe remaining around sides and rim. Bake at 275° for 1 hr. Mix condensed milk with chilled coffee. Add stiffly-beaten cream. Pour mixture into meringue shell, sprinkle generously with finely-chopped nuts and freeze. Serves 6-8.

CREAM CHEESE PIE

Mary Lois Yoder, Ruth Yoder

1 c. graham cracker crumbs
6 T. butter
3 T. sugar

12 oz. cream cheese
2 eggs
½ c. sugar
1 T. vanilla

1 c. sour cream
2 t. vanilla

2 t. sugar

Mix first 3 ingredients together; put into 9" pie pan and bake 10 min. at 350°; set aside. Cream together cream cheese, eggs, sugar and vanilla; pour into crust and bake 20 min.; cool. Then mix together 1 c. sour cream, 2 t. vanilla, and 2 t. sugar and put on cream cheese mixture. Bake 10 more min. Top with a strawberry topping:

2 T. cornstarch
1½ T. strawberry jello

½ c. water
½ c. sugar

Mix well and cook over medium heat until thickened. Cool and add ½ c. strawberries. Put on cooled Cream Cheese Pie. Serves 8.

CUSTARD PIE

Lela Brenneman, Mrs. Isaac Plank

2¾ c. milk
2 eggs, separated
5 T. sugar

2 T. flour
½ t. nutmeg

Scald 2½ c. milk. Beat egg yolks well. Add sugar, flour, nutmeg and stir. Add remaining ¼ c. milk, a little at a time, stirring to mix well. Add scalded milk and stir. Let set till no longer hot. Fold in stiffly-beaten egg whites and pour into unbaked 9" pie shell. Bake at 450° for 10 min., then reduce heat to 325° for 30 min., or until done. Do not allow to boil as custard will be watery.

CUSTARD PIE

Mrs. Crist Yoder, Sr.

2 c. milk
3 eggs, beaten separately
½ c. sugar

3 t. flour
Pinch of salt
Sprinkle nutmeg on top.
1 t. vanilla

Mix sugar and flour together, add to egg yolks and beat at least 5 min. Add milk and salt and beat a few min. more. Add beaten egg whites and vanilla. Pour in unbaked 9" pie shell, then sprinkle with nutmeg. Bake at 400° for 10 min., then 300° for 30 min. (total - 40 min. or until an inserted silver knife comes out clean.)

I usually add 1 egg white with the yolks and just beat 2 egg whites.

CUSTARD PIE

Ruth Yoder

2 c. milk
5 eggs
½ c. sugar

¼ t. salt
1 t. vanilla

Heat milk to a boiling point. Separate egg yolks from whites. Beat yolks of eggs **slightly**. Add sugar, salt and vanilla. Beat slightly again. Beat egg whites to a stiff peak. Add 1 T. sugar, continue beating a few seconds. Add egg whites to above mixture. Bake at 475° for 10 min., then at 300° till done. Put on topping just before serving.

TOPPING:
¼ c. brown sugar
½ c. flaked coconut

2 T. soft butter

Sprinkle on pie and broil 3 or 4 inches from heat for 2-4 min.

235

CUSTARD PIE

Mrs. Rufus L. Yoder, Mrs. Milton Yoder

½ c. sugar	3 eggs
½ t. flour	1 pt. milk
A little salt	½ t. vanilla

Mix dry ingredients. Add heated milk and vanilla. Beat eggs well. Add to above ingredients. Pour in unbaked 9" pie crust. Don't let it bake too long or it will be watery. Bake at 400° for 10 min., then reduce heat to 300° for 30 min.

ICE CREAM PIE

Mrs. Leslie Yoder

¼ c. corn syrup	¼ c. peanut butter
2 T. firmly-packed brown sugar	¼ c. fudge sauce for ice cream
3 T. margarine or butter	3 T. corn syrup
3-½ c. Rice Krispies	1 qt. vanilla ice cream

1. Combine the ¼ c. corn surup, the brown sugar and margarine in medium saucepan. Cook over low heat, stirring occasionally, until mixture begins to boil. Remove from heat. Add Rice Krispies, stirring until well-coated. Press evenly in 9" pie pan to form crust.
2. Stir together peanut butter, 3 T. corn syrup and fudge sauce. Spread ½ of peanut butter mixture over crust. Freeze until firm.
3. Allow ice cream to soften. Spoon into crust, spreading evenly. Freeze until firm. Let pie stand at room temperature about 10 min. before cutting. Warm remaining peanut butter mixture and spread over top.

A housewife, no matter how large the family,
can always get some time to be alone - by doing the dishes.

IMPOSSIBLE BROWNIE PIE

Esther R. Yoder

4 eggs
1-4 oz. bar sweet cooking
  chocolate (melted & cooled)
1/2 c. Bisquick baking mix
1/2 t. salt

1/2 c. packed brown sugar
1/2 c. granulated sugar
1/4 c. margarine or butter,
  softened
3/4 c. chopped nuts

Grease pie plate. Beat all ingredients except nuts until smooth, 2 min. in blender on high, stopping blender occasionally to stir, or 2 min. with hand beater. Pour into 9x1¼" plate, sprinkle with nuts. Bake at 350° for 30-35 min. until knife inserted in center comes out clean. Cool 5 min. Serve with ice cream, if desired. Serves 6-8.

LEMON MERINGUE PIE

Mrs. Harley Yoder

3 eggs, separated
14 oz. can Eagle Brand
  sweetened condensed milk
Juice of one lemon

¼t. cream of tartar
1/3 c. sugar
1-9" pie crust

Mix condensed milk, lemon juice and egg yolks together until thick. Pour in baked pie crust. Whip egg whites till stiff, add a pinch of cream of tartar and 3 T. sugar. Pour on pie. Bake at 350° for 15 min. until golden brown. Serves 6.

LEMON PIE

Mrs. Isaac Plank

1 lemon, juice & rind
1 c. sugar
3 eggs, separated
1 T. butter

2 c. water
1/2 t. salt
4 t. cornstarch

Mix lemon, 1½ c. water, butter and egg yolks; bring to boiling point. Add sugar and salt. Make a paste with ½ c. water and cornstarch, add to lemon mixture. Cook till thick. Pour into 9" baked pie crust. Top with meringue.

OLD-FASHIONED LEMON PIE

Mrs. Simon L. Yoder

Grated lemon rind from 2 sm. lemons
Juice from 2 sm. lemons
7 c. water

5 c. sugar
1 c. flour
5 eggs
Butter, the size of an egg

First grate lemons. Set aside. Boil 6 c. water and juice from 2 lemons with 4 c. of the sugar. Then stir together the flour, the fifth c. of sugar, the beaten eggs and the seventh c. of water, then add this mixture to the boiling water and sugar, stirring all the time until smooth and bubbly. Then add lemon rind and butter, the size of an egg. Makes 4-9" pies. Bake at 400°.

These are 2-crust pies. A little butter under top crust helps -they won't cook out so much.

MILLION DOLLAR PIE

Elsie N. Yoder

9 oz. Cool Whip
1 can Eagle Brand milk
1 sm. can crushed pineapple
(slightly drained)

Juice of 1 lemon
1 c. nuts

Mix all ingredients and pour into baked pie shells. Makes 2 pies.

MOCK MINCE PIE

Mrs. Elmer M. Yoder (Esther)

2 eggs, beaten
1 c. sugar
2 c. water
2 T. vinegar
2 lg. cupfuls bread crumbs
1 t. cinnamon

1 t. cloves
1 t. allspice
1 t. nutmeg
1/2 c. butter
1 c. light Karo
1 c. raisins

Mix together all ingredients. Cook until thickened; 15-20 min. Pour into 9" unbaked pie crust. Bake at 350° until crust is browned. This is a 2-crust pie.

MYSTERY PIE

Verna Mae Wingard

3 egg whites, beat till stiff
ADD:
1 c. sugar
1 t. vanilla

FOLD IN:
21 crushed Ritz crackers
1 c. chopped nuts

Pour into well-buttered 9" pie pan and bake at 300° for 25-30 min. Do not let it get brown. Top with whipped unsweetened cream. Serves 6.

NUTTY FUDGE PIE

Mrs. Rufus L. Yoder, Mrs. Paul E. Yoder

1/4 c. peanut butter
1/4 c. corn syrup
3 T. chopped salted cocktail
   peanuts
Chocolate syrup

2 c. Kellogg's honey and nut
   cornflakes cereal
1 qt. vanilla ice cream, slightly
   softened

Stir together peanut butter and corn syrup in medium-size mixing bowl. Add honey nut cornflakes cereal, stirring until well-coated. Press evenly in 9" pie or baking dish. Chill. Spoon softened ice cream into crust. Sprinkle with peanuts. Freeze until firm. Remove from freezer 10 min. before serving. Serve with chocolate syrup.

PEACH PIE FILLING

Lila Yoder

2 1/2 c. sugar
3 c. water
1/4 c. orange or peach jello
3/4 c. clear gel or cornstarch

1/2 t. salt
1 1/2 T. lemon juice
1/4 t. cinnamon
1/8 t. pepper
Fresh sliced peaches

Cook water, sugar, jello, and clear gel until thick and clear. Add next 4 ingredients and cool. Add as many freshly-sliced peaches as desired and pour into baked pie crust. Top with whipped cream. Makes 2 pies. Serves 12.

PEACH PIE

Alta Kauffman

FIRST:
Crumb Crust:
6 T. melted butter
1 c. graham cracker crumbs
3 T. sugar
SECOND:
Filling:
12 oz. cream cheese
1/2 c. sugar
2 eggs, beaten
1 T. vanilla

THIRD:
1 c. sour cream
3 t. sugar
1 t. vanilla
FOURTH:
Peace Glaze:
1 1/3 c. sugar
1/3 c. clear gel or cornstarch
1 1/3 c. water
1 sm. box peach jello
Dash of salt
1/2 t. vanilla
1/4 t. lemon juice

Mix ingredients in first step and press into 10" pie plate and chill. Mix step 2 and pour into crust and bake at 250° for 20-25 min. Cool slightly. Mix step 3 and cover filling and bake 10 min. longer. To prepare glaze: Mix sugar and clear gel and gradually add water. Bring this to a boil, stirring constantly. Remove from heat and stir in jello, salt, vanilla and lemon juice. Cool and add fresh peaches, enough to make a layer over the pie. Garnish with whipped cream.

You may substitute strawberries and strawberry jello for peach jello and fresh peaches.

PEANUT BUTTER PIE

Vernie Weaver

PUDDING:
4 c. milk
1 c. sugar
3 to 4 T. butter

4 egg yolks
1/2 c. clear gel or cornstarch
1/2 T. vanilla
1 t. salt

CRUMBS:
2/3 c. peanut butter

1 1/2 c. powdered sugar

Heat milk and 1/2 c. sugar. Mix beaten egg yolks and 1/2 c. sugar. Mix clear gel with water and add to egg mixture. Add to milk and boil until thick. Add vanilla. Put crumbs in bottom of a baked pie shell. (Reserve some for topping.) Pour pudding on crumbs and top with whipped cream. Sprinkle with crumbs. Makes 2 pies.

PEANUT BUTTER PIE

Esther Ruth Yoder

CRUMBS:
1/2 c. peanut butter   3/4 c. powdered sugar

PUDDING:
1/2 c. sugar   2 c. milk
1 T. flour   2 egg yolks
2 T. cornstarch   1 T. butter
1/2 t. salt   1 T. vanilla

Stir together sugar, flour, cornstarch, and salt with enough milk to
make a paste. Then add this and beaten yolks to the rest of hot milk.
Boil 1 min., or untl thickened and add butter and vanilla. Put crumbs
on crust, then pudding, then top with meringue. Save enough
crumbs to sprinkle a little on top. Makes 1-9" pie.

PEANUT BUTTER PIE

Mrs. Eli Hostetler

2 1/2 c. milk   3/4 c. sugar

Heat to boiling point.

MIX:
4 T. cornstarch   3 egg yolks
1/2 t. salt   1 t. vanilla
1/2 c. milk

Mix in given order. Pour into boiling milk and sugar and boil until
thick and smooth. Remove from heat and cool. Continue beating
occasionally while cooking. When cold, take baked pie shell, put a
layer of peanut butter crumbs. Then pudding and peanut butter
crumbs. Top with whipped topping.

PEANUT BUTTER CRUMBS:
2 c. powdered sugar   1/2 c. peanut butter

Mix together until crumbly. Makes 1 pie.

PEANUT BUTTER PIE

Mrs. Noah Yoder

1-9" pie shell, baked
1/2 c. peanut butter
2/3 c. powdered sugar
2/3 c. sugar (scant)
3 T. cornstarch

1/2 t. salt
3 c. milk, scalded
3 eggs, separated
1 T. butter
1 1/2 t. vanilla

Blend peanut butter and powdered sugar until crumbly. Sprinkle 2/3 of the mixture over bottom of the baked pie shell. Combine the beaten egg yolks, salt, cornstarch, and sugar and stir into the scalded milk. Cook until thick, stirring constantly. Add vanilla and butter and cool slightly. Pour into pie shell and top with meringue. Sprinkle remaining peanut butter mixture on top of meringue. Bake at 375° for 8-10 min., or until lightly browned.
MERINGUE: Beat the 3 egg whites with 1/4 t. cream of tartar and 6 T. sugar until sfiff and glossy.

PECAN PIE

Mrs. Crist Yoder, Jr.

1 c. white Karo
3/4 c. sugar
5 eggs

2 T. butter, melted
1 t. vanilla
1 c. pecans

Beat eggs lightly. Add sugar, Karo, and butter. Spread pecans over pie crust and pour filling over. Bake in a 9" pie pan at 400° for 10 min., then reduce heat to 325° and bake till done.

PECAN PIE

Mary Catherine Plank, Irene Yoder

6 eggs
1 1/3 c. sugar
1 t. salt

2/3 c. butter or margarine, melted
2 c. dark or light corn syrup
2 c. pecan halves or broken pieces

Beat eggs, sugar, salt, butter and syrup with rotary beater. Sprinkle 1 c. pecans evenly in each of 2-9" pastry-lined pie pans. Slowly pour 2 1/3 c. filling on pecans in each pan. Bake at 375° until filling is set; 40-45 min.

PECAN PIE

Mrs. Melvin (Katherine) Yoder

2½ c. sugar
2 c. corn syrup
6 c. pecans
5 eggs

2 T. butter
3½ c. milk
4 T. flour
½ t. salt
2 t. vanilla

Whip eggs; add other ingredients - all but pecans - and stir. Add pecans last. Pour into 4-9" unbaked pie crusts. Bake at 325° for 45 min.

PECAN PIE

Mrs. Eli Kauffman

2 eggs (slightly beaten)
1 c. light Karo
⅛ t. salt
1 c. light brown sugar

2 t. butter (melted)
1 t. each: vanilla and maple
flavoring
1 c. chopped pecans

Pour into unbaked pie shell and bake in hot oven (400°) for 15 min. Reduce heat to 300° and bake 45 min. longer. (Filling should appear less set in middle.) Serves 6-8.

PECAN CUSTARD PIE

Mrs. Ivan Yoder, Mrs. Rufus L. Yoder

2 eggs
½ c. white sugar
2 T. melted butter
3 level T. flour
1 c. white Karo

1 c. milk
¾ c. pecans
1 t. vanilla
⅛ t. salt

Combine all ingredients and pour into single 9" crust. Bake at 375° for 40 min. to 1 hr.

*When painting stairs, paint the even numbered steps one day
and the odd ones the next day.*

MIRIAM'S PECAN PIE

Ruth Yoder

3 eggs, slightly beaten
1 c. Karo
1 t. vanilla
2 t. butter, melted

1/2 c. brown sugar
1/8 t. salt
1 c. pecans

Mix all ingredients together, pecans last. Pour into unbaked 9" pie shell. Bake at 400° for 15 min., then 350° for 30-35 min. Serves 8.

MISSISSIPPI PECAN PIE

Mrs. Loretta Brenneman

1 c. dark corn syrup or
  cane syrup
3/4 c. sugar
3 T. butter

3 eggs, slightly beaten
1 t. vanilla
1 c. pecans, coarsely broken

Boil syrup and sugar together about 2 min. Pour slowly over eggs, stirring well. Add butter, vanilla and nuts. Bake in moderate oven (375°). Pie will be done when completely puffed across top.

You can add some water to fill up crust completely.

PUMPKIN PIE

Mrs. Crist Yoder, Sr.

1 c. white sugar
1 2/3 c. brown sugar
5 eggs, beat separately
4 c. milk
2 c. pumpkin

1 c. cream
3 T. flour
2 t. cinnamon
1 t. nutmeg
Pinch of salt

Add egg yolks, sugar, salt, spices and flour. Add milk, cream and pumpkin. Fold in beaten egg whites and pour in unbaked pie shell and bake at 400° for 10 min., then 350° for 45 min. or until done. Makes 3-9" pies.

*We have so much patience with ourselves,
why not borrow some of that and use it on others.*

BEST EVER PUMPKIN PIE   Ruth Yoder

1 c. pumpkin   1/2 t. salt
1 c. white sugar   1/2 t. nutmeg
1 c. brown sugar   1/2 t. cinnamon
3 T. flour   1 c. milk
3   eggs   1 c. evaporated milk

Scald milk. Mix pumpkin, sugar, flour, spices and salt. Add egg yolks. Beat egg whites and fold in last. Bake at 400° for 10 min., then 350° for 45 min. Makes 2-9" pies.

BEST EVER PUMPKIN PIE   Irene Yoder, Naomi Yoder

5   eggs (separated)   1 1/2 c. pumpkin
1/2 t. salt   1 1/2 t. cinnamon
1/2 c. brown sugar   1/2 t. cloves
1 c. white sugar   1/2 t. ginger
2 1/2 T. flour   1   can evaporated milk
                          3 c. milk

Beat egg whites till stiff. Heat 2 c. milk. Then add salt, brown and white sugar, flour, pumpkin, cinnamon, cloves, ginger and evaporated milk. Whip egg yolks and add to pumpkin mixture. Next, add egg whites and mix well. Pour into unbaked pie shells. Bake at 400° for 10 min., then 350° for 45 min. Makes 2-9" pies.

Also real good made with butternut squash.

Eat such things as are set before you. Luke 10:8

245

NEW ENGLAND PUMPKIN PIE
Mrs. Chris L. Miller

1 c. pumpkin
3/4 c. sugar
1 1/2 T. flour
1/2 t. salt

1 t. cinnamon
1/2 t. nutmeg
1 egg (separated)
1 1/2 c. hot milk

Mix pumpkin, sugar, flour, cinnamon, nutmeg, and salt. Separate egg, beat yolk, add with hot milk to pumpkin mixture. Beat egg white; fold carefully into mixture. Bake at 450° for 10 min., turn down to 250° and bake 10 min. more or till pie is firm. Makes 1 pie.

RAISIN PIE FILLING
Mrs. Crist Yoder, Sr.

1 c. raisins, cooked & drained
1 c. water
2 c. rich milk
2 egg yolks

1/2 c. brown sugar
3 T. flour or clear gel
2 T. butter

Add 1 c. water to raisins and cook for 20 min. Drain and add the raisin juice with 2 c. milk. Bring to a boil and add sugar, flour and egg yolks. Cook until thickened. Remove from heat and add butter. Pour into 9" baked pie shell, cover with whipped cream before serving.

RAISIN CRUMB PIE
Linda Kauffman

3/4 c. raisins
2 c. water
1 c. brown sugar
1 T. vinegar
1/4 t. salt
3 T. cornstarch

CRUMBS:
1 c. flour
1/2 c. brown sugar
1/4 c. butter
1 t. soda

Bring to boil raisins, water, brown sugar, vinegar and salt. Cook for 5 min., then thicken with 3 T. cornstarch in 1/3 c. water. Cool slightly, then pour into unbaked pie crust. Top with crumb mixture made from the flour, brown sugar, butter, and soda. Bake at 350° for 30-35 min. Makes 1-9" pie. Serves 6.

RAISIN MERINGUE BUTTERSCOTCH PIE   Ruth Yoder

RAISIN CRUNCH CRUST:
3/4 c. raisins, finely chopped
1/3 c. pecans, finely chopped
1/2 c. butter, soft
1/4 c. light brown sugar, firmly
   packed
1 c. flour

Blend all ingredients together. Press into greased 9" pan. Prick with fork and bake at 375° for 8-10 min., until lightly browned. (Do not overbake.)

BUTTERSCOTCH FILLING:
1 c. light brown sugar
6 T. cornstarch
1/2 t. salt
1 1/2 c. milk
3 eggs, beaten
2 T. butter
2 t. vanilla
1 c. raisins, chopped
1 c. dairy sour cream

In saucepan, blend brown sugar with cornstarch and salt. Stir in milk. Cook, stirring constantly, over moderate heat until mixture begins to thicken. Lower heat and cook until very thick, about 15 min., stirring constantly. Remove from heat, stir in beaten egg yolks. Stir in butter, vanilla and raisins, cover and cool until lukewarm. Stir in sour cream and turn into baked raisin crust; top with meringue.
MERINGUE: Beat 3 egg whites until foamy, add 1/4 t. cream of tartar and 1/8 t. salt. Gradually beat in 6 T. sugar, 2 T. at a time, until sugar is completely dissolved. Bake meringue-topped pie at 400° for 8-10 min. Serves 8.

RHUBARD PIE DELIGHT   Mrs. Melvin (Katherine) Yoder

1 1/2 c. diced rhubarb
1 c. sugar
4 T. water
1 pkg. raspberry jello
Dash of salt
1 c. whipping cream
1 t. vanilla

Simmer rhubarb, sugar and water till tender. Add jello and stir till dissolved; cool till partly set. Prepare whipped cream, add salt, and vanilla. Fold rhubarb mixture into whipped cream, put into a baked 9" pie shell and cool.

RHUBARD CUSTARD PIE

Mrs. Lloyd Swartzentruber

1 c. cut rhubarb
¾ c. cream
1 t. flour

1 c. sugar
3 eggs
Pinch of salt

Put rhubarb into prepared crust. Make custard with sugar, cream, eggs, salt and flour. Pour over rhubarb. Bake at 350° for 35 min. till custard sets. Do not let pie boil.

FRENCH RHUBARB PIE

Miriam Brenneman

1-9" unbaked pie shell
2 c. rhubarb, cut up
1 c. white sugar
1 egg
1 t. vanilla

2 T. flour
⅓ c. butter
½ c. brown sugar
¾ c. flour

Mix rhubarb, white sugar, egg, vanilla and 2 T. flour. Put in 9" pie shell. Make crumbs with butter, brown sugar, and ¾ c. flour. Sprinkle over top. Bake at 425° for 5 min., then at 350° for 30 min.

SHOO-FLY PIE

Mrs. L.D. Kauffman

CRUMB MIXTURE:
2 c. flour
¾ c. brown sugar
⅓ c. shortening or butter

½ t. nutmeg
1 t. cinnamon

Mix above ingredients together thoroughly in a bowl until crumbs are formed.

SYRUP MIXTURE:
1 c. light syrup (Karo)
½ c. brown sugar
2 eggs

1 c. hot water
1 t. soda dissolved in the hot water

Mix syrup ingredients. Pour into 2 prepared pie crusts, then divide the crumbs on top of syrup mixture. Bake at 350° for 50 min. Yield: 2 pies.

STRAWBERRY PIE
Mrs. Bertha Yoder

1 qt. water
2 c. sugar
3 T. clear gel or cornstarch

1 lg. box strawberry Jell-O
1/2 t. lemon juice
A little salt and pepper
1 qt. fresh strawberries

Bring water and sugar to boil. Thicken with clear gel. Add rest of ingredients. Pour in a 9" baked pie shell. Serves 6.

STRAWBERRY YOGURT PIE
Lena Swartzentruber

2-8 oz. containers strawberry
yogurt
1/2 c. crushed strawberries

1-8 oz. container Cool Whip
1 graham cracker crust

Mix well crushed fruit and yogurt. Fold in Cool Whip and blend well. Spoon into crust and freeze about 4 hrs. Remove from freezer and put into refrigerator 30 min. before serving.

FROSTY STRAWBERRY CREAM PIE
Mrs. Chris L. Miller

1/2 c. sugar
1 c. strawberries

1 egg white
1/2 c. cream (whipped)

Beat first 3 ingredients until fluffy, then fold in whipped cream. Then put into graham cracker crust and freeze.

SWEETHEART PIE
Mrs. William N. Yoder

CRUST:
18 graham crackers
1/2 c. sugar
1/2 c. melted butter

CUSTARD FILLING:
3 eggs, separated
1/2 c. sugar
4 t. cornstarch
2 c. milk
1 1/2 t. vanilla
1/4 t. nutmeg

CRUST: Combine cracker crumbs, sugar and melted butter. Keep 1 c. crumbs for top. Press the rest of crumbs in pie pan.
CUSTARD FILLING: Mix egg yolks, sugar, cornstarch and milk. Cook slowly until thick, add flavoring. Put in crumb-lined pan. Beat egg whites until stiff, add 1 T. sugar. Spread on top of custard, cover with remaining crumbs. Bake at 375° for 8-10 min. or until meringue is lightly browned. Yield: 1-9" pie.

EASY YOGURT PIE

Lena Yoder

2-8 oz. containers yogurt (your favorite)
8 oz. Cool Whip

1 pkg. graham crackers
1/2 c. white sugar
1 stick melted butter

Mix your favorite yogurt with 8 ounces of Cool Whip. Spoon into graham cracker crust. Cool and serve.

Delightful on a hot day!

SUNSHINE PIE

A pound of patience you must find mixed well with loving words so kind. Drop in 2 pounds of helpful deeds and thoughts of other people's needs. A pack of smiles to make the crust. Then stir and bake it well you must. And now I ask that you may try **The recipe of this Sunshine Pie.**

SALADS

ANGEL SALAD

Linda Yoder

1 sm. pkg. cherry Jell-O
3/4 c. boiling water
1 c. miniature marshmallows
1 can crushed pineapple (drained)

1 c. cottage cheese
1/3 c. nuts
1/2 c. whipped cream

Combine Jell-O and boiling water. Stir until completely dissolved. Add marshmallows. Mix and chill till partially set. Add pineapple, cottage cheese and nuts. Mix, then fold in whipped cream. Chill until set. Serves 6.

APRICOT JELLO DELIGHT

Alta Kauffman

2 sm. pkgs. apricot jello
3-1/2 c. boiling water
1-20 oz. can crushed pineapple
   (drained, reserve juice)
1 c. mini-marshmallows
2 bananas, mashed

1 c. sugar
2 T. flour
1 egg, beaten
1 T. butter
3 oz. pkg. cream cheese
1 pkg. Dream Whip

Dissolve jello in water and let set until syrupy. Add pineapple, marshmallows, and bananas to jello. Pour into 9x13" flat dish. In saucepan, combine sugar, flour, egg, butter and 1/2 c. pineapple juice. Cook until thick. Add cream cheese and cool. Prepare Dream whip and fold into cooled sauce, spread on congealed jello. Serves 12.

QUICK APPLE SALAD

Ruth Yoder

2 apples, cubed
2 bananas
1/3 c. celery
1/3 c. nuts
1/3 c. coconut

3 T. Cool Whip
1 T. peanut butter
1 T. mayonnaise

Mix together first 5 ingredients; set aside. Mix together Cool Whip, peanut butter, and mayonnaise, then add to apple mixture. Serves 6.

RAW APPLE SALAD

Malinda Wingard

8 ripe apples
1/2 c. diced celery

1/2 c. chopped nuts

DRESSING:
1 c. sugar
1 c. water
3 t. flour
1/8 t. salt

1 egg (beaten)
1 T. vinegar
1 t. vanilla

Stir together sugar, flour, salt, water, and beaten egg. Bring to a boil. Add vinegar and vanilla. Cool before pouring over apple mixture. Serves 8.

BLUEBERRY SALAD

Ruth Yoder

2 sm. pkgs. grape or lemon
  jello
2 c. boiling water
1-#2 can crushed pineapple
1 can blueberry pie filling

1-8 oz. cream cheese
1/2 pt. sour cream
1 t. vanilla
1/2 c. sugar
1/2 c. chopped nuts

Mix jello, water, pineapple and blueberry pie filling and congeal. Mix together cream cheese, sour cream, sugar and vanilla; add nuts and spread over congealed mixture. Seves 10.

If a nail in a plastered wall loosens,
wrap a little cloth around the nail,
saturate it with glue, and replace in the hole;
when the glue hardens, it'll hold firmly.

CHERRY-ORANGE SALAD
Mrs. Marlene Swartzentruber

1-6 oz. cn frozen orange juice concentrate, thawed & undiluted
1¼ c. water
1-3 oz. pkg. cherry-flavored gelatin
1-3 oz. pkg. orange-flavored gelatin
2 carrots, grated

2 c. crushed pineapple, drained
3 medium apples, grated
1 c. chopped pecans
2 c. miniature marshmallows
1 c. whipping cream (whipped)

Combine orange juice concentrate and water in a saucepan; stir well, and bring to a boil. Combine cherry and orange-flavored gelatins in a mixing bowl; add hot orange juice, stirring until gelatin dissolves. Stir in carrots and fruit. Chilll until mixture is the consistency of unbeaten egg whites. Fold in remaining ingredients into gelatin. Chill in 10-c. mold until firm. Makes 20 servings.

CHRISTMAS SALAD
Beulah Yoder

1-3 oz. pkg. lime jello
1-3 oz. pkg. raspberry jello
1-6 oz. pkg. lemon jello

1 sm. can crushed pineapple
1 pkg. Dream Whip, prepared or
2 c. whipped cream

Prepare first 2 jellos according to package directions in separate shallow pans. Let set. Cut into cubes. Prepare lemon jello. Let stand until slightly set. Beat until fluffy and mix with whipped cream and pineapple. Fold in cubed jello. Pour into mold and chill until firm. Serves 10-12.

CONGEALED BUTTERMILK SALAD
Lila Yoder

1-3 oz. pkg. lime jello
1 c. buttermilk
½ c. chopped nuts

½ c. crushed pineapple (undrained)
2 pkgs. whipped topping, prepared like on box

Mix gelatin and pineapple in saucepan and heat until jello dissolves. Allow to cool. Whip topping, then add buttermilk, jello mixture and nuts, just until blended. Refrigerate. Serves 12.

BRIDESMAID OR CONGEALED
STRAWBERRY BUTTERMILK SALAD

Mrs. Eli Kauffman,
Mrs. Levi Kauffman,
Mrs. Eli Hostetler

1 lg. pkg. strawberry gelatin
  (other flavors may be
  substituted)
2 c. buttermilk

1 c. chopped pecans
20 oz. can crushed pineapple
  (undrained)
1-9 oz. carton whipped topping

Mix gelatin and pineapple in large saucepan. Heat on stove until gelatin dissolves. (Do not boil.) Allow to cool. Mix in buttermilk, pecans and whipped topping until blended. Pour into 8x12" oblong dish or glass bowl. Refrigerate. Beautiful, light salad.

COTTAGE CHEESE SALAD

Ruby Swartzentruber,
Mrs. Isaac Plank

16 oz. cottage cheese
1 can drained mandarin oranges

1 pt. Cool Whip
1 pkg. dry orange gelatin

Mix dry jello into Cool Whip. Add other ingredients and serve.

CREAM CHEESE JELLO SALAD

Mrs. Daniel Swartzentruber

2 lg. boxes lime jello
1 lg. pkg. cream cheese
4 c. hot water
1/4 c. sugar

2 pkgs. Dream Whip (prepare as
  directions on box)
1/2 c. mayonnaise
1 can crushed pineapple
1/2 c. nuts

Dissolve jello and sugar in hot water and add cream cheese. Put in blender; then add the 4 c. ice water and gel slightly. Next add Dream Whip, mayonnaise, crushed pineapple and nuts. Serves 20.

Children need models more than they need critics.

CREAM CHEESE SALAD

Mrs. Harley Yoder

1³/4 c. hot water
1 sm. pkg. lime Jell-O
1-#2 can crushed pineapple
1/2 c. sugar
1 T. plain gelatin
1/2 c. water

1 c. pineapple juice
3 oz. pkg. cream cheese
1/2 pt. whipping cream, sweetened
2 to 3 sm. pkgs. strawberry Jell-O
1³/4 c. hot water to each pkg.

Mix Jell-O in hot water. Drain pineapple. Add sugar and cool in pan. While Jell-O sets, mix plain gelatin in 1/2 c. water. Boil pineapple juice, add gelatin and cool. Then add cream cheese, mix thoroughly. Next add whipping cream, spread on set lime Jell-O. After strawberry Jell-O sets slightly, spread over creamed mixture.

CREAMY JELLO SALAD

Ruth Yoder

2 c. boiling water
1-6 oz. pkg. orange or
   raspberry jello
1 pt. sherbet (orange or
   raspberry)

1 c. mandarin oranges
1 c. pineapple
1 c. marshmallows
1 c. coconut
1 c. sour cream

Dissolve jello in boiling water; add sherbet, pour into round jello ring, set until firm. Mix remaining ingredients together and put in center of inverted mold. Let set overnight.

DAIRY BERRY RIBBON SALAD

Mary Lois Yoder

RED LAYER:
1-3 oz.pkg. red raspberry jello
1 c. boiling water
1-16 oz. pkg. partially thawed
   raspberries

BLUE LAYER:
1-3 oz. pkg. black raspberry jello
1 c. boiling water
1¹/2 c. canned blueberries,
   drained
1/2 c. reserved juice

1-3 oz. pkg. lemon jello
1 c. boiling water

1-3 oz. pkg. cream cheese
1/2 c. whipping cream, whipped

Dissolve red raspberry gelatin in boiling water, add partially frozen berries and syrup. Stir gently until fruit thaws. Chill until thickened, pour into an oiled mold. Chill until set, but not firm. Dissolve lemon jello in boiling water and cool until partially set. Blend cream cheese and whipped cream, fold into jello, spoon over red layer in mold. Chill until set, but not firm. Dissolve black raspberry jello in boiling water. Add 1/2 c. blueberry juice and chill until partially set. Fold in blueberries, spoon on white layer and chill till firm. Unmold and serve.

255

DREAM SICKLE SALAD Mrs. Norman Yoder, Mrs. Daniel Yoder

2 sm. pkgs. orange jello
1/2 c. sugar
2 c. boiling water
1 c. cold water
1-8 oz. pkg. cream cheese
2 c. Cool Whip

Dissolve sugar and jello in boiling water. Add cold water. Let set until "syrupy" or "shaky." Beat cream cheese and add Cool Whip. Slowly pour jello in and mix well. Pour into dish and refrigerate till set. Serves 10-12.

For variation, use strawberry jello.

JELL-O SALAD Mrs. Rufus L. Yoder

1 lg. raspberry Jell-O
1-8 oz. pkg. cream cheese
1 qt. boiling water
1-20 oz. can crushed pineapple
1 c. pecans
10 to 12 oz. whipped topping

Melt Jell-O in boiling water. Cool. Cream the cream cheese in bowl. Slowly add cooled Jell-O. Add pineapple, nuts, and whipped topping. Yields 2 dessert bowls.

LAVENDER SALAD Mary Lois Yoder, Esther Ruth Yoder, and Susan Overholt

2 sm. boxes raspberry jello
2 c. boiling water
16 lg. marshmallows
2 c. cold water
1 c. crushed pineapple
1 c. cream (whipped)
1-8 oz. pkg. cream cheese
1/2 c. chopped nuts

Mix jello, water and marshmallows together and thicken in refrigerator. Next put pineapple, cream cheese and cream in blender. Then add this and nuts to jello mixture and put in serving bowls to thicken.

When using spray to spray plants on the inside,
spray inside of paper bag and place over plant.
This keeps fumes in, instead of all over the room.

LEMON SALAD ON LETTUCE

Malinda Wingard

1-8 oz. pkg. cream cheese
1-3 oz. pkg. lemon Jell-O
1/3 c. bottled lemon juice

1 t. vanilla

1-14 oz. Eagle Brand sweetened
condensed milk
1/8 c. chopped nuts

12 pieces of lettuce leaves

Prepare Jell-O as directed on package. Chill until slightly set, then beat until fluffy. Soften cream cheese, whip together with condensed milk, lemon juice and vanilla. Mix both mixtures together and beat. Pour into 9x9" buttered pan and sprinkle with nuts. Chill thoroughly. Cut into 9 pieces and place individually on lettuce leaves. Serves 9.

LEMON CHEESE SALAD

Mary M. Yoder

2-3 oz. pkgs. lemon jello
3 3/4 c. boiling water
1-6 oz. pkg. cream cheese
1/3 t. salt

1-8 1/2 oz. can crushed pineapple
1 c. diced celery
1/2 pt. cream (whipped)
1 c. chopped nuts

Dissolve gelatin in hot water; let cool. Cream cheese with salt, then add the gelatin. Add pineapple, nuts, and celery. Fold in whipped cream. Pour in mold and chill till firm. Serves 9-12.

ORANGE JELLO SALAD

Mrs. Allen M. Yoder

2 sm. boxes orange jello
1 sm. box orange-pineapple jello
1/2 c. drained, crushed
pineapple
3 c. hot water

2 c. cold water
1 lg. pkg. cream cheese
1 c. cream, whipped stiff
1 T. sugar

TOPPING:
2 beaten eggs
3 T. flour (level)
3/4 c. sugar

1/2 c. pineapple juice
1/2 c. water

Dissolve jello in 3 c. hot water and 2 c. cold water. Add pineapple. Pour in 9x13" dish. Let set. Whip the cream. Whip cream cheese and add a little milk, add sugar and beat together. Spread on top of jello. TOPPING: Mix all the topping ingredients together and bring to a boil. Cook until thick and spread on cheese mixture. Serves 15.

Jello can be substituted with lime and lemon.

257

ORANGE RICE SALAD

Mrs. Crist Yoder, Sr.

1 c. Minute rice
1-10½ oz. pkg. miniature
  marshmallows
1-3 oz. pkg. orange jello

1 can crushed pineapple, drained
½ c. pecans, chopped
1 pt. whipped cream of 2 pkgs.
  instant whipped topping

Cook rice - as it is cooling, add ½ of marshmallows and stir until blended. Prepare jello as directed on box, let congeal until amost set. In large bowl, combine rice and marshmallow mixture with jello and add rest of marshmallows, pecans and pineapple. Whip the cream and fold into the other ingredients. Serves 15.

PEACH PARTY SALAD

Miriam Brenneman, Ruth Yoder

2 sm. pkgs. orange gelatin
2 c. boiling ater
1-20 oz. can crushed pineapple
½ c. juice or water
1 T. butter
1 c. miniature marshmallows

1 c. whipped cream
2 c. drained frozen or fresh
  peaches
½ c. sugar
1 egg
3 T. flour
1 c. shredded Cheddar cheese

Dissolve gelatin in boiling water. Drain pineapple. Add water or peach juice to pineapple juice to make 1½ c. liquid. Add ¾ c. liquid to gelatin. Chill until syrupy. Spread peaches over bottom of 13x9" pan. Add gelatin and chill until firm. Combine sugar, flour, egg and remaining pineapple juice. Cook over low heat, stirring until thick and smooth. Stir in butter. Cool and chill, then fold pineapple, marshmallows, cheese and whipped cream into mixture. Spread over gelatin. Chill several hours before serving. Serves 12 to 15.

PINEAPPLE CHEESE JELLO

Verna Mae Wingard

1 sm. box lemon or orange jello
1 c. boiling water
½ c. cold water
1 c. pineapple (drain juice)

1 c. grated cheese
1 c. whipped cream
1 t. vanilla

Mix jello and water and let it cool till slightly set. Then stir in pineapple, cheese and whipped cream and vanilla. Chill until firm. Serves 6.

WHIPPED PINEAPPLE SALAD

Beulah Yoder

1 sm. pkg. lemon jello
1 c. boiling water
1 c. cold water
1 sm. can pineapple, drained

1 c. grated cheese
1 c. whipping cream
1 t. vanilla

Dissolve jello in boiling water. Add cold water and chill. When jello begins to thicken, whip it until light. Add whipped cream flavored with vanilla. Also add pineapple and cheese. Pour into mold and chill until firm. Serves 6.

PINK FLUFF

Alta Kauffman, Verda Overholt, Jr.,
and Ruth Yoder

1-20 oz. can crushed pineapple
1-13 oz. can evaporated milk
1/2 c. sugar

3 oz. pkg. strawberry jello
8 oz. pkg. cream cheese

Boil pineapple and sugar 5 min. Add dry jello and stir till dissolved. Cool till it starts to jell. Beat cream cheese and milk till fluffy. Fold in pineapple and jello mixture. Chill until firm. May be used as a salad or dessert. Serves 6.

RASPBERRY DELIGHT SALAD

Ruth Yoder

1-3 oz. box raspberry jello
1 c. hot water
1 c. vanilla ice cream

1 c. crushed pineapple
1/2 c. chopped nuts
1 medium-sized banana

Combine jello with hot water. Add ice cream and stir until thoroughly dissolved. Combine undrained pineapple, nuts and sliced banana. Add to jello mixture and pour into quart-size mold and chill until firm. Serves 6.

Sweeten whipped cream with powdered sugar
if dessert serving may be delayed.
Whip stays fluffy longer than when granulated sugar is used.

259

RIBBON SALAD

Mrs. Daniel Yoder

2 sm. pkgs. lime jello
2 sm. pkgs. strawberry jello
1 can crushed pineapple
2 pkgs. Knox gelatin

²/₃ c. warm water
1-8 oz. cream cheese
¹/₂ pt. whipping cream

Prepare jellos as directed on box. Drain juice from pineapple and boil. Dissolve gelatin in water and add to hot juice. Let cool. Add cream cheese. Whip cream, sweeten and add to mixture. Pour on lime jello and let set well. Put strawberry jello on top. Serves 12.

RIBBON SALAD

Naomi Yoder

6 oz. lime Jell-O
3 oz. lemon Jell-O
6 oz. raspberry Jell-O
3 c. boiling water
1¹/₂ c. cold water

6 oz. cream cheese
1 c. miniature marshmallows
¹/₂ c. mayonnaise
1 c. whipped cream
1 sm. can crushed pineapple

FIRST LAYER: Dissolve lime Jell-O in 2 c. boiling water and add 1¹/₂ c. cold water and let jell.

SECOND LAYER: Dissolve lemon Jell-O in 1 c. boiling water. Add cream cheese and marshmallows. Mix well. Set aside and slightly jell. Then add whipped cream, mayonnaise and pineapple.

THIRD LAYER: Dissolve raspberry Jell-O in 1 c. boiling water and add ³/₄ c. cold water. Let cool slightly. Pour over jelled lemon and refrigerate. Serves 18-20.

SEVEN-UP SALAD

Kathryn Yoder, Joyce Yoder

8 oz. pkg. cream cheese
1 sm. pkg. lime jello
¹/₄ c. sugar
³/₄ c. boiling water

1 sm. can crushed pineapple
1 t. vanilla
1 c. 7-Up
1 c. pecans

Mix jello, sugar and boiling water together. Beat cream cheese till smooth. Add jello mixture gradually to cream cheese. Add rest of ingredients and chill. Serves 6.

SWEETHEART SALAD

Esther Yoder

2 c. crushed pineapple
1/2 c. sugar
1 1/2 T. plain gelatin
1/4 c. cold water
6 oz. Philadelphia cream cheese

2 T. lemon juice
2 T. cherry juice
1 c. whipping cream
12 maraschino cherries (chopped)

Dissolve gelatin in cold water, add pineapple to sugar, bring to boiling point and add gelatin. Stir until gelatin is dissolved. Add lemon and cherry juice, cool. Mash cream cheese, add chopped cherries. Combine with pineapple mixture, adding a small amount at a time. Chill until slightly thickened. Whip cream and blend with salad mixture. Mold and chill. Serves 8.

SWEETHEART SALAD

Bertha Swartzentruber

5 c. crushed pineapple
3 c. water
4 c. sugar
7 pkgs. gelatin
1/4 c. cold water

24 oz. cream cheese
1 c. lemon juice
1/2 c. cherry juice
6 pkgs. Dream Whip
1/2 c. maraschino cherries

Dissolve gelatin in 1/4 c. cold water. Add pineapple to the 3 c. water and 4 c. sugar. Bring to boiling point and add gelatin. Stir until gelatin is dissolved. Add lemon and cherry juice. Cool. Mash cream cheese and add chopped cherries; combine with pineapple mixture, adding a small amount at a time. Chill until slightly thickened. Whip Dream Whip and blend with salad mixture. Mold and chill. Serves approximately 25.

SUNSET FRUIT SALAD

Ruth Yoder

1-6 oz. pkg. orange jello
2 c. boiling water
2 c. cold water
2 T. lemon juice

1/8 t. cinnamon
1 c. frruit (bananas, oranges, seedless grapes)
1-3 oz. pkg. cream cheese or
1/2 c. sour cream

Dissolve gelatin in boiling water. Add cold water and lemon juice. Let stand until slightly thickened. Stir occasionally. Set aside 1 c. jello. Add fruits to remaining jello; pour in serving bowl. Combine measured jello, cinnamon and cheese in blender; blend. Spoon over fruited jello. Chill until set. Serves 10.

YUM YUM SALAD
Linda Yoder

1-6 oz. box strawberry jello
2 c. boiling water
2 c. pineapple juice

1-#2 can crushed pineapple
1-8 oz. pkg. cream cheese
1/2 pt. cream

Mix jello and water and add pineapple juice. Combine pineapple and cheese with fork and add to jello. Fold in whipped cream and chill. Serves 12.

CLOCK WATCHER'S SALAD
Mrs. Chris L. Miller

3 c. shredded carrots
1-20 oz. can pineapple chunks, drained
1 c. miniature marshmallows

1/2 c. raisins
1/2 c. celery
2/3 c. salad dressing
Lettuce

Combine all ingredients except lettuce; mix lightly, chill. Serve in lettuce-lined bowl.

LUNSTROM SALAD
Verna Mae Wingard

1-16 oz. can fruit cocktail
1 can lemon pie filling
or for 2 recipes, use big

1 bag sm. marshmallows
1/2 pt. whipping cream (whipped)

container Cool Whip

Mix all ingredients together and let it set overnight in refrigerator. Serves 8-10.

PISTACHIO SALAD
Mrs. William N. Yoder, Delores Hostetler, and Mrs. Isaac Plank

1-3 oz. pkg. instant pistachio pudding
20 oz. can crushed pineapple, undrained

1 lg. container whipped topping
1/2 c. chopped nuts
1 c. miniature marshmallows

In large bowl, mix pudding mix with whipped topping. Add pineapple, nuts and marshmallows. Chill.

SALTINE CRACKER SALAD   Elsie N. Yoder

1 pack saltine crackers, crushed 3 hard-boiled eggs
1 c. onion, chopped   1 sm. jar pimentos
1 c. chopped celery or   1 c. mayonnaise
   bell peppers

Mix all ingredients and chill 1 hr. before serving.

GREEN BEAN SALAD   Mrs. L.D. Kauffman, Vernie Brenneman

1 onion, thinly sliced in rings   1 c. sugar
1 pepper, thinly sliced in rings   3/4 c. vinegar
1 can wax beans   1/2 c. oil
1 c. geen snap beans   1 t. salt
1 c. kidney or Great Northern   1/2 t. pepper
   beans

Mix all together and let stand at last 12 hrs.

GREEN SALAD   Barbara Jean Hershberger
                                    and Lena Swartzentruber

1-3 oz. pkg. lime jello   1/4 c. salad dressing
2 sm. pkgs. cream cheese,   1 to 1 1/2 c. drained, crushed
   softened   pineapple
1 c. cream, whipped, to which   1/2 c. nuts
   has been added 3 T. sugar
   and 1 t. vanilla

Dissolve jello in hot water according to directions on box. Beat in softened cream cheese. Chill until just beginning to jell. Add whipped cream, pineapple, salad dressing and nuts. Chill until firm.

Papa, are you growing taller?
No, my child. Why do you ask?
Cause the top of your head is poking up through your hair.

MARINATED CARROTS

Mrs. Levi Kauffman

2 lbs. carrots, peeled & sliced
1 green pepper, cut in rings
1 medium onion, thinly sliced
   & separated into rings
1 can tomato soup

1 c. sugar
1 c. corn oil
1/2 c. vinegar
1 T. dry mustard
1 t. salt

Cook carrots until crisp-tender. Drain. Combine carrots, pepper and onion in 13x9x2" pan. Mix thoroughly soup, sugar, oil, vinegar, mustard and salt and mix into the vegetables. Let marinate in refrigerator for 8 hrs. Serves 14.

COLESLAW

Mrs. Sol Yoder

1 lg. head cabbage (shredded),
   cut fine
1 c. celery
1 green mango
1/2. c. onion

1 1/2 c. sugar
1 t. salt
1 t. celery seed
1/2 t. mustard seed
1/2 c. white vinegar

Put all ingredients in large bowl and blend well. Will keep for 2 weeks in refrigerator. Makes about 2 quarts.

7 LAYER LETTUCE SALAD

Mrs. Crist Yoder, Jr., Marie King,
Mrs. Nelson Yoder, Mrs.Daniel Swartzentruber,
and Ruth Yoder

1 head lettuce, chopped
1 c. celery
4 cooked eggs
1-10 oz. frozen peas
1/2 c. green pepper

1 sweet onion, diced
1 pkg. bacon (fried & crumbled)
2 c. mayonnaise
2 T. sugar
4 oz. Cheddar cheese (shredded)

Place ingredients in pan in order given. Then mix 2 c. mayonnaise and 2 T. sugar and spread over salad. Then sprinkle cheese over dressing. This can be prepared several hours ahead before serving.

LETTUCE SALAD

Linda Weaver

1 head lettuce
1 onion, minced
½ c. grated cheese
1 t. salt
2½ T. sugar

½ c. salad dressing
1 t. mustard
2 T. cream
2 T. vinegar

DRESSING: Mix together salt, sugar, mustard, and cream. Add vinegar and salad dressing and stir until smooth. Mix dressing into lettuce just before serving.

MACARONI SALAD

Susan Overholt, Mrs. Ivan Yoder

1 lb. macaroni
4 hard-boiled eggs, chopped
1 family-size can tuna, drained
4 slices crisp-fried bacon, crushed

1 medium onion, minced
3 medium carrots, grated
2 stalks celery, chopped
½ c. olives, chopped (optional)

DRESSING:
2½ c. mayonnaise
1 c. sugar
¼ c. mustard

2 t. vinegar
¾ to 1 c. milk, enough to make salad moist

Cook macaroni as directed on package until tender; drain. Add rest of ingredients, flaking tuna as you add it. Then add the following dressing, which has been blended well. After the dressing has been mixed into salad, you may add a few tomato wedges to garnish. Serves 12-15.

*A smile is a light in the window of your face
to show your heart is at home.*

POTATO SALAD FOR A CROWD

Linda Kauffman

10 lbs. potatoes
1 stalk celery, diced
8 to 10 eggs, hard boiled
1 onion (optional)
2 c. sugar
2 c. salad dressing

6 T. vinegar
2 T. mustard
1 1/2 t. salt
1/2 t. pepper
1/2 t. celery seed

Cook potatoes till soft, then peel, and dice or shred, as preferred. Add celery, eggs, and onion. To make dressing, mix together remaining ingredients and pour over potato mixture, and mix lightly. Makes 2 gallons. Serves 50.

TACO SALAD

Ruth Yoder, Mrs. Crist Yoder, Sr. and Mrs. Daniel Yoder

1 head lettuce, chopped
1 lb. hamburger
8 oz. Cheddar cheese, coarsely grated
1 sm. can kidney beans

1 onion, chopped
4 medium tomatoes, diced
1 pkg. taco chips
1 pkg. taco seasoning

DRESSING:
8 oz. Thousand Island dressing
1/3 c. sugar

1 t. taco seasoning
1 t. taco sauce

Brown hamburger, add taco seasoning, reserving 1 t. for dressing. Put in salad bowl, allowing enough room to toss salad at serving time. Layer salad ingredients in salad bowl, starting with lettuce and ending with cheese; cover and refrigerate. At serving time, toss salad with dressing and taco chips. Also good served with sour cream. Serves 8.

Work smarter - not harder.

266

VEGETABLE SALAD

Malinda Wingard

1-16 oz. frozen mixed
  vegetables
1 c. raw celery, diced
1 sm. onion, chopped
1 sm. green pepper, diced
1 c. dark red kidney beans,
  drained

DRESSING:
3/4 c. sugar
3 T. flour
1 T. mustard (prepared)
1/2 c. vinegar
1/3 c. water

Cook, drain and cool mixed vegetables. (Do not overcook). Cook together all dressing ingredients. Cool well and pour over vegetable mixture. Refrigerate overnight. Serves 10.

COLESLAW DRESSING

Mrs. Norman Yoder

2 c. sugar
2 c. mayonnaise
3/4 c. vinegar
2 T. mustard

2 t. salt
1 t. celery salt
1/2 onion
1/4 t. pepper
1/4 t. garlic

Pour onion and vinegar in blender and chop onion real fine. Add the rest of the ingredients and blend well. Makes enough dressing for 3 heads of cabbage.

This will stay good in the refrigerator for several weeks.

COLESLAW DRESSING

Ruth Yoder

2 c. salad dressing
1 c. sugar
1 t. prepared mustard

1/4 c. vinegar
1 sm. can evaporated milk
1/2 t. celery seed

Beat together until creamy. Store in refrigerator.

Kindness is becoming at any age.

DILLY CUCUMBER DRESSING   Mrs. Marlene Swartzentruber

1½ c. peeled, seeded,   1 T. milk
   chopped cucumber   1 T. lemon juice
1 c. mayonnaise   2 t. dill weed
2 T. finely-chopped onion   ¼ t. salt

Mix all ingredients. Cover and chill. Makes 1½ c. of creamy, delicious dressing.

FRENCH DRESSING   Mary Cathrine Plank, Mrs. Eli Kauffman

2 c. mayonnaise   2 t. paprika
1½ c. sugar   ½ t. salt
¼ c. vinegar   4 t. water
½ c. catsup   ½ c. cooking oil
2 t. mustard

Put all ingredients in blender and blend. You may substitute Weight Watchers for regular mayonnaise if you want reduced calories.

FRENCH DRESSING   Mrs. Chris L. Miller

½ c. vegetable oil   1 c. white sugar
¼ c. vinegar   1 t. mayonnaise
⅓ c. catsup   1 t. lemon juice
1 t. salt   2 T. chopped onion

Put in blender and mix well.

FRENCH DRESSING   Lena Yoder

¼ c. sugar   1 c. oil
½ t. salt   ⅓ c. ketchup
2 T. chopped onion   ¼ c. vinegar
1 garlic clove, crushed   ½ t. Worcestershire sauce

In small bowl or blender, combine all ingredients. Blend until smooth. Cover and chill. Mix well before using. Makes 1¾ cups.

SWEET AND SOUR DRESSING Mrs. Chris L. Miller

1 c. sugar
1 c. oil
1 T. salad dressing
2 t. mustard
1 medium onion, chopped

1/4 c. water
1/4 c. vinegar
1 t. salt
1/4 t. pepper
1 t. celery seed

Mix all together in blender.

SWEET AND SOUR DRESSING Elsie N. Yoder

1 or 2 onions
1 1/2 c. sugar
2 t. dry mustard
1 t. salt

1 t. celery seed
2/3 c. vinegar
1 pt. salad oil

Put in blender.

TOSSED SALAD DRESSING Linda Yoder

1-10 1/2 oz. can tomato soup
1/2 c. corn oil
1/3 c. vinegar
1 t. salt

2 T. sugar
1 t. dry mustard
1 t. paprika
1 t. Worcestershire sauce

Blend and chill. Serve on tossed salad.

DRESSING FOR POTATO SALAD Mrs. Floyd E. Yoder

3/4 c. sugar
1 c. salad dressing
2 T. vinegar

1 T. mustard
1/2 t. salt

Mix all ingredients together till creamy.

POTATO SALAD DRESSING Mary Cathrine Plank

3/4 c. sugar
1 c. salad dressing
2 T. vinegar

1 T. mustard
1/2 t. salt
1/4 t. celery salt

Mix all ingredients together and add to cooked, chopped potatoes.
Chill and serve.

269

Notes

SOUP & SANDWICH

AMISH BEAN SOUP
Mrs. Eli Hostetler

1 qt. partially-cooked navy
 beans
Put ¼ lb. butter in a large
 kettle.
Melt butter, then add:

½ c. chopped onions
½ c. chopped celery
2 T. seasoning

Stir till all is mixed well. Add beans and enough water to cover all. Cook on slow heat until beans are soft. This can be kept in a covered container in refrigerator for a short length of time. Heat the amount of milk needed. Add beans to the milk. Bring to boil. Pour over cubed homemade bread.

BEEFY CHILI SOUP
Laura K. Yoder

3 lbs. hamburger
1 lg. onion
24 oz. catsup (homemade)*
1 qt. beef broth, or leftover gravy
½ pkg. chili seasoning mix
2 T. dark Karo or brown sugar
1 can pork and beans

1 can pinto beans
1 T. A.1. sauce
½ c. flour
1½ t. red pepper
½ t. black pepper
2 t. salt
1 T. seasoning salt

Fry hamburger, onion, and seasoning salt together till well-browned. Then stir in flour and fry a little longer, stirring constantly. Add rest of ingredients, and simmer on low heat for 30 min.
*If you don't have homemade catsup, use 2 cans tomato soup and 16 oz. regular catsup.
I also rinse my bean cans with hot water and add to the soup.

CARROT & ONION SOUP
Katie Hershberger

1 c. cooked rice
3 T. butter
4 to 5 medium carrots, grated
1 medium onion, minced

1 t. salt
1 T. sugar
4 c. chicken broth or vegetable
 stock
1 c. hot milk

Cook rice until very tender. Cook carrots and onions, add seasonings and butter. Add cooked rice. When ready to serve, add hot milk. Sometimes I put half of this in blender and make a puree.

This soup is very good. I add a little powdered milk for protein.

CELERY POTATO SOUP

Mrs. Bertha Yoder

1 c. diced potatoes
1 c. diced celery
Salt and pepper to taste

1 qt. milk
2 T. butter

Cook potatoes and celery together until soft. Add milk, butter and seasoning and bring to a boil. Serve with crackers or toasted bread. Serves 6.

CHICKEN CORN SOUP

Laura K. Yoder

2 lg. chickens (cooked & drained)
1 qt. corn
2 qts. stewed tomatoes (drained)
4 c. rice (prepared)
2 t. minced onion
Celery tops (optional)
1/2 gal. water
1/2 c. clear gel or cornstarch

Chicken broth from 2 chickens, or more
1/2 t. curry powder
3 T. chicken soup base
2 t. seasoned salt
1 t. salt
1/2 t. pepper
2 T. sugar

Add water to chicken broth and bring to boil. Mix together all seasonings, and clear gel or cornstarch, adding enough hot water to make a thin paste, then add to boiling liquid, stirring constantly, until boiling and thickened. Add celery tops and onion first, then add tomato, corn, rice and boned chicken. Makes 8 qts.

CHICKEN NOODLE SOUP

Lila Yoder

1 qt. chicken & broth (half & half)
1 qt. water
2 c. noodles (uncooked)
2 t. salt
1/8 t. pepper

2 t. chicken seasoning
1 T. minced onion
2 bay leaves
1 t. parsley flakes

Simmer all together until noodles are soft.

"Flattery is soft-soap, and soft-soap is ninety percent lye!"

272

CHICKEN GUMBO

Sadie A. Yoder

STEP I:
Saute in large heavy kettle:
1/4 c. oil or margarine
2 onions, sliced
1 clove garlic, minced

1 green pepper, diced
Blend in 2 T. flour
2 or 3 c. cooked, diced chicken

STEP II:
2 c. cooked tomatoes
2 c. cooked okra
2/3 c. tomato paste
3 c. broth or stock
1 1/2 T. salt
1/4 t. pepper

1 1/2 T. Worcestershire sauce
1/8 t. ground cloves
1/2 t. chili powder
Pinch of dried basil
1 bay leaf

Cooked rice

Cook and stir over low heat Step I until vegetables are tender, then add Step II and simmer 1 hr. Add cooked chicken. Simmer briefly. To serve, mound hot rice in center of soup bowls, using ice cream dipper or large spoon. Pour hot gumbo around the rice.

CLAM CHOWDER

Mrs. Loretta Brenneman

2 c. diced potatoes
1 medium onion, diced
1 c. diced celery
3 c. rich milk

2 oz. butter or margarine
3 T. flour
1 or 2-8 oz. cans minced clams

Simmer potatoes, celery and onion together in a small amount of water until tender. Melt butter or margarine in a small pan. Blend in 3 T. flour to make a smooth paste. Drain juice from minced clams and blend into flour mixture. Add to cooked potatoes, onion and celery, then stir in milk and clams. Heat to serving temperature **but do not boil**. Add pepper if desired. May be frozen.

COLD SOUP
Lorene Plank

Bread crumbs
1/2 c. sugar

Milk
Any kind of fresh fruit such as:
strawberries, bananas,
peaches, cherries

Put enough bread crumbs in a bowl to suit the size of your family. (make plenty - this is a deliciously refreshing soup.) Add fruit and sugar (more or less sugar can be used - whatever you desire). Add milk just before ready to serve. Bologna sandwiches, crackers and cheese, fresh tomatoes, or fried chicken is DELICIOUS with the soup.

CREAM OF ASPARAGUS SOUP
Mrs. Bertha Yoder

2 bunches asparagus
1 sm. onion
3 T. butter

3 T. flour
1 qt. milk
Salt and pepper to taste

Melt butter in saucepan, add flour and milk to make a cream sauce. Cook chopped asparagus for 20 min. in salt water. Fry minced onion in 1 T. of fat. Stir often. When brown, add to asparagus. Then add asparagus to cream sauce. Bring to a boil and serve. Serves 6.

CREAMY BROCCOLI SOUP
Sadie A. Yoder

2 T. minced onion
3 T. butter or margarine
3 T. flour
1 1/4 t. salt
Salt and pepper to taste

3 c. chicken broth
2 c. chopped fresh broccoli
2 c. thinly-sliced carrots
3 c. milk

Saute onion in butter until tender, stir in flour and 1 1/4 t. salt. Gradually add milk, stirring constantly; bring to a boil. Add broth, broccoli and carrots. Heat over low heat about 25 min., stirring occasionally. Be careful not to boil mixture. Add salt and pepper. Yields 2 qts.

HAMBURGER SOUP

Mrs. Elmer M. Yoder (Esther)

1 lb. hamburger
1 c. choped onion
1 c. diced potato
1 c. carrots
1 c. cabbage
1 c. celery
4 c. tomatoes

1/4 c. rice
3 c. water
4 t. salt
1/4 t. basil
1/4 t. thyme
1 bay leaf

Brown hamburger and onion together slightly. Add potatoes, carrots, cabbage, celery, tomatoes, rice, water, salt, basil, thyme, and bay leaf and simmer until done. Serves 10.

HAMBURGER SOUP

Ellen R. Brenneman

2 qts. milk
1 pt. canned hamburger

1 can peas
1 c. cooked, cubed potatoes

Mix all ingredients and heat. Season with salt and pepper.

HEARTY HAMBURGER SOUP

Mrs. Sol Yoder, Lila Yoder,
Mari Yoder, Marie King,
Mrs. Eli Hostetler, Linda Weaver

2 T. butter
1 c. sliced carrots
1 lb. ground beef
2 c. tomato juice
1 1/2 t. salt
1/8 t. pepper

4 c. milk
1 c. chopped onions
1/2 c. chopped green peppers
1 c. diced potatoes
1 t. seasoned salt
1/3 c. flour

Melt the butter in saucepan. Brown meat; add onions and cook till transparent. Stir in remaining ingredients except flour and milk. Cover and cook over low heat until vegetables are tender, about 20-25 min. Combine flour with 1 c. milk. Stir into soup mixture. Boil. Add remaining milk and heat, stirring frequently. Do not boil after adding remaining milk. This makes quite a large amount.

You can substitute celery for the green peppers.

Too much salt in gravy or soup may be remedied by adding a quartered white potato and boiling for 10 min.

POTATO SOUP

Elsie Yoder

1 c. celery, chopped
3 c. potatoes, cubed
3 c. water
1 can cream of celery soup

1 t. salt
1/4 t. pepper
1/4 t. thyme

Cook celery and potatoes in water until soft. Add remaining ingredients. Thicken with cornstarch and water if desired.

Delicious! Tastes like Shoney's.

SWISS POTATO SOUP

Laura Whitt

1/4 c. chopped onion
2 c. diced raw potato
1 t. salt
3 c. milk
1 T. chopped parsley

2 T. butter
1 c. boiling water
3 chicken bouillon cubes
2 T. flour
1 c. shredded cheese

Melt butter in large saucepan. Saute onion until tender. Add potatoes, water, salt and chicken bouillon cubes. Cover and simmer 10 min., or until potatoes are tender. Combine milk and flour. Stir into potato mixture. Cook over medium heat, stirring constantly until smoothly thickened and mixture comes to a boil. Stir in parsley and cheese.

RIVEL SOUP

Ruth Yoder

2 qts. milk
1 1/2 t. salt and a little pepper
1 heaping c. self-rising flour

1 lg. egg
A dash of salt
1/2 stick butter

Melt butter, then add milk to boiling point. To make Rivels, rub egg, flour and dash of salt. Drop Rivels no larger than peas into milk. Simmer a few minutes. Serve with crackers. Serves 6-8.

A wise wife will see that she has the ingredients on hand
for these meals or others like them
against the day when she will need them.

SPLIT PEA SOUP
Sadie A. Yoder

1 c. dried split peas
1 ham bone
3 qts. water
3 T. minced onion
Dash of pepper

3 T. butter
3 T. flour
1 t. salt
2 c. milk

Soak peas in water overnight. Drain in morning and cover with 3 qts. water. Add ham bone and onion, cook until soft. Rub through a sieve. Melt butter and stir in flour until well-blended and smooth. Add salt, pepper, and milk; cook, stirring constantly, until mixture thickens. Combine with strained liquid and cook until rather thick.

OLD-FASHIONED SPLIT PEA SOUP
Lila Yoder, Anna Yoder

1 c. split peas
1 ham bone or pieces of
   cubed ham
1 carrot, grated
2 medium onions, minced

1 potato, grated
1/4 c. diced celery
1/4 c. finely-chopped green
   peppers
Salt and pepper to taste

Cove split peas with 6 c. boiling water; let soak for 1 hr. Add ham bone, carrot, onions, potatoes, celery, and green pepper. Season with salt and pepper. Simmer until peas are tender. Add water, if needed; simmer for 5-10 min. longer. Pour into soup bowls; garnish with diced ham. Serves 4.

TOMATO SOUP
Barbara Jean Hershberger,
Mrs. Harley Yoder

3 T. butter
4 T. flour
2 c. tomato juice
1 T. minced onion

1/2 t. celery salt
1 T. sugar
1 t. salt
1/8 t. pepper
1 qt. milk

Brown onion and butter. Add tomato juice and seasonings. Boil milk, flour, and sugar, add some milk to thicken, bring to boil, add rest of milk. Serves 4.

Try putting peanut butter on radishes. Delicious.

CREAM OF TOMATO SOUP
Barbara Jean Hershberger

3 T. butter
4 T. flour
2 c. strained tomatoes
1 T. minced onion
1/4 t. celery salt

1 T. sugar
1 t. salt
1 qt. milk
1/8 t. pepper

Brown onions in butter. Add tomatoes, salt, and pepper. Mix flour and sugar in shaker, and enough milk to form creamy consistency. Shake. Bring tomatoes to boil and slowly stir in thickening. Boil a few minutes, stirring constantly. Very slowly add remaining milk. Heat (do not boil). Serves 6.

VEGETABLE SOUP
Mrs. Allen E. Yoder

3 lbs. hamburger
1 1/2 lg. onions, chopped
1 qt. snap beans
2 qts. whole kernel corn
1 1/2 pts. butter beans
1 qt. okra, cut
1 qt. tomato juice
2 qts. chunk tomatoes

6 sm. carrots, sliced
3 lg. potatoes, diced
6 beef bouillon cubes, dissolved
2/3 c. sugar
4 t. Shoney's Big Boy seasoning
Salt, pepper, Italian seasoning,
    and Accent to suit your taste.

Fry hamburger and onions. Drain off grease. add remaining ingredients and add water to cover. Boil till done. Serve. This may also be frozen for future use.

Delicious, tastes like Shoney's!

BEEF VEGETABLE SOUP
Mrs. Bertha Yoder

1 lb. ground beef
1/2 c. chopped onion
1 pkg. Hamburger Helper mix
    for beef noodle
5 c. water
1 bay leaf

1/4 t.salt
1/8 t. pepper
1-16 oz. can whole tomatoes
1-10 oz. pkg. frozen mixed
    vegetables or 2 c. cooked
    vegetables
1 sm. pkg. wide noodles

Cook and stir ground beef and onions in Dutch oven until beef is brown; drain. Stir in Hamburger Helper mix, water, bay leaf, salt, pepper, and tomatoes (with juice) - break up tomatoes with fork. Heat to boiling, stirring constantly. Reduce heat; cover and simmer, stirring constantly, 10 min. Stir in noodles and vegetables; cover and cook 10 min. longer. Serves 5 or 6.

BARBEQUE SANDWICHES

Sadie A. Yoder

3 lbs. hamburger
3 lbs. beef (boiled) or
  1 qt. canned chunk beef
1½ c. catsup
1 onion, chopped

¼ c. Worcestershire sauce
¼ c. brown sugar
2 cans chicken gumbo soup
Salt and pepper to taste

Brown hamburger and onion; drain. Boil beef until tender and break into string bits. Combine beef and hamburger and add other ingredients. Simmer for 45 min. to an hour over low heat. This lets the flavor become savory throughout mixture. This can be used right away for sandwiches or frozen for later use.

GOOEY LOUEY SANDWICHES

Mrs. Bertha Yoder

2 lbs. bologna
8 medium pickles
½ lb. Cheddar cheese

1 T. mustard
3 T. mayonnaise

Grind bologna, cheese, and pickles together, then add remaining ingredients. Mix well. Fill wiener buns. Wrap each in tin foil and bake. Makes 12 sandwiches.

GOOEY BUNS

Mrs. Sol Yoder

1 lb. big bologna
½ lb. American cheese

½ c. mustard
⅓ c. salad dressing
2 T. relish

Grind bologna and cheese, add remaining ingredients and mix well. Spread buns with mixture and wrap in foil. Heat in slow oven 325° for 25 min. Fills approximately 12 buns.

Insert a teaspoon in the toe of your nylons when hanging them on the line to prevent blowing and snagging.

HOT DOGS IN A BLANKET
Ruth Yoder

10 hot dogs   1 can crescent rolls
Pimento cheese

Slit hot dogs and put pimento cheese in middle. Securely wrap the roll around the hot dog and bake on cookie sheet at 425° until brown.

PIGS IN THE BLANKET
Lorene Plank

10 hot dogs   2 cans biscuits

Cut hot dogs in half. Take 1 biscuit to each half of a hot dog and wrap it securely. Bake on cookie sheet until brown (Oven temperature - same as on biscuit can). Eat with catsup, mustard, or barbeque sauce. This is very simple and delicious.

HOT SANDWICHES
Lela Brenneman

1 lb. hamburger   12 slices toast
1 onion   2 eggs
1 t. salt   1 c. milk
1/3 c. catsup   6 hot dogs
                               Cheese

Mix with hamburger, 1 onion, salt, catsup. toast 1/2 of bread and butter both sides. Put in cake pan. Put 1/3 c. hamburger on each toast, a slice of cheese, hot dogs, cut lengthwise. Butter the rest of toast and put on top, butter-side up. Beat eggs and add milk. Pour over toast before baking. Bake at 350° for 40-50 min. Serves 6.

HOT SPAM & CHEESE SANDWICHES
Ruth Yoder

1-12 oz. can Spam   1/2 lb. Cheddar cheese

Grind Spam and cheese and mix together. Put on open-face hamburger bun. Place under broiler until bubbly. 350°.

HOT SPAM PIZZA
Ruth Yoder

1 loaf Spam
1 sm. onion

½ lb. Cheddar cheese
1 can cream of mushroom soup

Grind together Spam, onion and cheese. Stir in mushroom soup. Fill hamburger buns with mixture and wrap in foil and heat for 1/2 hr. at 200°.

PIZZA BURGERS
Mrs. Sol Yoder

½ lb. luncheon meat (bologna)
⅓ c. Velveeta cheese
    or Swiss
1 lb. ground beef (brown)
1 T. dry parsley

1-#3 can spaghetti sauce
    (1½ c.)
½ t. salt
½ t. sage (optional)
2¼ t. oregano

Grind or chop the meat fine. Cut cheese in small pieces. Combine meat and cheese and remaining ingredients. Spread each half of bun face up. Broil in oven until done. Put buns together and serve. Makes enough for approximately 2 doz. buns.

PIZZA BURGERS NO. 2
Mrs. Cris Miller

2 lbs. hamburger
1 lb. bologna
1 lb. Velveeta cheese
¼ lb. pepperoni

1 pt. pizza sauce
1 T. sugar
1 t. salt
¼ t. pepper

Fry hamburger, drain, set aside to cool. Grind bologna, cheese, and pepperoni. Mix pizza sauce, sugar, salt and pepper. Mix all ingredients real well. Spread on halves of hamburger buns. Place in oven at 350° for 15 min.

Coat inside of cracked vases with hot paraffin.
It stops leaks.

PIZZA BURGERS   Mary M. Yoder

1 lb. ground beef   1 t. oregano
1/3 c. Parmesan cheese   1 t. salt
1/4 c. chopped onion   Dash of pepper
2/3 c. tomato paste

Mix all ingredients together and form into patties. Place on barbecue grill. When done, place patties in hamburger buns and top with a slice of mozzarella cheese.

PIZZA BURGERS Mrs. Ernest W. Yoder, Mrs. William N. Yoder,
Mrs. Leslie Yoder, Mrs. Noah Yoder,
Mrs. Milton Yoder, Kathy Hostetler

1 lb. ground beef   1/4 t. garlic salt
1 sm. onion, chopped   1/4 t. oregano
1-8 oz. can pizza sauce   1/2 lb. American cheese
1 sm. can mushrooms (drained)   (pizza cheese)
                                 Salt and pepper

Mix browned hamburger, onion, salt and pepper to taste. Add mushrooms, spices, and pizza sauce; cool before adding cheese. Spread on halves of hamburger buns or on English muffins. Place under broiler until cheese is bubbly and edges of buns are toasted.

SLOPPY JOES   Bertha Swartzentruber

2 lbs. ground beef   3/4 c. tomato juice
1/2 t. garlic salt   2 medium onions (chopped)
1 T. mustard   Salt and pepper to taste
1/4 c. brown sugar

Mix all this together and cook over low heat for 2 1/2 hrs. Serves 12.

*Correct a too salted dish - place a cloth over boiling pot,
sprinkle with flour and leave for a short while - as the steam
comes in contact with the flour, it will remove the salt.*

SLOPPY JOES

Mrs. Floyd E. Yoder

2 lbs. hamburger
1 onion
1/2 c. catsup
2 T. brown sugar

2 T. vinegar
2 t. prepared mustard
1 t. Worcestershire sauce
1 t. salt

Brown hamburger and onion. Stir until smooth and then add all the other ingredients. Simmer about 20 min. and serve with hamburger rolls. Serves 8.

SUPPER SANDWICH BAKE

Sadie A. Yoder

12 slices bread
Butter or margarine
1 lb. lean ground beef
1/4 c. catsup
1 T. salt

6 frankfurters
6 medium-sized onions, sliced
6 slices American cheese
2 beaten eggs
1 c. milk

Spread 6 slices of bread with butter, arrange in bottom of greased 13x9x2" pan. Toast in moderate oven, 350° for 15 min. Combine beef, catsup, and salt, and spread over toast, 1/3 c. per sandwich. Top with frankfurters, cut in thirds lengthwise. Add onion and cheese slices. Top with remaining slices. Combine eggs and milk, pour over bread. Bake in oven about 50 min. Serves 6.

TACO BURGERS

Mary Plank

1 env. Lipton onion, beefy
  onion, or beef flavor
  mushroom soup mix
2 lbs. ground beef

1/2 c. finely-chopped green pepper
1 medium potato, chopped
2 t. chili powder

In large bowl, combine all ingredients, mix thoroughly. Shape in 12 oblong burgers. Grill or broil until done. Serve, if desired, in taco shells or hot dog rolls and top with lettuce, Cheddar cheese and olives. Serves 12.

TUNA BURGERS

Mrs. Isaac Plank

1 lg. can tuna   1 T. chopped onion
1 can cream of mushroom soup   1 T. chopped green pepper

Mix together and spread on hamburger buns. Butter the top of each bun and place sandwich on cookie sheet. Put in oven at 350° till browned. Serves 8.

SANDWICH LOAF

Laura K. Yoder

SALMON FILLING:
1-7¾ oz. can salmon
⅓ c. dairy sour cream
¼ c. thinly-sliced celery
2 T. minced green onion
2 T. pickle relish
PARSLEY BUTTER FILLING:
1 stick butter
¼ c. snipped fresh parsley
2 t. fresh lemon juice

1 t. Worcestershire sauce
1 t. prepared mustard
2 hard-cooked eggs (finely
    chopped)
CHEDDAR CHEESE FILLING:
1½ c. (6 oz.) shredded
    Cheddar cheese
¼ c. butter
¼ c. chopped pecans
3 T. milk
Butter, softened
1 loaf unsliced white bread

To prepare Salmon Filling: Combine all ingredients and mix well. Chill.
To prepare Parsley Butter Filling: Cream butter, mix in parsley, lemon juice, Worcestershire sauce and mustard, gently fold in eggs, chill.
To prepare Sandwich Loaf: Remove crusts from bread. Cut into 4 slices lengthwise. Roll each slice with a rolling pin to flatten. Spread one side of each slice with butter. Top buttered side of bottom slice with Salmon Filling, spread second slice with Parsley Butter Filling and third slice with Cheddar Filling. Reassemble loaf. Place last slice of bread over Cheddar Filling. Frost and cover with plastic wrap. Chill thoroughly 2 hrs. before serving.

FROSTING:
2-8 oz. pkgs. cream cheese   ⅓ c. dairy sour cream

To prepare Frosting, beat cream cheese and sour cream until light and fluffy. Spread on sides and top of chilled Sandwich Loaf. Serves 16.

VEGETABLES

ASPARAGUS EGG MEDLEY   Mrs. Levi Kauffman

1-#2 can asparagus
5 hard-cooked eggs
4 T. butter
4 T flour

1½ c. rich milk
1 t. salt
⅛ t. pepper
3 c. buttered bread cubes

Brown bread crumbs in butter. Make a white sauce of 4 T. butter, 4 T. flour and milk. Add salt and pepper. Chop eggs and add eggs and asparagus to white sauce. Put half of bread cubes in 1 qt. casserole, pour asparagus mixture in bowl and cover with remaining bread cubes and bake at 350° for 45 min.

BAKED BEANS   Linda Weaver, Mrs. Ruth Weaver

1 lg. can pork & beans
1 T. Worcestershire sauce
2 to 3 T. brown sugar

¾ to 1 c. tomato catsup
1 lg. onion (cut fine)
1 to 1½ t. mustard

Mix in 3 strips of bacon (broken in small pieces). Bake at 350° for 1½ hrs. After baking 1 hr. watch so it won't get too brown on top.

BAKED BEANS   Mrs. Samuel Nisly

1 lg. can pork and beans
3 T. brown sugar
¼ t. dry mustard
½ c. chopped onions

1 T. molasses
1 t. Worcestershire sauce
1-6 oz. can tomato paste

Mix well. Top with bacon. Bake at 350° for 1 hr.

Write your grocery list on an envelope.
Carry coupons in the envelope.
Bring trading stamps home in it.

MOM'S BAKED BEANS

Verda Overholt

1 lb. Great Northern beans
or 4 sm. cans Great Northern
beans, drained
1 lb. bacon

2 c. catsup
1 1/2 c. brown sugar
3/4 c. pancake syrup

Soak dried beans overnight in cold water. In the morning drain and add 2 qts. fresh water. Cook till almost tender; drain off liquid. Fry. Cut up bacon lightly, add to beans, bacon and drippings, catsup, sugar and syrup. If using canned beans, drain and add rest of ingredients and bake at 350° for 1 1/2 hrs.

LIMA BEAN CASSEROLE Mrs. Alva Yoder, Lena Swartzentruber

2 slices bacon, diced
1 medium onion, chopped
1/2 green pepper, chopped

1-17 oz. can lima beans
1 c. cooked tomatoes
2 t. sugar
1/2 t. salt - dash of pepper

Saute bacon, onion and pepper until slightly browned. Pour undrained lima beans and tomatoes in casserole dish. Add sugar, salt, pepper and bacon mixture. Mix well and bake at 300° for 40 min.

MEXICAN REFRIED BEANS

Lena Yoder

16 oz. pinto beans
1/2 lb. bacon or ham fat

2 qts. water
Salt to taste
Hot sauce

Wash beans thoroughly, soak overnight. Add 1/2 lb. bacon or ham fat and 2 qts. water. Simmer for 1 to 1 1/2 hrs. Salt to taste. Mash and continue simmering 1/2 hr. Serve with hot sauce and flour tortillas. Serves 6.

Sad fact of life - square meals make round people.

286

MEXICAN REFRIED BEANS

Sadie A. Yoder

1 lb. dried pinto, or kidney
   beans - soak overnight
Add 6 c. water

2 c. onions
½ c. hot bacon grease
Salt to taste

Bring to boil the beans and onions, cover and simmer slowly until beans are tender; about 3 hrs. Mash beans with potato masher, then add bacon grease (hot) and salt. Mix well, continue cooking, stirring frequently, until beans are thickened and grease is absorbed. Serve at once or refrigerate for later use.

BROCCOLI CASSEROLE

Christ Inhulsen

2 boxes chopped broccoli
1 pkg. cream cheese
¼ c. bacon bits

1 can cream of onion soup
1 c. crushed Ritz crackers

Cook broccoli and drain. Mix all ingredients (except crackers), put in casserole. Cover with Ritz crackers, dot with butter and bake at 350° for 30 min.

BROCCOLI CASSEROLE

Bertha G. Yoder

2-10 oz. pkgs. frozen broccoli
1 can cream of mushroom soup
1 c. grated cheese

¾ c. mayonnaise
2 eggs, beaten
2 T. chopped onions

Cook broccoli for 10 min. and drain. Pour into buttered casserole and layer cream of mushroom soup, cheese, mayonnaise, eggs and onions. Sprinkle ½ c. crushed soda crackers on top. Bake in medium-size casserole at 350° for 30 min. Serves 4 to 5.

*The girl who searches too long for a smart cookie
is apt to wind up with a crumb.*

BROCCOLI CASSEROLE

Ruby Swartzentruber

1 pkg. chopped broccoli
1/2 c. chopped celery
1/2 c. chopped onions
1/4 c. margarine

1 can cream of mushroom soup
1-8 oz. Cheez Whiz
1 1/2 c. Minute rice
Ritz cracker crumbs

Pour 1 c. boiling water over broccoli and let stand. Fry celery and onions in margarine until tender. Add broccoli with water and soup. Pour in 1 1/2 qt. casserole dish. Sprinkle Ritz cracker crumbs over top and bake at 350° for 30-40 min.

BROCCOLI CASSEROLE

Lena Swartzentruber

1 lb. Velveeta cheese
1 c. butter

4 boxes frozen broccoli, well
  drained
8 oz. Ritz crackers

Melt 1 stick butter and cheese. Add to broccoli. Crush crackers. Melt 1 stick butter and mix with crackers. Put broccoli mixture in baking dish and put cracker crumbs on top and bake at 350° for 1 hr.

BROCCOLI & BEAN BAKE

Mrs. Paul E. Yoder
and Mrs. Ernest W. Yoder

1-10 oz. pkg. frozen lima beans
1-20 oz. pkg. chopped broccoli
1-10 1/2 oz. can cream of
  mushroom soup

8 oz. commercial sour cream
1/2 pkg. dry onion soup mix

TOPPING:
3 c. Rice Krispies, browned in butter

Cook lima beans and broccoli until tender. Pour other ingredients into vegetables and mix together. Pour into 2 qt. casserole and top with browned Rice Krispies. Cover and bake at 350° for 45 min.

BROCCOLI-CORN BAKE
Alma Yoder

1 lb. cream-style corn
1-10 oz. pkg. frozen chopped broccoli, cooked & drained
1 egg, beaten
1/2 c. coarse cracker crumbs

1/4 c. chopped onion
1/2 t. salt
Dash of pepper
5 T. melted butter or oleo, divided
1 c. bread cubes

In mixing bowl, combine corn, cooked broccoli, egg, cracker crumbs, onion, salt, pepper and 3 T. melted butter. Pour into 2 qt. casserole. Combine bread cubes and remaining 2 T. butter. Sprinkle on top of corn mixture. Bake, uncovered, at 350° for 35-40 min. Serves 6 to 8.

BROCCOLI-RICE CASSEROLE
Ruth Yoder

1/2 c. mayonnaise
1 onion, chopped
2 cans cream of mushroom soup
8 oz. Cheez Whiz

1 c. water
2 pkgs. frozen broccoli
2 c. uncooked Minute rice

Cook broccoli according to directions. Saute onions in margarine, add all ingredients and bake at 300° for 30 min.

BAKED CORN
Ruth Yoder

1 pt. cream-style corn
2 eggs, well beten
2 T. sugar
2 T. flour

1 t. baking powder
1 t. salt
1 c. milk
2 T. butter

Mix corn, eggs, sugar, flour, baking powder and salt. Gradually add milk. Put in greased baking dish. Dot with butter. Bake at 350° for 50 min.

No one has ever choked to death from swallowing his pride.

BAKED CORN

Mrs. Sol Yoder

1 qt. frozen corn
1 c. cracker crumbs
1/2 c. celery
1/2 c. onion (chopped)

2/3 c. Velveeta cheese
1 t. salt
2 beaten eggs
1 c. milk (use less milk
   if corn has liquid)

Put first 6 ingredients in layers in 2 qt. casserole; pour milk and eggs over it. Bake at 350° for 20 min.

SCALLOPED CORN

Ruth Yoder

2 c. cooked corn
1 c. milk
3 T. melted butter
1/2 t. salt
2/3 c. cracker crumbs

1/8 t. pepper
1 T. sugar
2 eggs
1 t. minced onion

Beat the eggs and add milk and crumbs. Add the corn, onion, seasoning, and melted butter. Mix together well and pour in a greased casserole. Bake at 350° for 40 min. Serves 6.

FRITTATA

Laura Whitt

1/2 c. finely-chopped onions
1 T. butter
8 eggs
1/2 c. milk
1 t. salt
1 t. Worcestershire sauce

4 to 5 drops hot pepper sauce
   (optional)
2 c. rice (cooked)
1-4 oz. can green chilies
   (undrained)
1 medium tomato, chopped
1/2 c. shredded Cheddar cheese

In 10" skillet, over medium-high heat, cook onions in butter until tender. Beat eggs with milk and seasoning. Stir in 2 c. cooked rice, chilies, and tomato. Pour in pan. Reduce heat to medium-low. Cover. Cook until top is almost set, 12-15 min. Sprinkle with cheese, cover, remove from heat, and let set 10 min. Serves 4.

OKRA AND TOMATOES
Mary Lois Yoder

3 slices bacon
2 lbs. okra, sliced
1 medium green pepper
(chopped)

1 sm. onion, chopped
2 lbs. fresh tomatoes, peeled
and cubed)
Salt and pepper to taste

Fry bacon until crisp; cook okra in drippings, add pepper, onion, tomatoes and bacon. Add salt and pepper. Cover and simmer 15 min. Serves 8.

BAKED FILLED POTATOES
Ellen R. Brenneman

8 medium potatoes
5 T. butter
Salt and pepper to taste

½ c. milk
1 c. grated cheese

Cut off tops of potatoes after baking them in 9x13" pan at 350° for 1 hr. Scoop out pulp and mix with rest of ingredients. Fill potato shells, then bake for 20 min. again. Serves 8.

BAKED STUFFED POTATOES
Bertha Swartzentruber

3 lg. baking potatoes
Vegetable oil
¼ c. butter, melted
¼ c. milk
3 T. sour cream
2 T. chopped onion

1½ t. parsley flakes
¼ t. dry mustard
⅛ t. salt
⅛ t. pepper
2 slices American cheese (grated)
Paprika

Scrub potatoes well and rub skins with oil; bake at 400° for 1 hr., or until done. Allow potatoes to cool to touch. Cut potatoes in half lengthwise, carefully scoop out pulp, leaving shells intact. Spoon pulp in a mixing bowl. Add remaining ingredients except cheese snd paprika. Beat till fluffy. Stuff shells with potato mixture, garnish with cheese and sprinkle with paprika. Bake at 400° for 15 min. Serves 6.

STUFFED POTATOES

Ruth Yoder

4 baked potatoes
4 slices bacon
4 T. butter

$\frac{1}{2}$ c. sour cream
Salt and pepper to taste
Cheese

Cut potatoes in half and scoop out pulp. Mix with sour cream and butter, salt and pepper. Mix well. Add more milk if desired. Add bacon, and stuff potato shells with mixture. Dot with butter and sprinkle with paprika. Place under broiler until warm and brown. These may be prepared ahead and heated before serving. Serves 8.

MAKE-AHEAD POTATOES

Mrs. Elmer M. Yoder (Esther)

12 lg. potatoes, peeled &
  boiled in salt water
1-8 oz. pkg. cream cheese,
  softened
1-8 oz. carton sour cream

1 t. onion powder
$\frac{1}{4}$ c. melted margarine
Paprika

Combine cooked potatoes, sour cream, cream cheese and onion powder and whip or mash until fluffy. Add a small amount of milk if necessary. Spread in a buttered 9x13" pan and refrigerate or freeze until needed. When ready to use, drizzle melted margarine over top and sprinkle with paprika. Bake at 350° for 1 hr. Delicious with any meat and no gravy is needed.

REFRIGERATOR MASHED POTATOES

Alta Kauffman

5 lbs. potatoes
6 oz. cream cheese
1 c. sour cream
2 T. butter

2 t. onion salt
1 t. salt
$\frac{1}{4}$ t. pepper

Cook and mash potatoes. Add all ingredients except butter. Put in a casserole, dot with butter. You may mix this and keep up to a week in the refrigerator or it may be frozen also. When ready to use, bake at 325° till heated through.

A well-beaten egg white added to mashed potatoes will add to the looks and taste of the dish.

"Seven prayerless days makes one weak."

SCALLOPED POTATO BAKE
Kathryn Yoder

3 T. butter or margarine
3 T. flour
2 c. milk
4 to 5 lg. baking potatoes

1 lg. onion, chopped
1 c. cubed, cooked ham
1 t. salt
1/4 t. pepper
4 c. (1 lb.) shredded American
cheese

Melt butter in a heavy saucepan over low heat; add flour, stirring until smooth. Cook 1 min., stirring constantly. Gradually stir in milk; cook over medium heat, stirring constantly, until thickened and bubbly. Peel and cut potatoes into 1/4' slices. Layer 1/2 of potato slices, onion, ham, salt, pepper, cheese and white sauce in order given in 1 1/2 qt. casserole dish; repeat. Cover and bake at 350° for 2 hrs. Serves 8.

SCALLOPED POTATOES
Ruth Yoder

2 cans cream of mushroom
soup
1/2 c. milk
1/4 t. pepper
1/2 t. salt

8 c. thinly-sliced potatoes
1/3 c. onions
2 c. Cheddar cheese
2 T. butter

Mix all ingredients together and bake at 375° for 1 hr., uncover, add paprika, and bake 15 more min.

SKILLET HASH BROWNS
Lila Yoder

3 c. cooked potatoes, diced
3 T. flour
1 T. finely-chopped onion

1/4 c. light cream
1 t. salt
1/4 t. pepper

Combine cooked, diced potatoes with flour, onion, cream, salt and pepper and toss lightly to coat. Heat shortening in skillet, enough to cover bottom of skillet. Add potatoes and press down with a spatula. Brown slowly on one side, then turn and brown other side. Serves 4.

You'll have delicious golden fried potatoes if you sprinkle them slightly with flour before frying.

SKILLET-SCALLOPED POTATOES

Shirley Yoder

6 medium potatoes
4 T. shortening
1 medium onion, chopped
1 t. salt

¼ t. pepper
4 T. light cream
⅓ c. sharp cheese

Peel potatoes; slice thinly. Heat shortening in large skillet. Add potatoes, onion and seasonings. Fry potatoes slowly over low heat till golden brown, turning frequently. Pour on cream; add cheese, stirring gently to mix. Cover; cook slowly 10 min. or until potatoes are tender.

CANDIED SWEET POTATOES

Linda Yoder

5 medium sweet potatoes
1 t. salt
1 c. brown sugar
2 T. butter

3 T. flour
1 c. thin cream
½ c. nuts (chopped)
8 marshmallows

Cook potatoes till tender, drain and cool. Cut lengthwise and arrange in greased dish. Mix salt, sugar and flour. Pour over sweet potatoes. Dot with butter, marshmallows and nuts. Pour cream over all. Bake at 350° for 30 min.

ORANGE GLAZED SWEET POTATOES

Mrs. Melvin (Katherine) Yoder

6 medium sweet potatoes
1 T. cornstarch
2 t. grated orange peel
2 T. butter

⅔ c. brown sugar
1 t. salt
1 c. orange juice
Add pecans

Heat oven to 350°. Pare sweet potatoes, cut each lengthwise in half. Arrange in ungreased casserole. In small saucepan, stir together sugar, cornstarch, salt, and orange peel. Slowly stir orange juice into sugar mixture, add butter. Cook, stirring constantly, until mixture thickens and boils. Boil and stir 1 min. Pour hot orange juice mixture over sweet potatoes in casserole. Cover, bake 1 hr. Serves 4 to 6.

*Grease the lip of the cream or milk pitcher with butter
to prevent the drip.*

SUNDAY SWEET POTATOES   Mrs. Eli Hostetler

STEP 1:
3 c. mashed sweet potatoes
1 c. sugar
½ c. milk
2 eggs
1 t. vanilla

STEP 2:
1 c. coconut
1 c. chopped nuts
1 c. brown sugar
⅓ c. flour
⅓ c. melted butter

Combine Step 1 ingredients and put in casserole dish. Top with Step 2. Blend Step 2, add butter last. Sprinkle mixture over mashed potatoes. Bake at 350° until brown.

SWEET POTATO CASSEROLE Katie Hershberger

2 c. mashed sweet potatoes
½ stick butter or margarine
1 c. sugar
2 T. flour
½ t. salt
1 t. vanilla
2 eggs

1 t. cinnamon
¼ t. nutmeg
2 T. concentrated orange juice
TOPPING:
¾ stick oleo
1¼ c. brown sugar
1 c. chopped nuts

Mix all together and put topping on top. Bake in 2 qt. casserole at 350° for 1 hr.

SWEET POTATO SOUFFLE CRUNCH   Kathryn Yoder,
Lena Swartzentruber, Mrs. Leslie Yoder,
Mrs. Ivan Yoder, Mrs. Nelson Yoder,
and Mrs. Eli Kauffman

3 c. cooked mashed sweet
   potatoes
1 c. sugar
½ t. salt
2 eggs, slightly beaten
2½ T. melted butter
½ c. milk
1 t. vanilla

CRUNCH:
2½ T. melted butter
1 c. brown sugar
⅓ c. flour
1 c. chopped pecans

Mix all together and pour into a 9x13″ baking dish. Cover with Crunch and bake at 350° for 45 min. Serves 6 to 8.

SWEET POTATO SOUFFLE

Mrs. Milton Yoder

3 lbs. sweet potatoes
2 T. melted butter
1/2 c. cream *whipping*
1/2 c. brown sugar

1/2 t. vanilla
3 beaten eggs
Dash of salt
Cinnamon and nutmeg

TOPPING:
1/4 c. flour
Pecans

1/4 stick butter
3/4 c. brown sugar

Cook, peel, and mash potatoes. Add remaining ingredients, except Topping, and put in greased 9x13" baking dish. Spread Topping on top of potatoes. Bake at 325° for 1/2 hr.

BROWN RICE

Laura Whitt

1 stick butter
1 can beef broth

1 c. uncooked rice
1 can onion soup

Brown rice in butter. Add broth and onion soup. Pour into baking dish and bake at 350° for 45 min., or until rice is soft.

RICE CASSEROLE

Elsie N. Yoder

1 c. uncooked rice
1 can broth bouillon soup
1 stick butter

1 onion, chopped
1 sm. can mushrooms, cut in
  small pieces

Mix all ingredients and put in casserole and bake at 350° for 45 min.

RICE AND MUSHROOMS

Mrs. Allen M. Yoder

1 lb. rice (2 c.)
2 sm. onions, chopped
1/4 c. bell peppers
1 stick butter

1 sm. can mushrooms
1 can beef consomme
2 soup cans of water
1 cube beef bouillon

Fry onions and peppers in butter. Mix all ingredients together and put in 3 qt. pan. Bake at 350° for 1 hr. and 15 min. Serves 15.

The fire you kindle for your enemy
often burns yourself more than him.

MEXICAN RICE

Miriam Brenneman

2 T. cooking oil
1 c. uncooked rice
2 c. tomato juice
2 c. water
1½ t. garlic salt
1 t. cumin

Brown uncooked rice in cooking oil in skillet. Mix tomato juice, water, garlic salt and cumin. Add to rice. Cook slowly, without stirring, until light and fluffy.

RICE SQUARES

Lila Yoder

3 c. cooked rice
1 c. shredded cheese
⅓ c. chopped onion
½ c. chopped celery
1 T. salt
3 eggs
1½ c. milk
1 T. parsley flakes

Mix all together and turn into buttered 2 qt. baking dish. Bake at 350° for 30 min. or until set. Serve with chicken and gravy.

SQUASH CASSEROLE

Mary M. Yoder

3 c. cooked squash
2 eggs
1 T. margarine
2 c. crushed Ritz crackers
1 can cream of chicken soup
1 medium mild onion, chopped
2 c. mild American cheese, grated
1 T. milk
½ t. salt

Mix all ingredients together (drain squash). Grease 3 qt. baking pan or casserole dish. Bake at 350° for 30-40 min. until browned on top.

SQUASH CASSEROLE

Bertha G. Yoder

2 c. cooked squash
1 can cream of chicken soup
2 beaten eggs
½ c. chopped onions
2 T. margarine
7 to 8 slices bread (crumbled)
½ c. grated cheese
Salt and pepper to taste

Cook squash (not using much water). Mix squash, soup, eggs, onions, margarine, salt and pepper, bread and ¼ c. cheese together. Pour into buttered medium casserole and top with remaining cheese. Bake at 350° for 30 min. Serves 4 to 5.

SQUASH CASSEROLE   Mrs. Crist Yoder, Jr., Vernie Weaver

2 c. cooked and mashed squash
1 c. milk
1 stick butter, melted
2 eggs, beaten
1 c. soda cracker crumbs

1/2 t. salt
1/4 t. pepper
1 T. sugar
1 sm. onion, chopped
1 c. grated cheese

Mix in order given and bake in 2 qt. casserole at 350° for 30-40 min. until firm. Keep 1/2 of cheese to put on top after baked and return to oven till melted. Use more or less cheese to suit your taste. Serves 12.

SQUASH CASSEROLE Mrs. Rufus L. Yoder, Mrs. Bertha Yoder, Verda Overholt, Jr.

1 qt. cooked squash
3 T. onion
1/2 c. milk
1 can cream of mushroom soup
Salt and pepper to taste

2 eggs
1/2 c. butter or margarine
1 c. cracker crumbs (preferable Ritz)
1 c. grated cheese (save 1/2 c. for top)
Bread crumbs

Put crackers and milk together. Drain squash. Add everything together and add bread crumbs and 1/2 c. cheese on top. Bake in 9x9" pan or 2 qt. casserole at 350° for 30 min. Serves 12.

BAKED TOMATOES   Mrs. Melvin (Katherine) Yoder

2 c. peeled tomatoes
1/2 c. brown sugar
Salt and pepper

Butter (1/2 stick)
1/2 c. water
2 T. clear gel or cornstarch

Cook the tomatoes with sugar, pepper, salt, and oleo; thicken with clear gel and water. Bake with bread crumbs and cheese at 350° for 30 min.

Rub chigger bites with an aspirin tablet, slightly dampened.

BAKING POWDER

Ruth Yoder

2 t. cream of tartar
1 t. baking soda

1 t. cornstarch

Mix well and store in airtight container.

BEST-EVER BARBECUE SAUCE

Alma Yoder

1/3 c. salad oil
1/3 c. melted butter
1/3 c. vinegar
1 c. orange juice
1/4 c. catsup
1/4 c. finely-chopped onion

1/4 c. Worcestershire sauce
2 t. hot sauce
2 t. salt
1 t. cayenne pepper
1/4 t. oregano
1/8 t. chili powder (optional)
2 T. sugar

Combine all ingredients in 1 1/2 qt. saucepan and bring to a boil. Lower heat and simmer 10 min. Makes 2 1/2 c. of barbecue sauce.

"Sauce is good on chicken, pork chops or ribs."

BARBECUE SAUCE

Naomi Yoder

1/4 c. oil
1/4 c. chopped onions
1 T. brown sugar
1 T. Worcestershire sauce
1/4 t. paprika

1/2 t. salt
1/4 c. lemon juice
1 c hot water
1 c. catsup

Fry onions in oil till brown. Add remaining ingredients and bring to a full boiling point. Cook 2 min.

This sauce is good to pour over grilled hamburgers or cubed raw steaks, then bake for 1 1/2 hrs.

"Whether therefore ye eat, or drink, or whatsoever ye do,
do all to the Glory of God."
I Cor. 10:31

Notes

MISCELLANEOUS

BASTING SAUCE FOR BARBECUED CHICKEN

The Allen E. Yoder Family

1 c. water	1 c. oil
2 c. vinegar	2 T. salt
2 t. pepper	

Mix all ingredients and bring to a good boil. Before putting on the grill, coat chicken real well with this sauce. Grill 10 min. on a side and turn. After turning twice, baste with Dad's Barbecue Sauce and keep turning and brushing with barbecue sauce till tender.

DAD'S BARBECUE SAUCE:

1 c. butter	2 t. salt
1 c. vinegar	3 T. mustard
2¼ c. catsup	Dash of red pepper
7 T. Worcestershire sauce	Juice of 1 lemon
3 T. hot sauce	

Melt margarine; add vinegar and other ingredients. Bring to boil and let simmer for a few min.

One batch will barbecue 1½ chickens.

SAUCE FOR GRILLED CHICKEN

Mrs. Stanley Yoder,
Naomi Yoder

1 c. vinegar	7 t. salt
1 c. water	1 t. pepper
¼ lb. butter	¼ c. Worcestershire sauce

Put all ingredients in saucepan and heat till hot. Dip chicken in sauce and put on grill. Keep dipping chicken in sauce every few minutes till chicken is done. Steam chicken in oven on low heat ½ to 1 hr.

BEEF STROGANOFF MIX

Mrs. Chris L Miller

¼ c. flour	1 T. nonfat dry milk
1 T. grated Parmesan cheese	2 t. dehydrated onion
2 t. instant bouillon	Pinch of garlic salt

Mix all ingredients in blender. Store in airtight container.

CARAMEL POPCORN Mrs. Levi Kauffman, Miriam Brenneman,
Mrs. Elmer M. Yoder (Esther)

2 c. brown sugar
1/2 c. white Karo
1 c. margarine
1 c. pecans or peanuts

1 t. salt
1/2 t. soda
8 qts. popped corn

Bring all ingredients to a boil, except soda and popcorn. Cook for 5 min. Remove from heat and add soda and stir thoroughly. Pour over popcorn and nuts in a large pan or roaster and stir well. Bake uncovered at 250° for 1 hr. Stir while cooling. Store in airtight container. Freezes well.

CHEESE SPREAD Mrs. Henry Overholt, Sr.

2 lb. box Velveeta cheese
2-8 oz. pkgs. cream cheese
2 T. liquid smoke
1 T. Worcestershire sauce

1 t. minced onion
1/2 t. or more smoked or
seasoned salt
1 pkg. smoked beef, cut fine

Take 1-2 lb. box Velveeta cheese and 2-8 oz. pkgs. cream cheese. Put in bowl, place over hot water till cheese is soft. Add liquid smoke, Worcestershire sauce, minced onion, and salt. Mix well with mixer. Add smoked beef or anything else you prefer (Lebanon bologna, etc.). Mix again. Put in small dishes or cups, sprinkle with paprika and parsley. Spread on crackers to eat. Serves 8 to 12.

CHEX SNACK MIX Mrs. Levi Kauffman

2 c. Corn Chex
2 c. Rice Chex
2 c. Wheat Chex
2 c. Bran Chex
1 c. salted mixed nuts

1 c. pretzel sticks
1/2 c. butter or margarine
1 1/4 t. seasoned salt
1 T. soy sauce
1/4 t. onion powder
1/4 t. garlic powder

Melt butter in electric skillet. Stir in seasonings. Blend well. Add Chex, nuts and pretzels. Mix until all pieces are coated. Cover skillet, leaving lid vents open. Heat at 250° for 15 min. Cool on paper towels. Serves 12.

CHOCOLATE SYRUP   Verna Mae Wingard

¹/₂ c. cocoa   1 c. water
2 c. sugar   Pinch of salt

Bring to a boil. Remove from heat and add a little vanilla. Use for chocolate milk or cocoa.

CHOCOLATE SYRUP   Elsie N. Yoder

2 c. sugar   2 c. water
²/₃ c. cocoa   2 T. butter
¹/₄ c. flour   1 T. vanilla
¹/₄ t. salt

Heat to a boiling point.

A thick syrup - good over ice cream.

CORN MEAL MUSH   Mrs. Norman Yoder

2¹/₂ c. water   2 c. plain corn meal (rounded full)
2¹/₂ c. milk   1 t. salt

Bring water to a boil. Mix corn meal and salt into milk and pour into boiling water. Turn to medium heat and stir constantly till thickened. Turn to low heat and boil about 20-25 min. Pour out in 9x5" pan and let cool overnight. Slice in pieces about ¹/₂" thick and fry till golden brown on each side. Serve with tomato gravy or syrup. Makes 1 panful, serves 3 to 4 people.

COUNTRY FRIED CHICKEN BATTER   Verda Overholt, Jr.

2 c. flour   3 t. baking powder
¹/₂ t. salt   1¹/₂ c. milk

Mix well. Dip drained, cooked chicken pieces in batter, then roll in cracker crumbs. Deep fry in hot oil till brown. Celery salt may be added to batter for a more seasoned taste.

EAGLE BRAND MILK

Ramona Yoder

1 c. instant nonfat dry milk solids
²/₃ c. sugar

¹/₃ c. boiling water
3 T. melted butter

In your blender, combine dry milk, sugar, water and butter. Blend until smooth. Store in refrigerator until ready to use. Yields about 14 ounces. Same as canned milk.

GOOD EARTH GRANOLA

Mrs. Henry Overholt, Sr.

3 lbs. rolled oats
¹/₂ lb. rye flakes
¹/₂ lb. triticale flakes (optional)
¹/₂ lb. soy flakes
¹/₂ lb. sesame seeds
1 lb. sunflower seeds
¹/₂ c. almonds
¹/₂ c. peanuts

¹/₂ c. pumpkin seeds
1 c. coconut
2 c. wheat germ
1 c. bran flakes
1¹/₄ c. vegetable oil
1¹/₂ c. raw honey
1¹/₂ c. raisins
1 c. water

Heat and blend water, oil, and honey. Pour over and mix well with dry ingredients. Do not add raisins, wait till cereal is cold. Bake in slow oven, 300° to 325° for ¹/₂ hr. stirring often.

GRANOLA

Ruth Yoder

12 c. rolled oats
6 c. wheat germ
3 c. coconut
3 c. brown sugar

³/₄ t. salt
2 sticks butter (melted)
1 c. water
2 c. nuts

Mix all ingredients together and bake at 300° for 1¹/₂ hrs., stirring every 15 min. Cool, crumble into pieces. Store in containers. Serve with milk.

GRANOLA CEREAL

Mrs. Crist Yoder, Sr.

5 c. quick oats
1/2 c. brown sugar
1/2 c. sesame seeds
1 c. chopped pecans
2 T. water

3/4 c. wheat germ
1/2 c. coconut
1/2 c. honey
2/3 c. vegetable oil
1 1/2 t. vanilla

In a bowl, combine quick oats, brown sugar, wheat germ, coconut, sesame seeds, and nuts, then combine honey, vegetable oil, water and vanilla. Add to oat mixture. Stir to coat ingredients well. Pour into 2 large shallow pans and bake at 300° for 25-30 min. It may take more than 30 min. as it should be slightly toasted. Stir several times while in oven and also while cooling. Crumble into pieces. Store in tight containers.

GRAPE-NUTS

Mrs. Chris L. Miller

4 lbs. brown sugar
8 lbs. whole wheat flour
1 1/4 T. salt
3/4 lb. oleo, melted

1 1/2 t. maple flavoring
2 T. vanilla
2 T. soda
1 1/2 qts. buttermilk or sour milk

Put dry ingredients in bowl. Add milk, oleo and flavorings. Mix well. (May need a little more milk.) The dough should be fairly thick, put in pans and spread evenly. Bake in 350° oven until done - rub Grape-Nuts over 1/4 wire mesh. Spread crumbs in pans and toast to a golden brown, stirring occasionally.

GREASE FOR CAKE PANS

Verda Overholt, Jr.

1 c. cooking oil
1 c. shortening

1 c. flour

Mix well and keep in a tight container in refrigerator.

PLANT FOOD

Mrs. Levi Kauffman

African violets take more water than you think. Give them warm water in a saucer. The following is a good tonic, especially recommended for violets: 1 t. baking powder, 1 t. epsom salts, 1 t. salt petre, 1/2 t. household ammonia in 1 gal. of water. Use this solution once a month.

PLAY DOUGH

Linda Kauffman

1 c. flour
1/2 c. salt
2 t. cream of tartar

1 T. cooking oil
1 c. water
Food coloring

Mix together flour, salt and cream of tartar. Add oil, water and coloring. Cook, stirring for 1 to 3 min. or until thick. Knead almost immediately. Keep in airtight container in refrigerator. This makes a nice, soft play dough and will last up to a year.

PLAY DOUGH FOR CHILDREN

Sadie A. Yoder

2 c. flour
1/2 c. salt

1 T. alum
1 T. liquid shortening

Mix together, then bring 2 c. of water to a boil. Add food color, then pour over flour mixture and stir. It will be lumpy. Knead thoroughly as soon as it is cool enough to handle. Keep in airtight container when not in use. Stays nice for a long time.

RECIPE FOR LIFE

Verda Overholt

1 c. good thoughts
1 c. kind deeds
1 c. consideration

2 c. sacrifice for others
3 c. forgiveness
Then add 2 c. well-beaten faults.

This is to mix thoroughly with tears of joy ad sorrow, as well as plenty of sympathy. Flavor the mixture well with little gifts of love and kindness. Use 4 c. of prayer and faith to lighten the other ingredients and raise the texture to great heights in daily living. Bake well in the heat of human kindness and serve with a smile.

SEASONED SALT

Mrs. Chris L. Miller

1 c. salt
2 T. paprika
1 t. parsley flakes
1 t. dried chives (or onions)
1 t. black pepper
1/2 t. dried marjoram leaves
1/2 t. celery seed

1/2 t. curry powder
1/4 t. garlic powder
1/8 t. cayenne red pepper
1 t. turmeric
1 t. Accent
1 T. sugar

Mix all together in blender and blend about 30 seconds, or until all herbs and seeds are finely chopped.

STAINLESS STEEL CLEANER
Lorene Plank

3 qts. water   3 T. Ivory or Lux soap flakes

Fill a gallon aluminum kettle with 3 qts. of water. Add soap flakes. Bring to a boil and add flatware. Cook for 10 min. Remove from water and rinse in hot water. Rub thoroughly with soft, dry towel.

This is especially good for pieces of silverware difficult to clean.

SOFT MARGARINE
Alta Kauffman

1 lb. Superbrand margarine   3/4 c. corn oil
3/4 c. buttermilk   Dash of salt

Have all ingredients at room temperature, then mix thoroughly in electric mixer. Refrigerate.

SOUR CREAM DRESSING
FOR POTATOES
Lela Brenneman,
Mrs. Floyd E. Yoder, Mrs. Daniel Yoder,
Delores Hostetler, Elsie N. Yoder,
and Mrs. Eli Kauffman

1 c. mayonnaise   1 1/2 T. parsley flakes
1 c. sour cream   1 heaping t. dill weed
1 1/2 T. onion powder   1 1/2 t. seasoned salt

Mix together and serve on baked potatoes.

Any recipe of life must contain a goodly amount of seasoning.

SPAGHETTI SAUCE

Mrs. Marlene Swartzentruber

2 lbs. lean ground beef
1 lg. onion, chopped
1 clove garlic, minced
2-1 lb. cans tomatoes, cut up
1-8 oz. can tomato sauce
1-12 oz. can tomato paste
1 c. beef bouillon

1 T. brown sugar
1 t. dried oregano leaves
1 t. dried basil leaves
1 t. salt
¼ t. pepper
¼ c. chopped bell peppers
2 T. minced parsley

Brown meat with onions and peppers. Drain. Combine remaining ingredients and cook slowly, about 2 to 3 hrs. It also does well in a crock pot, on low for 6 to 8 hrs. can be frozen.

NOODLES

Mrs. Eli Hostetler

1 c. egg yolks
½ c. water
1 T. salt

1 T. oil
Flour

Add enough flour for a **very** stiff dough. Put through noodle roller surfaces 2 times, or until the thickness desired. Then dry the dough a little, then pass it quickly through the cutter rollers.

TOMATO GRAVY

Ruth Yoder

1½ c. tomato juice
A pinch of soda
1 t. salt

1 T. sugar
1½ c. milk
3 T. cornstarch

Boil tomato juice, add a pinch of soda, salt and sugar. Mix cornstarch and milk together, and pour into tomato mixture. Bring to a boil. Serve on scrambled eggs or fried mush. Serves 8.

Freely receive; then freely give.

WINDOW CLEANER
Becky Plank

1 pt. rubbing alcohol   2 t. dishwashing liquid
2 T. ammonia   Food coloring

Mix above ingredients and put in 1 gal. container. Fill with water.

YOGURT
Chris Inhulsen

1 qt. milk   1 t. plain yogurt
1/2 c. powdered milk

Bring milk and powdered milk to a boil. Let cool to 110° to 120° F.
Then add yogurt, stir well, and pour in pre-warmed wide-mouth
thermos and let set overnight.

This makes plain yogurt. Fruits may be added as desired.

MOTHER'S MEDITATIONS

When we are in the kitchen
Busy with cooking and baking
With sugar and cream to enrich
Whatever we are making -

Let us not forget to be thankful.
Let not our minds go astray.
When we fail in one or other,
Or feel our life is all dismay.

We ask Thee not for riches, Lord
Or luxuries and food that's rare.
But to be a better mother
Is our eager earnest prayer.

Make our words a little kinder
Than the ones we spoke today.
Teach us love and understanding
In all we think and do or say.

We ask Thee simply to humble
And lead us in the right road.
Help to guide our children rightly.
Give strength for the day's load.

Notes

INDEX

APPETIZERS & BEVERAGES:

CASSEROLES:
Breakfast Casseroles:

Beef Casseroles:

Fish Casseroles:

Pork Casseroles:

COOKIES & CANDY:
Cookies:

DESSERTS:

MEATS:
Beef:

ORIENTAL FOODS:

PASTRIES & PIES:

SALADS:

SOUPS & SANDWICHES:
Soups:

Sandwiches:

YODER'S DEITSCH HAUS

Hwy. 26 - 3 Miles East of Montezuma

RT. #1, MONTEZUMA, GA
912-472-2024

OPEN TUES. THRU SAT.

SPECIALIZING IN PENNSYLVANIA DUTCH STYLE COOKING
CHURCH GROUPS, MEETINGS, CLUBS

YODERS CATERING SERVICE

MELVIN & RUTH YODER
Montezuma, Georgia
912-472-8921
912-472-6462

HOUSEHOLD HINTS

TABLE OF CONTENTS

INDEX

I. THE KITCHEN

GENERAL

Salt

1. If stew is too salty, add raw cut potatoes and discard once they have cooked and absorbed the salt. Another remedy is to add a teaspoon each of cider vinegar and sugar. Or, simply add sugar.

2. If soup or stew is too sweet, add salt. For a main dish or vegetable, add a teaspoon of cider vinegar.

Gravy

3. For pale gravy, color with a few drops of Kitchen Bouquet. Or to avoid the problem in the first place, brown the flour well before adding the liquid. this also helps prevent lumpy gravy.

4. To make gravy smooth, keep a jar with a mixture of equal parts of flour and cornstarch. Put 3 or 4 tablespoons of this mixture in another jar and add some water. Shake, and in a few minutes you will have a smooth paste for gravy.

5. To remedy greasy gravy, add a small amount of baking soda.

6. For quick thickener for gravies, add some instant potatoes to your gravy and it will thicken beautifully.

Vegetables

7. If fresh vegetables are wilted or blemished, pick off the brown edges. Spinkle with cool water, wrap in towel and refrigerate for an hour or so.

8. Perk up soggy lettuce by adding lemon juice to a bowl of cold water and soak for an hour in the refrigerator.

9. Lettuce and celery will crisp super fast if you place it in a pan of cold water and add a few slices potatoes.

10. If vegetables are overdone, put the pot in a pan of cold water. Let it stand from 15 minutes to 1/2 hour without scraping pan.

11. By lining the crisper section of your refrigerator with newspaper and wrapping vegetables with it, moisture will be absorbed and your vegetables will stay fresher longer.

12. Store leftover corn, peas, green beans, carrots, celery, potatoes and onions in a container in the freezer. Add to other ingredients when making stew.

13. To keep the flavor in the vegetables, add a small amount of sugar to the water after cooking carrots, peas, beets, and corn.

14. Onions, broccoli and Brussels sprouts will cook faster if you make an X-shaped cut at the base of the vegetable.

Eggs

15. If you shake the egg and you hear a rattle, you can be sure it's stale. A really fresh egg will sink and a stale one will float.

16. If you are making deviled eggs and want to slice it perfectly, dip the knife in water first. The slice will be smooth with no yolk sticking to the knife.

17. The white of an egg is easiest to beat when it's at room temperature. So leave it out of the refrigerator about a half an hour before using it.

18. To make light and fluffy scrambled eggs, add a little water while beating the eggs.

19. Add vinegar to the water while boiling eggs. Vinegar helps to seal the egg, since it acts on the calcium in the shell.

20. STORING EGGS: 1. Place your eggs in those tight-sealing egg containers and they will last longer in the refrigerator. You really shouldn't keep eggs longer than 11 days. 2. Cover them with oil on the top in a sealed contained in the refrigerator. 3. For long-term storage: If there's a special on eggs at your local supermarket, you can take advantage of it. Just crack all the eggs open and put them in the freezer unit. To use one egg at a time, put single eggs in the ice tray. When frozen, put the egg cubes in a sealed pastic bag. You can take out the cubes one at a time for daily use. If you use eggs in twos or threes, freeze them that way in a plastic sack.

21. To make quick-diced eggs, take your potato masher and go to work on a boiled egg.

22. If you wrap each egg in aluminum foil before boiling it, the shell won't crack when it's boiling.

23. To make those eggs go further when making scrambled eggs for a crowd, add a pinch of baking powder and 2 teaspoons of water per egg.

24. A great trick for peeling eggs the easy way. When they are finished boiling, turn off the heat and just let them sit in the pan with the lid on for about five minutes. Steam will build up under the shell and they will just fall away.

25. Or, quickly rinse hot hard-boiled eggs in cold water, and the shells will be easier to remove.

26. When you have saved a lot of egg yolks from previous recipes, use them in place of whole eggs for baking or thickening. Just add 2 yolks for every whole egg.

27. Fresh or hard-boiled? Spin the egg. If it wobbles, it is raw - if it spins easily, it's hard boiled.

28. Add a few drops of vinegar to the water when poaching an egg to keep it from running all over the pan.

29. Add one tablespoon of water per egg white to increase the quantity of beaten egg white when making meringue.

30. Try adding eggshells to coffee after it has perked, for a better flavor.

31. Fresh eggs are rough and chalky in appearance. Old eggs are smooth and shiny.

32. Pierce the end of an egg with a pin, and it will not break when placed in boiling water.

33. Beaten egg whites will be more stable if you add 1 teaspoon cream of tartar to each cup of egg whites (7 or 8 eggs).

34. A small funnel is handy for separating egg whites from yolks. Open the egg over the funnel and the white will run through and the yolk will remain.

35. For baking it's best to use medium to large eggs. Extra large may cause cakes to fall when cooled.

36. Brown and white shells are the same quality.

37. Egg whites can be kept up to 1 year. Add them to a plastic container as you "collect them" for use in meringues, angel food cake . . . 1 cup equals 7 or 8 egg whites. You can also refreeze defrosted egg whites.

38. For fluffier omelets, add a pinch of cornstarch before beating.

Potatoes

39. Overcooked potatoes can become soggy when the milk is added. Sprinkle with dry powdered milk for the fluffiest mashed potatoes ever.

40. To hurry up baked potatoes, boil in salted water for 10 minutes, then place in a very hot oven. Or, cut potatoes in half and place them face down on a baking sheet in the oven to make the baking time shorter.

41. When making potato pancakes, add a little sour cream to keep potatoes from discoloring.

42. Save some of the water in which the potatoes were boiled - add to some powdered milk and use when mashing. This restores some of the nutrients that were lost in the cooking process.

43. *Use a couple of tablespoons of cream cheese in place of butter for your potatoes; try using sour cream instead of milk when mashing.*

Onions
44. *To avoid tears when peeling onions, peel them under cold water or refrigerate before chopping.*
45. *For sandwiches to go in lunchboxes, sprinkle with dried onion. They will have turned into crisp pieces by lunchtime.*
46. *Peel and quarter onions. Place one layer deep in a pan and freeze. Quickly pack in bags or containers while frozen. Use as needed, chopping onions while frozen, with a sharp knife.*

Tomatoes
47. *Keep tomatoes in storage with stems pointed downward and they will retain their freshness longer.*
48. *Sunlight doesn't ripen tomatoes. It's the warmth that makes them ripen. So find a warm spot near the stove or dishwasher where they can get a little heat.*
49. *Save the juice from canned tomatoes in ice cube trays. When frozen, store in plastic bags in freezer for cooking use or for tomato drinks.*
50. *To improve the flavor of inexpensive tomato juice, pour a 46-ounce can ot it into a refrigerator jar and add one chopped green onion and a cut-up stalk of celery.*

A quick way to whip cream
51. *A pinch of salt added to the cream before whipping strengthens the fat cells and makes them more elastic. This helps the cream stiffen much more quickly.*

Cream that will not whip
52. *Chill cream, bowl and beater well. Set bowl of cream into a bowl of ice water while you're whipping. Add the white of an egg. Chill and then whip. If the cream still does not stiffen, gradually whip in 3 or 4 drops of lemon juice. Cream whipped ahead of time will not separate if you add a touch of unflavored gelatin (1/4 teaspoon per cup of cream). To elminate a lot of mess when whipping cream with an electric beater, try this: Cut 2 holes in the middle of a piece of waxed paper, then slip the stems of the beaters through the holes and attach the beaters to the machine. Simply place paper and beaters over the bowl and whip away.*

Rock-hard brown sugar
53. *Add a slice of soft bread to the package of brown sugar, close the bag tightly, and in a few hours the sugar will be soft again. If you need it in a hurry, simply grate the amount called for with a hard grater. Or, put brown sugar in a cup of water (do not add to the sugar, set it alongside of it) in a covered pan. Place in the oven (low heat) for a while. Or, buy liquid brown sugar.*

Thawing frozen meat
54. *Seal the meat in a plastic bag and place in a bowl of very warm water. Or, put in a bag and let cold water run over it for an hour or so.*

Caked or clogged salt
55. *Tightly wrap a piece of aluminum foil around the salt shaker. This will keep the dampness out of the salt. To prevent clogging, keep 5 to 10 grains of rice inside your shaker.*

Soggy potato chips, cereal and crackers
56. *If potato chips lose their freshness, place under the broiler for a few moments. Care must be taken not to brown them. You can crisp*

soggy cereal and crackers by putting them on a cookie sheet and heating for a few minutes in the oven.

Pancake syrup
57. To make an inexpensive syrup for pancakes, save small amounts of leftover jams and jellies in a jar. Or, fruit-flavored syrup can be made by adding 2 cups sugar to 1 cup of any kind of fruit juice and cooking until it boils.

Easy topping
58. A good topping for gingerbread, coffeecake, etc., can easily be made by freezing the syrup from canned fruit and adding 1 tablespoon of butter and 1 tablespoon of lemon juice fo 2 cups of syrup. Heat until bubbly, and thicken with 2 tablespoons of flour.

Tasty cheese sandwiches
59. Tasty cheese sandwiches in a frying pan lightly greased with bacon fat for a delightful new flavor.

No spattering or sticking
60. To keep frying food from spattering, invert a metal colander over the pan, allowing steam to escape.
61. Always heat the frying pan before adding oil or butter. This will keep things from sticking to the pan.
62. Boil vinegar in a brand new frying pan to keep things from sticking to it.

Hurry-up hamburgers
63. Poke a hole in the middle of the patties while shaping them. The burgers will cook faster and the holes will disappear when done.

Shrinkless links
64. Boil sausage links for about 8 minutes before frying and they will shrink less and not break at all. Or, you can roll them lightly in flour before frying.

Frozen bread
65. Put frozen bread loaves in a clean brown paper bag and place for 5 minutes in a 325° oven to thaw completely.

Removing the corn silk
66. Dampen a paper towel or terry cloth and brush downward on the cob of corn. Every strand should come off.

Nuts
67. To quickly crack open a large amount of nuts, put in a bag and gently hammer until they are cracked open. Then remove nutmeats with a pick.
68. If nuts are stale, place them in the oven at 250° F. and leave them there for 5 or 10 minutes. The heat will revive them.

Preventing boil-overs
69. Add a lump of butter or a few teaspoons of cooking oil to the water. Rice, noodles or spaghetti will not boil over or stick together.

Softening butter
70. Soften butter quickly by grating it. Or heat a small pan and place it upside-down over the butter dish for several minutes. Or place in the microwave for a few seconds.

Measuring sticky liquids
71. Before measuring honey or syrup, oil the cup with cooking oil and rinse in hot water.

Scalded milk
72. Add a bit of sugar (without stirring) to milk to prevent it from scorching.
73. Rinse the pan in cold water before scalding milk, and it will be

much easier to clean.

Tenderizing meat
74. Boiled meat: Add a tablespoon of vinegar to the cooking water.
75. Tough meat or game: Make a marinade of equal parts cooking vinegar and heated bouillon. Marinate for 2 hours.
76. Steak: Simply rub in a mixture of cooking vinegar and oil. Allow to stand for 2 hours.
77. Chicken: To stew an old hen, soak it in vinegar for several hours before cooking. It will taste like a spring chicken.

Instant white sauce
78. Blend together 1 cup soft butter and 1 cup flour. Spread in an ice cube tray, chill well, cut into 16 cubes before storing in a plastic bag in the freezer. For medium-thick sauce, drop 1 cube into 1 cup of milk and heat slowly, stirring as it thickens.

Unpleasant cooking odors
79. While cooking vegetables that give off unpleasant odors, simmer a small pan of vinegar on top of the stove. Or, add vinegar to the cooking water. To remove the odor of fish from cooking and serving implements, rinse in vinegar water.

Don't lose those vitamins
80. Put vegetables in water after the water boils - not before - to be sure to preserve all the vegetables' vitamins.

Clean and deodorize your cutting board
81. Bleach it clean with lemon juice. Take away strong odors like onion with baking soda. Just rub it in.

Keep the color in beets
82. If you find that your beets tend to lose color when you boil them, add a little lemon juice.

No-smell cabbage
83. Two things to do to keep cabbage smell from filling the kitchen: don't overcook it (keep it crisp) and put half a lemon in the water when you boil it.

A great energy saver
84. When you're near the end of the baking time, turn the oven off and keep the door closed. The heat will stay the same long enough to finish baking your cake or pie and you'll save all that energy.

Grating cheese
85. Chill the cheese before grating and it will take much less time.

Special looking pies
86. Give a unique look to your pies by using pinking shears to cut the dough. Make a pinked lattice crust!

Removing ham rind
87. Before placing ham in the roasting pan, slit rind lengthwise on the underside. The rind will peel away as the ham cooks, and can be easily removed.

Sluggish catsup
88. Push a drinking straw to the bottom of the bottle and remove. this admits enough air to start the catsup flowing.

Unmolding gelatin
89. Rinse the mold pan in cold water and coat with salad oil. The oil will give the gelatin a nice luster and it will easily fall out of the mold.

Leftover squash
90. Squash that is left over can be improved by adding some maple syrup before reheated.

No-spill cupcakes
91. *An ice cream scoop can be used to fill cupcake papers without spilling.*

Slicing cake or torte
92. *Use dental floss to slice evenly and cleanly through a cake or torte - simply stretch a length of the floss taut and press down through the cake.*

Ice cream
93. *Buy bulk quantities of ice cream and pack in small margarine containers. These provide individual servings.*

Canning peaches
94. *Don't bother to remove skins when canning or freezing peaches. They will taste better and be more nutritious with the skin on.*

Angel food cookies
95. *Stale angel food cake can be cut into 1/2" slices and shaped with cookie cutters to make delicious "cookies." Just toast in the oven for a few minutes.*

How to chop garlic
96. *Chop in a small amount of salt to prevent pieces from sticking to the knife or chopping board. Then pulverize with the tip of the knife.*

Excess fat on soups or stews
97. *Remove fat from stews or soups by refrigerating and eliminating fat as it rises and hardens on the surface. Or add lettuce leaves to the pot - the fat will cling to them. Discard lettuce before serving.*

Broiled meat drippings
98. *Place a piece of bread under the rack on which you are broiling meat. Not only will this absorb the dripping fat, but it will reduce the chance of the fat catching on fire.*

Fake sour cream
99. *To cut down on calories, run cottage cheese through the blender. It can be flavored with chives, extracts, etc., and used in place of mayonnaise.*

Browned butter
100. *Browning brings out the flavor of the butter, so only half as much is needed for seasoning vegetables if it is browned before it is added.*

Cooking dried beans
101. *When cooking dried beans, add salt after cooking; if salt is added at the start, it will slow the cooking process.*

Tasty carrots
102. *Adding sugar and horseradish to cooked carrots improves their flavor.*

Carrot marinade
103. *Marinate carrot sticks in dill pickle juice.*

Clean cukes
104. *A ball of nylon net cleans and smooths cucumbers when making pickles.*

Fresh garlic
105. *Peel garlic and store in a covered jar of vegetable oil. The garlic will stay fresh and the oil will be nicely flavored for salad dressings.*

Leftover waffles
106. *Freeze waffles that are left; they can be reheated in the toaster.*

Fluffy rice
107. *Rice will be fluffier and whiter if you add 1 teaspoon of lemon juice to each quart of water.*

Nutritious rice
108. *Cook rice in liquid saved from cooking vegetables to add flavor and nutrition. A nutty taste can be achieved by adding wheat germ to the rice.*

Perfect noodles
109. *When cooking noodles, bring required amount of water to a boil, add noodles, turn heat off and allow to stand for 20 minutes. This prevents overboiling and the chore of stirring. Noodles won't stick to the pan with this method.*

Easy croutons
110. *Make delicious croutons for soup or salad by saving toast, cutting into cubes, and sauteeing in garlic butter.*

Baked fish
111. *To keep fish from sticking to the pan, bake on a bed of chopped onion, celery and parsley. This also adds a nice flavor to the fish.*

Non-sticking bacon
112. *Roll a package of bacon into a tube before opening. This will loosen the slices and keep them from sticking together.*

Tasty hot dogs
113. *Boil hot dogs in sweet pickle juice and a little water for a different taste.*

Golden-brown chicken
114. *For golden-brown fried chicken, roll it in powdered milk instead of flour.*

Double boiler hint
115. *Toss a few marbles in the bottom of a double boiler. When the water boils down, the nose will let you know!*

Flour Puff
116. *Keep a powder puff in your flour container to easily dust your rolling pin or pastry board.*

Jar labels
117. *Attach canning labels to the lids instead of the sides of jelly jars, to prevent the chore of removing the labels when the contents are gone.*

Different meatballs
118. *Try using crushed cornflakes or corn bread instead of bread crumbs in a meatball recipe. Or use onion-flavored potato chips.*

* * * * * * *

CLEAN-UP TIPS

Appliances
119. *To rid yellowing from white appliances try this: Mix together: 1/2 cup bleach, 1/4 cup baking soda and 4 cups warm water. Apply with a sponge and let set for 10 minutes. Rinse and dry thoroughly.*
120. *Instead of using commercial waxes, shine with rubbing alcohol.*
121. *For quick clean-ups, rub with equal parts water and household ammonia.*
122. *Or, try club soda. It cleans and polishes at the same time.*

Blender
123. *Fill part way with hot water and add a drop of detergent. Cover and turn it on for a few seconds. Rinse and drain dry.*

Breadboards
124. *To rid cutting board of onion, garlic or fish smell, cut a lime or lemon in two and rub the surface with the cut side of the fruit.*
125. *Or, make a paste of baking soda and water and apply generously. Rinse.*

Copper pots

126. Fill a spray bottle with vinegar and add 3 tablespoons of salt. Spray solution liberally on copper pot. Let set for a while, then simply rub clean.

127. Dip lemon halves in salt and rub.

128. Or, rub with Worcestershire sauce or catsup. The tarnish will disappear.

129. Clean with toothpaste and rinse.

Burnt and scorced pans

130. Sprinkle burnt pans liberally with baking soda, adding just enough water to moisten. Let stand for several hours. You can generally lift the burned portions right out of the pan.

131. Stubborn stains on non-stick cookware can be removed by boiling 2 tablespoons of baking soda, 1/2 cup vinegar and 1 cup water for 10 minutes. Re-season pan with salad oil.

Cast-iron skillets

132. Clean the outside of the pan with commercial oven cleaner. Let set for 2 hours and the accumulated black stains can be removed with vinegar and water.

Can opener

133. Loosen grime by brushing with an old toothbrush. To thoroughly clean blades, run a paper towel through the cutting process.

Enamelware or casserole dishes

134. Fill a dish that contains stuck food bits with boiling water and 2 tablespoons of baking soda. Let it stand and wash out.

Dishes

135. Save time and money by using the cheapest brand of dishwashing detergent available, but add a few tablespoons of vinegar to the dishwater. The vinegar will cut the grease and leave your dishes sparkling clean.

136. Before washing fine china and crystal, place a towel on the bottom of the sink to act as a cushion.

137. To remove coffee or tea stains and cigarette burns from fine china, rub with a damp cloth dipped in baking soda.

Dishwasher

138. Run a cup of white vinegar through the entire cycle in an empty dishwasher to remove all soap film.

Clogged drains

139. When a drain is clogged with grease, pour a cup of salt and a cup of baking soda into the drain followed by a kettle of boiling water. The grease will usually dissolve immediately and open the drain.

140. Coffee grounds are a no-no. They do a nice job of clogging, especially if they get mixed with grease.

Garbage disposal

141. Grind a half lemon or orange rinds in the disposal to remove any unpleasant odor.

Glassware

142. Never put a delicate glass in hot water bottom side first; it will crack from sudden expansion. The most delicate glassware will be safe if it is slipped in edgewise.

143. Vinegar is a must when washing crystal. Rinse in 1 part vinegar to 3 parts warm water. Air dry.

144. When one glass is tucked inside another, do not force them apart. Fill the top glass with cold water and dip the lower one in hot water. They will come apart without breaking.

Grater

145. For a fast and simple clean-up, rub salad oil on the grater before using.

146. Use a toothbrush to brush lemon rind, cheese, onion or whatever out of the grater before washing it.

Meat grinder

147. Before washing, run a piece of bread through it.

Oven

148. Following a spill, sprinkle with salt immediately. When oven is cool, brush off burnt food and wipe with a damp sponge.

149. Sprinkle bottom of oven with automatic dishwasher soap and cover with wet paper towels. Let stand for a few hours.

150. A quick way to clean oven parts is to place a bath towel in the bathtub and pile all removable parts from the oven onto it. Draw enough hot water to just cover the parts and sprinkle a cup of dishwasher soap over it. While you are cleaning the inside of the oven, the rest will be cleaning itself.

151. An inexpensive oven cleaner: Set oven on warm for about 20 minutes, then turn off. Place a small dish of full strength ammonia on the top shelf. Put a large pan of boiling water on the bottom shelf and let it set overnight. In the morning, open oven and let it air a while before washing off with soap and water. Even the hard baked-on grease will wash off easily.

Plastic cups, dishes and containers

152. Coffee or tea stains can be scoured with baking soda.

153. Or, fill the stained cup with hot water and drop in a few denture cleanser tablets. Let soak for 1 hour.

154. To rid foul odors from plastic containers, place crumpled-up newspaper (black and white only) into the container. Cover tightly and leave overnight.

Refrigerator

155. To help eliminate odors fill a small bowl with charcoal (the kind used for potted plants) and place it on a shelf in the refrigerator. It absorbs odors rapidly.

156. An open box of baking soda will absorb food odors for at least a month or two.

157. A little vanilla poured on a piece of cotton and placed in the refrigerator will eliminate odors.

158. To prevent mildew from forming, wipe with vinegar. The acid effectively kills the mildew fungus.

159. Use a glycerine-soaked cloth to wipe sides and shelves. Future spills wipe up easily. And after the freezer has been defrosted, coat the inside coils with glycerine. The next time you defrost, the ice will loosen quickly and drop off in sheets.

160. Wash inside and out with a mixture of 3 tablespoons of baking soda in a quart of warm water.

Sinks

161. For a sparkling white sink, place paper towels across the bottom of your sink and saturate with household bleach. Let set for 1/2 hour or so.

162. Rub stainless steel sinks with lighter fluid if rust marks appear. After the rust disappears, wipe with your regular kitchen cleanser.

163. Use a cloth dampened with rubbing alcohol to remove water spots from stainless steel.

164. Spots on stainless steel can also be removed with white vinegar.

165. Club soda will shine up stainless steel sinks in a jiffy.

Sponges
166. *Wash in your dishwasher or soak overnight in salt water or baking soda added to water.*

Teakettle
167. *To remove lime deposits, fill with equal parts of vinegar and water. Bring to a boil and allow to stand overnight.*

Thermos bottle
168. *Fill the bottle with warm water, add 1 teaspoon of baking soda and allow to soak.*

Tin pie pans
169. *Remove rust by dipping a raw potato in cleaning powder and scouring.*

Fingerprints off the kitchen door and walls
170. *Take away fingerprints and grime with a solution of half water and half ammonia. Put it in a spray bottle from one of these expensive cleaning products, you'll never have to buy them again.*

Formica tops
171. *Polish them to a sparkle with club soda.*

* * * * * * * *

KEEPING FOODS FRESH AND FOOD STORAGE
Celery and lettuce
172. *Store in refrigerator in paper bags instead of plastic. Leave the outside leaves and stalks on until ready to use.*

Onions
173. *Wrap individually in foil to keep them from becoming soft or sprouting.*

174. *Once an onion has been cut in half, rub the leftover side with butter and it will keep fresh longer.*

Cheese
175. *Wrap cheese in a vinegar-dampened cloth to keep it from drying out.*

Milk
176. *Milk at room temperature may spoil cold milk, so don't pour milk back into the carton.*

Brown sugar
177. *Wrap in a plastic bag and store in refrigerator in a coffee can with a snap-on lid.*

Cocoa
178. *Store cocoa in a glass jar in a dry and cool place.*

Cakes
179. *Putting half an apple in the cake box will keep cake moist.*

Ice cream
180. *Ice cream that has been opened and returned to the freezer sometimes forms a waxlike film on the top. To prevent this, after part of the ice cream has been removed press a piece of waxed paper against the surface and reseal the carton.*

Lemons
181. *Store whole lemons in a tightly sealed jar of water in the refrigerator. They will yield much more juice than when first purchased.*

Limes
182. *Store limes, wrapped in tissue paper, on lower shelf of the refrigerator.*

Smoked meats
183. *Wrap ham or bacon in a vine-*

gar-soaked cloth, then in waxed paper to preserve freshness.

Strawberries
184. Keep in a colander in the refrigerator. Wash just before serving.

Soda crackers
185. Wrap tightly and store in the refrigerator.

Vegetables with tops
186. Remove the tops on carrots, beets, etc. before storing.

Bread
187. A rib of celery in your bread bag will keep the bread fresh for a longer time.

Cookies
188. Place crushed tissue paper on the bottom of your cookie jar.

Cottage cheese
189. Store carton upside-down. It will keep twice as long.

Garlic
190. Garlic cloves can be kept in the freezer. When ready to use, peel and chop before thawing.
191. Or, garlic cloves will never dry out if you store them in a bottle of cooking oil. After the garlic is used up, you can use the garlic-flavored oil for salad dressing.

Honey
192. Put honey in small plastic freezer containers to prevent sugaring. It also thaws out in a short time.

Marshmallows
193. They will not dry out if stored in the freezer. Simply cut with scissors when ready to use.

Olive oil
194. You can lengthen the life of olive oil by adding a cube of sugar to the bottle.

Parsley
195. Keep fresh and crisp by storing in a wide-mouth jar with a tight lid. Parsley may also be frozen.

* * * * * * *

SUBSTITUTES
For bread crumbs
197. Use crushed corn or wheat flakes, or other dry cereal. Or use potato flakes.

For butter
198. Use 7/8 cup of solid shortening plus 1/2 teaspoon of salt.

For fresh milk
199. To substitute 1 cup of fresh milk, use 1/2 cup each of evaporated milk and water.
200. For 1 cup of whole milk, prepare 1 liquid cup of nonfat dry milk and 2-1/2 teaspoons butter or margarine.

For sugar
201. Use brown sugar, although it will result in a slight molasses flavor.

For superfine sugar
202. Process regular granulated sugar in your blender.

For red and green sweet pepper
203. Use canned pimientos.

For vanilla extract
204. Use grated lemon or orange rind for flavoring instead. Or try a little cinnamon or nutmeg.

For flour
205. Use 1 tablespoon cornstarch instead of 2 tablespoons of flour. Or try using instant potatoes or cornmeal.

For buttermilk
206. *Use 1 tablespoon of lemon juice or vinegar and enough fresh milk to make 1 cup. Let it stand 5 minutes before using.*

For catsup
207. *Use a cup of tomato sauce added to 1-1/4 cups of brown sugar, 2 tablespoons of vinegar, 1/4 teaspoon of cinnamon and a dash of ground cloves and allspice.*

For unsweetened chocolate
208. *Use 1 tablespoon of shortening plus 3 tablespoons of unsweetened cocoa to equal 1 square of unsweetened chocolate.*

For corn syrup
209. *Use 1/4 cup of water or other type of liquid called for in the recipe, plus 1 cup of sugar.*

For eggs
210. *Add 3 or 4 extra tablespoons of liquid called for in the recipe. Or, when you're 1 egg shy for a recipe that calls for many, substitute 1 teaspoon of cornstarch.*

For cake flour
211. *Use 7/8 cup of all-purpose flour for each cup of cake flour called for in a recipe.*

For fresh herbs and spices
212. *Use 1/3 the amount of dried herbs or spices. Dried herbs are more concentrated.*

For honey
213. *To substitute 1 cup of honey, use 1-1/4 cups of sugar and 1/4 cup of water or other liquid called for in the recipe.*

* * * * * * * *

II. TO REMOVE STAINS FROM WASHABLES

Alcoholic beverages
214. *Pre-soak or sponge fresh stains immediately with cold water, then with cold water and glycerine. Rinse with vinegar for a few seconds if stain remains. These stains may turn brown with age. If wine stain remains, rub with concentrated detergent; wait 15 minutes; rinse. Repeat if necessary. Wash with detergent in hottest water safe for fabric.*

Blood
215. *Pre-soak in cold or warm water at least 30 minutes. If stain remains, soak in lukewarm ammonia water (3 tablespoons per gallon water). Rinse. If stain remains, work in detergent, and wash, using bleach safe for fabric.*

Candle wax
216. *Use a dull knife to scrape off as much as possible. Place fabric between two blotters or facial tissues and press with warm iron. Remove color stain with non-flammable dry cleaning solvent. Wash with detergent in the hottest water safe for fabric.*

Chewing gum
217. *Rub area with ice, then scrape off with dull blade. Sponge with dry cleaning solvent; allow to air dry. Wash in detergent and hottest water safe for fabric.*

Chocolate and cocoa
218. *Pre-soak stain in cold or warm water. Wash in hot water with detergent. Remove any greas stains with dry cleaning solvent. If color remains, sponge with hydrogen peroxide, wash again.*

Coffee
219. *Sponge or soak with cold water as soon as possible. Wash, using detergent and bleach safe for fabric. Remove cream grease stains with non-flammable dry cleaning solvent. Wash again.*

Crayon
220. *Scrape with dull blade. Wash in hottest water safe for fabric, with detergent and 1-2 cups of baking soda. NOTE: If full load is crayon stained, take to cleaners or coin-op dry cleaning machines.*

Deodorants
221. *Sponge area with white vinegar. If stain remains, soak with denatured alcohol. Wash with detergent in hottest water safe for fabric.*

Dye
222. *If dye transfers from a non-colorfast item during washing, immediately bleach discolored items. On whites use color remover. CAUTION: Do not use color remover in washer, or around washer and dryer as it may damage the finish.*

Egg
223. *Scrape with dull blade. Pre-soak in cold or warm water for at least 30 minutes. Remove grease with dry cleaning solvent. Wash in hottest water safe for fabric, with detergent.*

Fruit and fruit juices
224. *Sponge with cold water. Pre-soak in cold or warm water for at least 30 minutes. Wash with detergent and bleach safe for fabric.*

Grass
225. *Pre-soak in cold water for at least 30 minutes. Rinse. Pre-treat with detergent. Wash, using detergent, hot water, and bleach safe for fabric. On acetate and colored fabrics, use 1 part of alcohol to 2 parts water.*

Grease, oil, tar
226. *Method 1: Use powder or chalk absorbents to remove as much grease as possible. Pre-treat with detergent or non-flammable dry cleaning solvent, or liquid shampoo. Wash in hottest water safe for fabric, using plenty of detergent.*
227. *Method 2: Rub spot with lard and sponge with a non-flammable dry cleaning solvent. Wash in hottest water and detergent safe for fabric.*

Ink—ball-point pen
228. *Pour denatured alcohol through stain. Rub in petroleum jelly. Sponge with non-flammable dry cleaning solvent. Soak in detergent solution. Wash with detergent and bleach safe for fabric.*

Lipstick
229. *Loosen stain with a non-flammable dry cleaning solvent. Rub detergent in until stain outline is gone. Wash in hottest water and detergent safe for fabric.*

Meat juices
230. *Scrape with dull blade. Pre-soak in cold or warm water for 30 minutes. Wash with detergent and bleach safe for fabric.*

Mildew
231. *Pre-treat as soon as possible with detergent. Wash. If any stain remains, sponge with lemon juice and salt. Dry in sun. Wash, using hottest water, detergent and bleach safe for fabric. NOTE: Mildew is very hard to remove; treat promptly.*

Milk, cream, ice cream
232. *Pre-soak in cold or warm water*

for 30 minutes. Wash. Sponge any grease spots with non-flammable dry cleaning solvent. Wash again.

Nail polish
233. Sponge with polish remover or banana oil. Wash. If stain remains, sponge with denatured alcohol to which a few drops of ammonia have been added. Wash again. Do not use polish remover on acetate or triacetate fabrics.

Paint
234. Oil base: Sponge stains with turpentine, cleaning fluid or paint remover. Pre-treat and wash in hot water. For old stains, sponge with banana oil and then with non-flammable dry cleaning solvent. Wash again.
235. Water base: Scrape off paint with dull blade. Wash with detergent in water as hot as is safe for fabric.

Perspiration
236. Sponge fresh stain with ammonia; old stain with vinegar. Pre-soak incold or warm water. Rinse. Wash in hottest water safe for fabric. If fabric is yellowed, use bleach. If stain still remains, dampen and sprinkle with meat tenderizer, or pepsin. Let stand 1 hour. Brush off and wash. For persistent odor, sponge with colorless mouthwash.

Rust
237. Soak in lemon juice and salt or oxalic acid solution (3 tablespoons oxalic acid to 1 pint warm water). A commercial rust remover may be used. CAUTION: **Handle poisonous rust removers carefully. Keep out of reach of children. Never use oxalic acid or any rust remover around washer or dryer as it can damage the finish. Such chemicals may also remove permanent press fabric finishes.**

Scorch
238. Wash with detergent and bleach safe for fabric. On heavier scorching, cover stain with cloth dampened with hydrogen peroxide. Cover this with dry cloth and press with hot iron. Rinse well. CAUTION: Severe scorching cannot be removed because of fabric damage.

Soft drinks
239. Sponge immediately with cold water and alcohol. Heat and detergent may set stain.

Tea
240. Sponge or soak with cold water as soon as possible. Wash using detergent and bleach safe for fabric.

* * * * * * *

III. CARPETS AND FLOORS

Flattened shag carpets
241. Raise flattened spots in your carpeting where heavy furniture has stood by using a steam iron. Hold the iron over the spot and build up a good steam. Then brush up the carpet.

Candle drippings
242. For spilled wax on carpet, use a brown paper bag as a blotter and run a hot iron over it, which will absorb the wax.

Dog stains
243. Blot up excess moisture with paper towel. Pour club soda on the spot and continue blotting. Lay a towel over the spot and set a heavy object on top in order to absorb all the moisture.

Rug care
244. When washing and drying foam-backed throw rugs, never

wash in hot water, and use the "air only" dryer setting to dry. Heat will ruin foam.

Cleaning rugs
245. If the rug is only slightly dirty, you can clean it with cornmeal. Use a stiff brush to work the cornmeal into the pile of the rug. Take it all out with the vacuum.

What to do with new carpet
246. Wait about three months before attempting to clean your new carpet. It needs that amount of time to spring up and keep its normal nap.

Spills on the rug
247. When spills happen, go to the bathroom and grab a can of shaving cream. Squirt it on the spot, then rinse off with water.

Liven up your carpet
248. Give your carpet a new lease on life. Sprinkle some salt on it right before you vacuum. The rug will be much brighter when you have finished vacuuming.

Ballpoint ink marks
249. Saturate the spots with hairspray. Allow to dry. Brush lightly with a solution of water and vinegar.

Glue
250. Glue can be loosened by saturating the spot with a cloth soaked in vinegar.

Repairing braided rugs
251. Braided rugs often rip apart. Instead of sewing them, use clear fabric glue to repair. It's that fast and easy.

Repairing a burn
252. Remove some fuzz from the carpet, either by shaving or pulling out with a tweezer. Roll into the shape of the burn. Apply a good cement glue to the backing of the rug and press the fuzz down into the burned spot. Cover with a piece of cleansing tissue and place a heavy book on top. This will cause the glue to dry very slowly and you will get the best results.

Spot remover for outdoor carpeting
253. Spray spots liberally with a pre-wash commercial spray. Let it set several minutes, then hose down and watch the spots disappear.

Blood on the rug
254. When you get blood on your rug, rub off as much as you can at first, then take a cloth soaked in cold water and wet the spot, wiping it up as you go. If a little bit remains, pour some ammonia onto the cool, wet cloth and lightly wipe that over the spot, too. Rinse it right away with cold water.
255. Use silver polish to remove from vinyl tile or linoleum.

Spilled nail polish
256. Allow to almost dry, then peel off of waxed floors or tile.

Tar spots
257. Use paste wax to remove tar from floors. Works on shoes, too.

Dusting floors
258. Stretch a nylon stocking over the dust mop. After using, discard the stocking and you will have a clean mop.

Varnished floors
259. Use cold tea to clean woodwork and varnished floors.

Spilled grease
260. Rub floor with ice cubes to

solidify grease. Scrape up excess and wash with soapy water.

Quick shine
261. Put a piece of waxed paper under your dust mop. Dirt will stick to the mop and the wax will shine your floors.

Unmarred floors
262. Put thick old socks over the legs of heavy furniture when moving across floors.

Wood floor care
263. Never use water or water-based cleaners on wood floors. Over a period of time, warping and swelling will develop.

Floor polisher
264. When cleaning the felt pads of your floor polisher, place the pads between layers of newspaper and press with an iron to absorb built-up wax.

Garage floors
265. In an area where a large amount of oil has spilled, lay several thicknesses of newspaper. Saturate the paper with water; press flat against the floor. When dry, remove the newspaper and the spots will have disappeared.

Basement floors
266. Sprinkle sand on oily spots, let it absorb the oil, and sweep up.

Fix those loose linoleum edges
267. Take a knife with some tile adhesive and work it under the loose part. Put a heavy weight, such as a big stack of books, over the whole area and keep it weighed down for the amount of time it says on the can of adhesive.

Stop squeaking floors
268. Just dust some talcum powder between the cracks and it should do the job. If you have really serious spueaking, it could be that you need to wedge in some slivers of wood to the underneath side.

Heel marks
269. Just take a pencil eraser and wipe them off.

* * * * * * *

IV. WINDOWS

Window cleaning
270. Newspaper is much cheaper to use for drying freshly-washed windows than paper toweling.

Drying windows
271. Dry the inside panes with up-and-down strokes, and the outside with back-and-forth motions to see which side has smudges.

Window cleaning solution
272. The best mixture for cleaning windows is 1/2 cup of ammonia, 1 cup of white vinegar, and 2 table-spoons of cornstarch in a bucket of warm water.

Cold weather window cleaning
273. Add 1/2 cup of rubbing alcohol to the above mixture on cold days to prevent ice from forming on your windows.

Clean window sills
274. To remove spots on window sills, rub the surface with rubbing alcohol.

Puttying windows
275. Mix some putty to match the woodwork before puttying windows.

Loosening window panes

276. Dig through old putty with a very hot instrument to loosen a window pane.

Aluminum window frames

277. Use cream silver polish to clean aluminum window frames.

Grease spots

278. Any cola drink will remove grease spots from windows.

Numbered windows

279. When cleaning, painting or changing windows, number each with a ballpoint pen and put the corresponding number inside the proper window frame.

Window shade tears

280. Repair with colorless nail polish. This works wonders on small tears.

Cleaning screens

281. For a thorough job, brush on both sides with kerosene. Wipe with a clean cloth. this method will also prevent rust from forming. Be sure to dust the screens with a small paintbrush before you begin.

282. For small jobs, rub a brush-type hair roller lightly over the screen and see how easily it picks up all the lint and dust.

* * * * * * *

V. FURNITURE

Fantastic polish

283. Use 1/3 cup each boiled linseed oil, turpentine and vinegar. Mix together and shake well. Apply with a soft cloth and wipe completely dry. Wipe again with another soft cloth. Do not try to boil you own linseed oil - it is not the same. Buy it at a hardware or paint store.

To remove polish build-up

284. Mix 1/2 cup vinegar and 1/2 cup water. Rub with a soft cloth that has been moistened with solution, but wrung out. Dry immediately with another soft cloth.

Polishing carved furniture

285. Dip an old soft toothbrush into furniture polish and brush lightly.

Cigarette burns

286. For small minor burns, try rubbing mayonnaise into the burn. Let set for a while before wiping off with a soft cloth.

287. Burns can be repaired with a wax stick (available in all colors at paint and hardware stores). Gently scrape away the charred finish. Heat a knife blade and melt the shellac stick against the heated blade. Smooth over damaged area with your finger. But always consider the value of the furniture. It might be better to have a professional make the repair.

288. Or, make a paste of rotten-stone (available at hardware stores) and salad oil. Rub into the burned spot only, following the grain of the wood. Wipe clean with a cloth that has been dampened in oil. Wipe dry and apply your favorite furniture polish.

Scratches

289. Make sure you always rub with the grain of the wood when repairing a scratch. Walnut: Remove the meat from a fresh, unsalted walnut or pecan nut. Break it in half and rub the scratch with the broken side of the nut.

290. Mahogany: You can either rub the scratch with a dark brown crayon or buff with brown paste wax.

291. Red Mahogany: Apply ordinary iodine with a number 0 artist's brush.

292. *Maple:* Combine equal amounts of iodine and denatured alcohol. Apply with a Q-tip, then dry, wax and buff.

293. *Ebony:* Use black shoe polish, black eyebrow pencil or black crayon.

294. *Teakwood:* Rub very gently with 0000 steel wool. Rub in equal amounts of linseed oil and turpentine.

295. *Light-finished furniture::* Scratches can be hidden by using tan shoe polish. However, only on shiny finishes.

296. For all minor scratches: Cover each scratch with a generous amount of white petroleum jelly. Allow it to remain on for 24 hours. Rub into wood. Remove excess and polish as usual.

297. For larger scratches: Fill by rubbing with a wax stick (available in all colors at your hardware or paint store) or a crayon that matches the finish of the wood.

Removing paper that is stuck to a wood surface

298. *Do not scrape with a knife. Pour any salad oil, a few drops at a time, on the paper. Let set for a while and rub with a soft cloth. Repeat the procedure until the paper is completely gone.*

299. *Old decals can be removed easily by painting them with several coats of white vinegar. Give the vinegar time to soak in, then gently scrape off.*

Three solutions to remove white water rings and spots

300. *Sprinkle salt on a fresh-cut lemon. Rub very lightly over stain. Do not rub hard or you will ruin the polished surface. Wash off with soap and water.*

304. *Scour with a water and baking soda paste. Let stand for a few minutes before rinsing with warm water.*

Removing candle wax from wooden finishes

305. *Soften the wax with a hair dryer. Remove wax with paper toweling and wash down with a solution of vinegar and water.*

Plastic table tops

306. *You will find that a coat of Turtle Wax is a quick pick-up for dulled plastic table tops and counters.*

307. *Or, rub in toothpaste and buff.*

Glass table tops

308. *Rub in a little lemon juice. Dry with paper towels and shine with newspaper for a sparkling table.*

309. *Toothpaste will remove small scratches from glass.*

Chrome cleaning

310. *For sparkling clean chrome without streaks, use a cloth dampened in ammonia.*

Removing glue

311. *Cement glue can be removed by rubbing with cold cream, peanut butter or salad oil.*

Wicker

312. *Wicker needs moisture, so use a humidifier in the winter.*

313. *To prevent drying out, apply lemon oil occasionally.*

314. *Never let wicker freeze. This will cause cracking and splitting.*

315. *Wash with a solution of warm salt water to keep from turning yellow.*

Metal furniture

316. *To remove rust, a good scrub-*

bing with turpentine should accomplish this job.

Vinyl upholstery
317. Never oil vinyl as this will make it hard. It is almost impossible to soften again. For proper cleaning, sprinkle baking soda or vinegar on a rough, damp cloth, then wash with a mild dishwashing soap.

Leather upholstery
318. Prevent leather from cracking by polishing regularly with a cream made of 1 part vinegar and 2 parts linseed oil. Clean with a damp cloth and saddle soap.

Grease stains
319. Absorb grease on furniture by pouring salt on the spill immediately.

Soiled upholstery
320. Rub soiled cotton upholstery fabric with an artgum eraser or squares (purchased at stationery store).

* * * * * * *

VI. LAUNDRY

Spot removal
321. Two parts water and one part rubbing alcohol are the basic ingredients in any commercial spot remover.

Clean machine
322. Fill your washer with warm water and add a gallon of distilled vinegar. Run the machine through the entire cycle to unclog and clean soap scum from hoses.

Too sudsy
323. When your washer overflows with too many suds, sprinkle salt in the water - the suds will disappear.

Final rinse
324. Add a cup of white vinegar to the final rinse when washing clothes to make sure the alkalines in the soap are dissolved.

Hand-washed sweaters
325. Add a capful of hair cream rinse to the final rinse water when washing sweaters.

Whiter fabric
326. Linen or cotton can be whitened by boiling in a mixture of 1 part cream of tartar and 3 parts water.

Whitest socks
327. Boil socks in water to which a lemon slice has been added.

Clean work clothes
328. To your wash water, add 1/2 cup of household ammonia.

Freshen feather pillows
329. Put feather pillows in the dryer and tumble, then air outside.

Lintless corduroy
330. While corduroy is still damp, brush with clothes brush to remove all lint.

Ironing tip
331. When pressing pants, iron the top part on the wrong side. Iron the legs on the right side. This gives the pockets and waistband a smooth look.

Creaseless garments
332. Take an empty cardboard paper towel roll and cut through it lengthwise. Slip it over a wire hanger to prevent a crease from forming in the garment to be hung on the hanger.

Remove creases from hems
333. Sponge material with a white

vinegar solution and press flat to remove creases in hems.

Bedroom Ironing
334. A good place to iron is in the bedroom. Closets are nearby to hang clothes up immediately, and the bed makes a good surface on which to fold clothes and separate items into piles.

Ironing board cover
335. When washing your ironing board cover, attach it to the board while it is still damp. When it dries, the surface will be completely smooth.
336. Starch your ironing board cover. This helps the cover stay clean longer.

Lint remover
337. Add a yard of nylon netting to your dryer with the wet clothes - it will catch most of the lint.

Washer advice
338. Button all buttons on clothing and turn inside out before putting into the washer. Fewer buttons will fall off and garments will fade less if turned inside out.

Soiled collars
339. Use a small paintbrush and brush hair shampoo into soiled shirt collars before laundering. Shampoo is made to dissolve body oils.

Faster ironing
340. Place a strip of heavy-duty aluminum foil over the entire length of the ironing board and cover with pad. As you iron, heat will reflect through to the underside of the garment.

Ironing embroidery
341. Lay the embroidery piece upside-down on a Turkish towel before ironing. All the little spaces between the embroidery will be smooth when you are finished.

* * * * * * *

VII. BATHROOM

Bathroom tile
342. Rub ordinary car wax into your ceramic bathroom tiling to clean and refinish. Let it stand 10 minutes and buff or polish.
343. Use a typewriter eraser to clean spaces between bathroom tiles.

Metal shower head
344. To clean mineral deposits from a clogged shower head, boil it with half a cup of white vinegar and one quart of vinegar for awhile.

Plastic shower head
345. Soak a plastic shower head in a hot vinegar and water mixture to unclog it.

Shower curtains
346. Before hanging shower curtains, soak them in a salt water solution to prevent mildew.
347. To remove mildew on shower curtains, wash them in hot soapy water, rub with lemon juice, and let them dry in the sun.

Bathroom fixtures
348. Dip a cloth in kerosene or rubbing alcohol to remove scum from your bathroom fixtures.

Removing film and scum
349. Use a piece of very fine steel wool to remove film from the shower stall.

Porcelain cleaners
350. Restore whiteness to a yellowed bathtub by rubbing with a salt and turpentine solution.

Yellowed bathtub
351. *Restore whiteness to a yellowed bathtub by rubbing with a salt and turpentine solution.*

Shower mat tip
352. *Dip a stiff brush in a kerosene and warm water solution to clean the bath mat.*

Rust stains
353. *Spread a paste of hydrogen peroxide and cream of tartar over the area, and add a few drops of ammonia. Let it stand for 2 or 3 hours.*

Rusty tile
354. *Rust stains on tile can be removed with kerosene.*

Cleaning shower doors
355. *Rub glass shower doors with a white vinegar-dampened sponge to remove soap residue.*

Steam-free mirror
356. *If your medicine cabinet has two sliding mirrors, slide one side open before taking a bath or shower. After the bath, you'll have one clean mirror instead of two that are steamed and foggy.*

Steamy bathrooms
357. *If you run about an inch of cold water before adding hot water to your bath, there will be absolutely no steam in your bathroom.*

Medicine cabinet
358. *It's a good idea to go through your medicine cabinet several times a year and throw away medicines that are old or outdated. They could be dangerous.*

Easy bathroom cleaning
359. *Clean your bathroom after a steamy bath or shower. the walls, fixtures, etc., will be much easier to clean because the steam will have loosened the dirt.*

Sink cleaners
360. *Light stains can often be removed by simply rubbing with a cut lemon.*
361. *For dark stains, and especially rust, rub with a paste of borax and lemon juice.*

Dripping faucet
362. *If the drip occurs during the night and you can't sleep, simply wrap a cloth around the opening of the faucet.*

Sweet-smelling bathroom
363. *Place a fabric softener sheet in the wastepaper basket. Or, add a touch of fragrance by dabbing your favorite perfume on a light bulb. When the light is on, the heat releases the aroma.*

* * * * * * *

VIII. HANDYPERSON

Leaky vase
364. *Fix a leaky vase by coating the inside with paraffin and letting it harden.*

Plywood cutting
365. *Put a strip of masking tape at the point of plywood where you plan to begin sawing to keep it from splitting.*

Locating wall studs
366. *Move a pocket compass along the wall. When the needle moves, usually the stud will be located at that point. Studs are usually located 16" apart.*

Fraying rope
367. *Shellac the ends of the rope to prevent fraying.*

Fraying nylon cord
368. *Heat the cut end of nylon cord over a match flame to bond the end together.*

Loosening rusty bolts
369. *Apply a cloth soaked in any carbonated soda to loosen rusted bolts.*

Sandpaper hint
370. *By dampening the backing on sandpaper, it will last longer and resist cracking.*

Tight screws
371. *Loosen a screw by putting a couple of drops of peroxide on it and letting it soak in.*

Screwdriver tip
372. *Keep a screwdriver tip from slipping by putting chalk on the blade.*

Loosening joints
373. *Loosen old glue by applying vinegar from an oil can to the joint.*

Rule to remember
374. *Left is loose and right is tight.*

Sticking drawers
375. *Rub the runners of drawers with a candle or a bar of soap so they will slide easily.*

Stubborn locks
376. *Dip key into machine oil or graphite to loosen up a lock.*

Loose draw knobs
377. *Before inserting a screw into the knob, coat with fingernail polish to hold it tightly.*

Slamming doors
378. *Reduce the noise level in your home by putting self-sticking protective pads on the inside edges of cabinet doors, cupboards, etc.*

Icy sidewalk tip
379. *Sprinkle sand through a strainer on an icy sidewalk to distribute evenly.*

Garbage can tip
380. *Garbage cans will last longer if they are painted. Use primer on galvanied metal, then paint with matching house paint.*

Towel rack tip
381. *Replace the bottom screws of towal racks with cup hooks. Small towels and washcloths may be hung from them.*

Screen repair
382. *Use clear cement glue to repair a small hole in wire screening.*

Hairdryer hint
383. *Thaw a frozen pipe with a portable hairdryer.*

Finding a gas leak
384. *Lather the pipes with soapy water. The escaping gas will cause the soapy water to bubble, revealing the damaged areas. You can make a temporary plug by moistening a cake of soap and pressing it over the spot. When the soap hardens, it will effectively close the leak until the gasman comes.*

Hanging pictures
385. *Before you drive nails intothe wall, mark the spot with an X of cellophane tape. This trick will keep the plater from cracking when you start hammering.*
386. *when the landlady says, "no*

nails in the wall," hang pictures with sewing machine needles. They will hold up to 30 pounds.

* * * * * * *

IX. BEAUTY

Natural facial
387. A good and inexpensive facial to try: mash half an avocado, spread thickly on face, and remove with warm water 20 minutes later.

Cuticle treatment
388. Apply a mixture of equal parts of castor oil and white iodine to your cuticles every night.

Sunburn relief
389. A wonderful relief for sunburn pain is the application of mint-flavored milk of magnesia to the skin.
390. Dab on some apple cider vinegar. The pinkness and pain will disappear.
391. For a super bad burn, put on a paste of water and baking soda.

Hair shiner
392. These hair rinses will remove soap film and shine hair: For blondes, rinse water containing a few tablespoons of lemon juice. For brunettes and redheads, a few tablespoons of apple cider vinegar in the rinse water.

Broken lipstick
393. Hold a match under the broken ends until they melt enough to adhere to each other. Cool in the refrigerator.

Nail polish
394. Don't throw away that gummy nail polish. Place the bottle in boiling water to bring it back to its original consistency.

395. Instead of storing the nail polish bottle right-side-up, put in on its side. Stir it up with the brush when you need some.
396. Before you put on polish, put vinegar on your nails. It will clean them completely and help nail polish stick longer.

Deodorant
397. To make you own pump-spray deodorant, just add 4 tablespoons of alum to 1 quart of water. Mix it up and put into a spray bottle. If you want a scent, add your favorite cologne.

Your own manicure
398. Soak your hands in warm water with lemon juice added. Take them out after about 8 minutes. Rub some lemon peel over the nails while you gently push back the cuticle. Then buff with a soft cloth.

Baking soda for teeth
399. Baking soda instead of toothpaste does as good a job. It also works on dentures.

Cleaning combs and brushes
400. A solution of baking soda and hot water cleans hair brushes and combs.

Hair conditioner
401. Mayonnaise gives dry hair a good conditioning. Apply 1/2 cup mayonnaise to dry, unwashed hair. Cover with plastic bag and wait for 15 minutes. rinse a few times before shampooing thoroughly.

Homemade dry shampoo
402. Mix together 1 tablespoon salt and 1/2 cup cornmeal for your own homemade dry shampoo. Transfer to a larger-holed shaker, sprinkle it on oily hair lightly and brush out dirt and grime.

403. *Baby powder or cornstarch can also be used as dry shampoos.*

Tired eyes
404. *Place fresh cold cucumber slices on your eyelids to rid them of redness and puffiiness.*

* * * * * * *

X. SEWING

Threading needles
405. *Apply some hair spray to your finger and to the end of the thread, stiffening it enough to be easily threaded.*

Sharp machine needles
406. *Sharpen sewing machine needles by stitching through sandpaper.*

Buttons
407. *Coat the center of buttons with clear nail polish and they'll stay on longer.*
408. *On a four-hole button, sew through two holes at a time, knotting the thread and tying off for each set of holes.*
409. *Use dental floss or elastic thread to sew buttons on children's clothing. The buttons will take a lot of wear before falling off.*

Dropped needles and pins
410. *Instead of groping around your floor for fallen needles and pins, keep a magnet in your sewing kit. Simply sweep it across your rug to pick up those strays.*

Sewing machine oil
411. *Stitch through a blotter after oiling your sewing machine to prevent extra oil from damaging your garments.*

Patterns
412. *Instead of trying to fit used patterns back into their envelopes, stor them in plastic bags.*
413. *Keep patterns from tearing and wrinkle-free by spraying with spray starch.*

Recycled elastic
414. *Remove elastic waistband from used pantyhose for use in other sewing projects.*

Heavy seams
415. *Rub seams with a bar of soap to allow a sewing machine needle to easily pass through.*

Sewing on nylon
416. *When repairing seams on nylon jackets or lingerie, make the job a lot simpler by placing a piece of paper underneath the section you are going to sew. Stitch through the fabric and paper. When finished, tear the paper off.*